Bollywood and Postmodernism

Bollywood and Postmodernism
Popular Indian Cinema in the 21st Century

Neelam Sidhar Wright

For my parents, Kiran and Sharda
In memory of Rameshwar Dutt Sidhar

Edinburgh University Press is one of the leading university presses in the UK. We publish academic books and journals in our selected subject areas across the humanities and social sciences, combining cutting-edge scholarship with high editorial and production values to produce academic works of lasting importance. For more information visit our website: edinburghuniversitypress.com

© Neelam Sidhar Wright, 2015, 2017

Edinburgh University Press Ltd
The Tun – Holyrood Road
12 (2f) Jackson's Entry
Edinburgh EH8 8PJ
www.euppublishing.com

First published in hardback by Edinburgh University Press 2015

Typeset in 11/13 Monotype Ehrhardt by
Servis Filmsetting Ltd, Stockport, Cheshire

A CIP record for this book is available from the British Library

ISBN 978 0 7486 9634 5 (hardback)
ISBN 978 1 4744 2094 5 (paperback)
ISBN 978 0 7486 9635 2 (webready PDF)
ISBN 978 1 4744 0356 6 (epub)

The right of Neelam Sidhar Wright to be identified as author of this work has been asserted in accordance with the Copyright, Designs and Patents Act 1988 and the Copyright and Related Rights Regulations 2003 (SI No. 2498).

Contents

Acknowledgements	vi
List of Figures	vii
List of Abbreviations of Film Titles	viii
1 Introduction: The Bollywood Eclipse	1
2 Anti-Bollywood: Traditional Modes of Studying Indian Cinema	21
3 Pedagogic Practices and Newer Approaches to Contemporary Bollywood Cinema	46
4 Postmodernism and India	63
5 Postmodern Bollywood	79
6 Indian Cinema: A History of Repetition	128
7 Contemporary Bollywood Remakes	148
8 Conclusion: A Bollywood Renaissance?	190
Bibliography	201
List of Additional Reading	213
Appendix: Popular Indian Film Remakes	215
Filmography	220
Index	225

Acknowledgements

I am grateful to the following people for all their support, guidance, feedback and encouragement throughout the course of researching and writing this book: Richard Murphy, Thomas Austin, Andy Medhurst, Sue Thornham, Shohini Chaudhuri, Margaret Reynolds, Steve Jones, Sharif Mowlabocus, the D.Phil. student organisers of the MeCCSA postgraduate conference 2008, staff at the BFI library, the British Library, the University of Sussex library and the Prince of Wales Museum in Mumbai, Leena Yadav, Pollyana Ruiz, Iain M. Smith, Michael Lawrence and his Indian cinema undergraduate students, Rachael Castell and Eliot Grove from Raindance East, Asjad Nazir, Bobby Friction, Jeremy Wooding, Herbert Krill, Paulo Mantovani, Ian Huffer, Niall Richardson, Rosalind Galt, Corey Creekmur, Abhiji Rao, Kay Dickinson, Richard Dyer, Ian Garwood, Stephen Barber, André Rinke, Sara Schmitz, Catherine Reynolds and Helen Wright. I am also very grateful to Gillian Leslie and the editorial team at Edinburgh University Press for their advice in preparing this book for publication. Thank you to Exotic India Art Pvt. Ltd for permitting me use of two artworks from their collection ('Shri Krishna' and 'Mumtaz Mahal' by Kailash Raj), and to Nidhi Chopra at Pop Goes the Art for allowing me to use her original artwork for my cover design. I would also like to thank my parents, my brother Vikram, and my husband Christopher for accompanying me in sitting through all those Bollywood films, and for always sharing my enthusiasm, interest and belief in this project. Finally, thanks to Annapurna and Amenic, whose births during the times of writing have given this book its greatest purpose and meaning.

Figures

1.1	Bollywood actress Madhuri Dixit as Mona Lisa in *Gaja Gamini*	1
1.2	Bollywood actor Shah Rukh Khan in *Dilwale Dulhania Le Jayenge* and post-millennium in *Om Shanti Om*	8
2.1	A (hi)story of Indian cinema	22
2.2	Critical comments on Indian cinema	42
5.1	Key features of the postmodern in contemporary Bollywood.	82
5.2	Film City billboards in 1977 and 2007 from *Om Shanti Om*	96
5.3	The recursive structural framework of *Om Shanti Om*	98
5.4	Jadoo in *Koi . . . Mil Gaya* as the sci-fi incarnation of Lord Krishna	104
5.5	Moments of spectacle in *KMG* and *E.T.*	110
5.6	Reality is fictionalised and pictures come to life in *Abhay*	119
5.7	Abhay murders Sharmilee in a hyperrealistic animated sequence in *Abhay*	121
5.8	Cartoon comic aesthetics in *Cash* and *Krrish*	122
6.1	Farah Khan's postmodern parody of *The Matrix* and *Mission: Impossible* in *Main Hoon Na*	137
7.1	Ornately decorated and framed, Paro in *Devdas* resembles a figure in a fine Indian miniature painting	157
7.2	'Wo Ladhki Hai Kahan?' A parodic journey through popular Hindi cinema in the 1950s, 1960s and 1980s in *Dil Chahta Hai*	170
7.3	Exploiting Hollywood conventions in the opening sequence of *Kaante*	175
7.4	Bhaiyyaji's postmodern-esque makeover in *Tashan*	180
8.1	Shah Rukh Khan's self-simulation in *Billu Barber*	199

Abbreviations of Film Titles

DCH	*Dil Chahta Hai* (2001)
DDLJ	*Dilwale Dulhaniya Le Jayenge* (1995)
E.T.	*E.T.: The Extra Terrestrial* (1982)
KANK	*Kabhi Alvida Naa Kehna* (2006)
K3G	*Kabhi Kushi Kabhie Gham* (2001)
KHNH	*Kal Ho Naa Ho* (2003)
KMG	*Koi . . . Mil Gaya* (2003)
K2H2	*Kuch Kuch Hota Hai* (1998)
MNIK	*My Name Is Khan* (2013)
OSO	*Om Shanti Om* (2007)

CHAPTER 1

Introduction: The Bollywood Eclipse

Figure 1.1: Bollywood actress Madhuri Dixit as Mona Lisa in *Gaja Gamini* (Dashaka Films, 2000).

In May 1998, the Indian Government announced that it would grant the Bombay film industry (commonly referred to as Bollywood) the right to finance its films through foreign funding, bank loans and commercial investment. With this new industry status, Indian filmmakers would no longer need to seek money from the government or resort to black money laundering via the criminal underworld, but could instead have their productions backed by global sponsors and multinational corporations such as Coca-Cola and Nokia. Within this climate of economic restructuring, Bollywood also opened itself up to several aesthetic makeovers. In 1998 it adopted the frenetic editing techniques of popular Music Television (MTV) to re-image its song sequences (*Dil Se*, 1998). A year later, in 1999, the release of Sanjay Leela Bhansali's film *Hum Dil De Chuke Sanam* marked the beginnings of a new, visually 'excessive' style of filmmaking. This novel aestheticism was achieved not only through Bhansali's designer *mise-en-scène* and extravagant cinematography, but also through the careful casting of Miss World contest winner Aishwarya Rai – a rising star who would exhibit a kind of hyper-femininity and visual perfection previously unknown to the cinema.[1] Rai was soon branded as 'the new face of film' by *Time* magazine,[2] and her unique star quality was soon matched by that of male star Hrithik Roshan in 2000. Roshan's hyper-masculine physique and almost superhumanly fluid dancing abilities in his first feature *Kaho Naa . . . Pyaar Hai* made him an astonishing overnight success, with the Indian press describing the Indian public's feverishly fanatical response to his cinematic debut as 'Hrithik mania'. In this same year, India also witnessed the revival of its biggest film star Amitabh Bachchan, who (previously representative as a working-class hero and socialist political figure, both in and outside of his films) now returned with a new, internationalised affluent image – an iconic white goatee beard and designer suit – as a pop star and television show host.[3] Bachchan also used this time to relaunch his film career by starring as a cynical headmaster in Bollywood's *Dead Poets Society*-inspired *Mohabbatein*, and was subsequently voted the biggest star of the millennium in a BBC poll. Since that time, Bachchan has worked on over seventy films and has often appeared in middle-class patriarchal or darker anti-heroic (sometimes even villainous) lead roles. The year 2000 also saw the release of M. F. Hussain's *Gaja Gamini*, a film with avant-garde qualities which was one of the first commercially released art films with a major Bollywood cast (including superstars Madhuri Dixit and Shah Rukh Khan) to display an explicitly postmodern aesthetic style: an abstraction of realism through the fusion of historical events and mythology, a blending of canvas art, theatre and cinema aesthetics, temporal and spatial suspension (with the collapsing together of different historical eras), the intersection of multiple story worlds, and the subordination of narrative coherence and meaning in favour of image saturation. This film aimed to communicate a pseudo-feminist politics by questioning modes of representation of women throughout history and playfully drawing attention to Dixit's female star persona – most famously by reconstructing her image in the form of Leonardo da Vinci's Mona Lisa.[4]

A year later, 2001 saw Bollywood's industry status finally take effect and saw its global circulation realised. Santosh Sivan's *Asoka* was marketed across the UK and screened at London's Empire Leicester Square. Karan Johar's big-budget family melodrama *Kabhi Kushi Kabhie Gham* followed soon after, proving to be the industry's highest international grosser, with many non-Indian European audiences flocking to see the film. This film, coupled with Farhan Akhtar's smart and stylish tale of urban youth *Dil Chahta Hai*, marked the beginning of a new generation of young directors in Bollywood who promised to challenge old-fashioned attitudes and promote a newer, more modernised India. Meanwhile in Hollywood, Baz Luhrmann also helped draw attention to Bollywood with his homage to the cinema in his Oscar-nominated *Moulin Rouge*. Further global awareness was received in 2002 with Hollywood's first fully-fledged Bollywood-themed film *The Guru*, and a similar tribute in the West End in the form of Andrew Lloyd Webber's musical *Bombay Dreams*. While the West showed its critical appreciation of Indian culture largely through East–West hybridised productions such as BAFTA, and Golden Globe nominated *Bend It Like Beckham* and Golden Lion winner *Monsoon Wedding*, Bollywood orchestrated its own international publicity by exhibiting Bhansali's even more visually operatic follow-up film *Devdas* at the Cannes Film Festival. This hype was further exceeded in the same year by the Oscar nomination of the colonial-period sports film *Lagaan: Once Upon a Time in India* and the promotion of Bollywood fashion by *Vanity Fair* and major department stores in London and New York. Meanwhile, in India, Sanjay Gupta inaugurated a new era of cross-cultural remakes in Bollywood with his Hindi adaptation of Quentin Tarantino's *Reservoir Dogs*. A year later, Bollywood produced another indirect Hollywood remake in the form of *Koi . . . Mil Gaya* – a formally unacknowledged reinterpretation of Steven Spielberg's *E.T.: The Extra Terrestrial*.

While the West continued to play with mixing Hollywood and Bollywood conventions in *Bride and Prejudice*, 2004 brought about further hybridity and creativity in Hindi filmmaking. Farah Khan's *Main Hoon Na* wowed audiences with its *Matrix*-inspired special effects action choreography, while *Hum Tum*, one of the biggest hits of the year, experimented with inserting animation sequences into its live-action diegesis.

In 2005, Bollywood released its first full-length feature animation *Hanuman*, again something novel that was received well by Indian audiences. One more landmark film came in the form of yet another Bhansali production, *Black* – a film which lacked the so-called 'essential' song and dance elements required for a film to be commercially successful in India. *Black* presented a remarkably unglamorous role to its lead actress Rani Mukherjee (one of the industry's top stars), who took on a deaf, blind and mute character, earning her several awards and the film critical acclaim. Most importantly, the film's commercial success in India signalled the changing and diversifying tastes of the Indian viewing public. At the same time, India demonstrated the power and influence Bollywood stars had over their audiences when the *Times of India* group launched 'India Poised' – a government-supported initiative which combined politics with entertainment media in order to reinvigorate the country's future leadership. Following the model of Western panel shows such as *Pop Idol*, the campaign ran a television show called *Lead India*, inviting members of the Indian public to apply and compete for a place in India's assembly elections.[5] Audiences were able to vote for their favourite contestants via an SMS text or online ballot. Most significantly, despite the serious politics behind this campaign, the judges' panel on the programme comprised Bollywood industry professionals such as lyricist Javed Akhtar and movie star Akshay Kumar. The India Poised publicity campaign also included adverts starring Bollywood megastars such as Amitabh Bachchan and Shah Rukh Khan, which were displayed on TV channels[6] and before film screenings in Cineplex theatres across the country.

In 2006, Bollywood production companies realised the potential for mass profit through film franchises and launched their first blockbuster movie sequels, *Krrish* and *Dhoom 2*. This year also marked a first in the industry for self-adaptation,[7] producing two big-budget remakes of landmark Hindi films from previous eras: *Don* and *Umrao Jaan*. Interestingly, these new sequels and remakes challenged assumptions regarding Bollywood's supposed moral high ground, instead casting their lead stars in negative roles: Hrithik Roshan as a master-thief in *Dhoom 2*, Shah Rukh Khan as a ruthless Mafia boss in *Don: The Chase Begins*, and Amitabh Bachchan as a torturing psychopath in *Aag* (a 2008 remake of the legendary seventies 'curry Western' *Sholay*). Bollywood's trend for recycling continued to increase in the following years. In 2007 – the same year that the word 'Bollywood' entered the *Oxford English Dictionary*, veteran Indian actor Anupam Kher appeared in Ang Lee's Chinese espionage thriller *Lust, Caution*, and Indian film actress Shilpa Shetty won the public's vote on *Big Brother* in the UK – the industry's previous record for highest-grossing film was broken by *Om Shanti Om*, a postmodern remake of 1980s Indian film *Karz*. Other films in the top ten of highest grossers that year included formally unacknowledged versions of Hollywood's *Three Men and a Baby* and *Hitch*. The next year, 2008, followed in similar vein with two more hit sequels (*Golmaal Returns* and *Sarkar Raj*) and *Ghajini*, which, despite being a Bollywood remake of a South Indian film adaptation of Christopher Nolan's *Memento*, then became the most successful Indian film of all time. This was also the year American rap star Snoop Dog fashioned a turban and produced the theme song for the Bollywood hit film *Singh Is Kinng*. In 2009, Warner Bros Pictures released its first Hindi film – martial arts comedy *Chandni Chowk to China* – while Bollywood was drawn into the Hollywood awards limelight once more with Shah Rukh Khan presenting at the Golden Globes and, more indirectly, through Danny Boyle's award-winning *Slumdog Millionaire*. Despite its grittier aesthetics, Boyle's film paid homage to the Bollywood style with an end-credit dance sequence, and by employing for its soundtrack Bollywood composer A. R. Rahman (who subsequently won an Oscar for his collaboration). The film also launched the international career of

Bollywood actor Anil Kapoor, who would go on to appear in major US film and television projects (the Fox network's *24* and *Mission Impossible: Ghost Protocol*). Thus, 2009 marked a significant increase in global casting, with Australian pop star Kylie Minogue appearing in a song sequence with Akshay Kumar in Bollywood underwater action film *Blue* and Sylvester Stallone evoking his action-star persona in *Kambakkht Ishq*, a romantic comedy set in LA (also featuring Hollywood actress Denise Richards). Aishwarya Rai added another film to her list of international productions by starring in Hollywood's *Pink Panther 2*, while transnational productions came in the form of the attempted revival by Jennifer Lynch (daughter of surrealist director David Lynch) of the Indian snake film genre in *Hisss* and Indian company UTV Motion Pictures' financing of the Hollywood film *ExTerminators*.

The above shifts in Bollywood's film production all take place after its economic liberalisation, and many of them point towards a new, consumer-centred, cross-cultural, self-reflexive, visually spectacular and nostalgic style of filmmaking in India. Bollywood's increased impulse to repeat and recycle, to excessively express and visualise, to commercialise and self-commodify, to appropriate other cultural works and to de-differentiate binaries or blur distinctions through such processes also suggests that the cinema has, in its restructuring, acquired strikingly postmodern qualities.

NEW BOLLYWOOD

Some scholars have already gone further in demonstrating recent changes within the Hindi film industry by hailing an entirely new form of cinema, which is sometimes described as 'New Bollywood'.[8] Sangita Gopal (2011) distinguishes this new cinema by pointing to the increased capitalisation, regulation and restructuring of the Hindi film industry and its altered distribution and exhibition processes, the commercialisation and branding of Bollywood and its immersion in a global economy, and the rise of the urban middle classes and 'transnational' audiences. In terms of film content, she observes 'radically novel styles of filmmaking' making a greater use of 'high-end technology' (including steadicams), a merging of popular and parallel cinema, a digression from the song-sequence formula (in the form of multi-plex or *Hatke* films[9]), genre diversity (particularly Hollywood-style horror and comedy), a 'triumphant' use of Hinglish, an obsession with remakes, and most significantly, the cinema's shifting focus towards the subjectivity of the 'conjugated couple' (Gopal, 2011). As regards the difference between New Bollywood and earlier cinematic periods, Gopal distinguishes classical Hindi cinema's 'self-imposed homogeneity enforced by the all-embracing format of the social film and the *masala*' (3). She acknowledges that many of the above filmmaking processes have been present in earlier forms of the cinema (particularly films from the 1970s), but asserts that this filmmaking style has since 'solidified' (14) from 1991 onwards, and 'only begins to emerge as a distinctive product in the post-liberalization era' (3). As she stresses, '*New* is necessary in order to emphasise that post-liberalization Mumbai film, while owing much to changes in the previous two decades, is nonetheless a radically new art form that must be analysed on its own terms' (14). However, the innovative style Gopal refers to often corresponds to a type of cinema (*Hatke*) that is seen as somewhat alternative to the commercial blockbusters that this book will investigate as part of 'New Bollywood'.

Although it aims equally to demonstrate a significant shift in Bollywood cinema aesthetics in recent years, my study of popular Indian cinema does not intend to create an explicit binary of 'New' and 'Old' Bollywood. Rather, it exposes a postmodern dialogue between the Hindi cinema of the present and that of the past, which has ultimately allowed the cinema to reinvent itself. The 'New' in this case resides in the postmodern sense of the word; Bollywood's 'postmodern turn' implies a shift that reworks or revisits previous aesthetic trends in order to produce an aesthetic that is altogether different. As with all postmodern works, we are not talking about a clear-cut break from the 'classical' in the traditional sense. Rather, we are discussing a transformation and change that takes place *through* a special kind of continuity – a reworking of the past.[10] 'New Bollywood' here refers to contemporary films which exhibit a strong postmodern aesthetic style which was not as present in the 1990s (when popular Indian cinema officially became 'Bollywood'). After 2000, this aesthetic style came to dominate the cinema and has been used as a means of internally commenting on and critiquing the industry in its current form.

DEFINING THE 'CONTEMPORARY'

A certain widespread disregard for post-1990s popular Indian films has been evident, from popular film journalism (an October 2007 issue of *Total Film* magazine offers an introductory timeline of Bollywood cinema, stopping at 1996), reference compendiums and introductory film guides (such as the *BFI 100 Bollywood Films* [2005], which reveals a bias towards earlier periods of the cinema's history), to established film societies and organisations such as the British Film Institute (in 2007 its web archive provided a canonical list of the 'greatest Indian films of all time', which included only one post-millennium release).[11] In this book I will reveal how film institutions, scholars and educators concerned with Indian cinema have (until very recently) habitually refrained from moving their focus beyond issues surrounding national identity or diaspora politics, and therefore films released after the mid-1990s. Such accounts would have us believe that popular Indian cinema is anything but 'contemporary'. As I demonstrate in the following chapter, there seems to be a shared sense among many film scholars that newer Bollywood films display a certain 'lack' of critical appeal and are in some way of lesser value than their canonised predecessors. I challenge this assumption, and instead suggest that the problem lies in the fact that these newer films often do not fit existing models and established theories, and are thus often left unacknowledged in the hope that we may never assume their significance. Indian cinema has ultimately been a platform for exploring cultural *tradition* in India. The 'contemporary', it seems, then, poses a threat to our precious established definitions of popular 'traditional' Indian cinema.

We must be wary of the limitations inherent in purely offering definitions of a cinema that no longer dominates, and of the dangers posed by this elision of contemporary filmmaking processes. Let us consider, for example, the inadequacy of conceptualising contemporary Hollywood cinema without acknowledging any of the developments that have taken place after 1996. Could one justifiably describe popular American cinema without considering the impact of CGI after *The Matrix* (1999), the Internet and its influence on film marketing strategies, recent shifts in the global economy, the emergence of DVD and digital filmmaking, or the aftermath of 9/11? Likewise, in television, could we claim to understand the medium today if we overlooked its shift from analogue to digital broadcasting formats? Like its Western counterpart, popular Indian cinema has changed dramatically in the last fifteen years. The pleasures on offer in 1990s Indian cinema no longer suffice – they no longer wholly embrace the needs of today's Bollywood audience. A lead character's charm alone is no longer enough to push a movie to the box-office top spot. The leading actor must now be more marketable as a superstar and be able to do his own stunts. He must be measured and approved, exhibiting an actual talent in acting and dancing. He must sponsor a decent haircut, display the muscles of a superhero, and be the face of an internationally renowned consumer brand. He must offer everything a Hollywood A-list actor does – and more. The much talked-about rebranding of Bollywood megastar Shah Rukh Khan demonstrates this shift perfectly. Khan is famously known for having initially gained popularity in the 1990s despite his scruffy hair, dark skin and ordinary stature. He originally won audiences over because of his mischievous smile and 'cheeky yet charming' character (see Chopra, 2007). However, the actor himself has recently discussed his need to reinvent his image (through hair extensions, chest waxing, intensive body building and skin-lightening[12]) in order to meet the demands of current younger Bollywood audiences – including his own son. In a television interview with director Farah Khan on the Indian celebrity talk show *Koffee with Karan* (hosted by Bollywood director and producer Karan Johar), the three discuss Shah Rukh Khan's radical makeover for the then-upcoming film

Figure 1.2: Bollywood actor Shah Rukh Khan in *Dilwale Dulhania Le Jayenge* (Yash Raj Films, 1995) and post-millennium in *Om Shanti Om* (Red Chillies Entertainment, 2007).

Om Shanti Om, for which he physically trained for months to achieve a leaner, muscular body. Farah Khan declares the film to have launched an entirely new look for Khan, which she describes as an 'item boy' image.[13] In Bollywood film, an 'item number' usually refers to the objectification of a seductive female performer (the 'item girl') in a singular, highly-sexualised song sequence which is inserted in a film independently of its narrative context, but this has been extended across gender in recent years, with actors Abhishek Bachchan, Hrithik Roshan and Shah Rukh Khan occupying similar roles in films (see Bachchan in *Rakht* [2004] and Roshan in *Krazzy 4* [2008]). Such shifts on the level of star image and on-screen sexuality are prime examples of how films have changed in terms of their aesthetics in the post-millennial era – signalling a New Bollywood cinema with a more contemporary visual style.

Like 'New Bollywood', 'contemporary Bollywood' here also refers to a cinema beyond the aforementioned period of first-generation NRI movies, specifically films released post-millennium. I shift between the terms 'New' and 'contemporary' – the former helping to emphasise the cinema as aesthetically distinct and innovative, and the latter accentuating the post-millennial era. While hesitant to confine my research to a fixed historical period, I have found that the most significant factors solidifying change within the industry emerge from 2001 on. The year 2001 in particular beckoned a change with regard to the 'polish' of Bollywood cinema in terms of its actor-stars as well as its general production. The release of Farhan Akhtar's *Dil Chahta Hai* that year is almost unanimously seen as a landmark moment in this sense, and thus is a key text which I explore in more depth (see Chapter 7).

THE POSTMODERN

Despite 'postmodernism' being a highly debated and perplexing descriptive term, the phenomenon has already brought much to cinema and its academic study in the West. As a mode of film practice, it allows texts to inscribe and subvert prevailing conventions and question ideology, subjectivity and historical knowledge, allowing us to 'reconsider the operations by which we both create and give meaning to our culture through representation' (Hutcheon, 1989: 117). In doing so, it draws our attention to certain films' consciously mimetic and anti-original qualities and to how contemporary films now seek to 'rework' rather than invent stories. Postmodern films facilitate an act of looking from both sides of the screen (Degli-Eposti, 1998: 5) and will (mis)represent identity in a way that exposes it as something to be understood as decentred and complex rather than whole and fixed. Postmodernism also increases the tension between, and closeness of, the political and the aesthetic, paradoxically creating texts that are at once culturally resistant and yet seem politically barren (Connor, 1989: 180). Postmodernism has helped us to understand and create shifts in knowledge and thinking, economic and social ordering, and aesthetic debates in the contemporary Western climate. It has offered us a means to investigate how capitalism and globalisation have impacted upon our society, pushing our artistic cultural practice towards profit-driven eclecticism and a saturation of media images and signs. The concept has also proved useful in helping to reveal how even the most commercial and trivial art forms can have the potential to interrogate: to be oppositional, contestatory, aesthetically diverse and ideologically ambivalent (Hill, 1998: 101–2). We are able to appreciate how popular cinema can use irony as a means of questioning truth, reality and artificiality, how it can manipulate images for commercial ends while problematising image-creation itself (Harvey, 1990: 323).

Postmodernism has thus provided us with new reading strategies and different systems of interpreting films (Degli-Eposti, 1988: 16). With this in mind, this book attempts to apply the concept to Bollywood cinema in order to enrich our understanding of its contemporary filmmaking processes and shed light on a range of issues and questions concerning popular Indian film. My study of New Bollywood explores reasons behind the lack of scholarly attention paid to post-millennial Bollywood films, particularly in existing Indian film criticism and Western film studies courses. Within this, I consider the issue of non-Indian audiences' lack of interest in – even rejection of – popular Hindi film texts, suggesting that Hindi cinema may have a more unusually unique film language and logic of pleasure compared to other, more accessible Asian cinemas. This study also argues that contemporary Indian popular cinema should not be dismissed as crass, mindless entertainment, or considered unworthy of intellectual engagement. Rather, it suggests that there is a credible, academically engaging cinema to be found beyond high art, political and diasporic Indian cinema, and that current popular Indian cinema can be found to be equally fascinating and revealing in a *postmodern* sense.

In addition, far from declaring it a straightforward continuation of previous eras of filmmaking, I demonstrate how post-millennial Bollywood has mutated away from certain modes of representation, so much so that it can be described as representing a kind of renaissance period for the cinema. Among the cinema's many formal aesthetic changes, the 'noughties' decade saw the emergence of a new genre of contemporary Hindi cinema in the form of the remake. In studying this recent phenomenon, I reveal how Bollywood uses postmodern methods of appropriation in order to reinvigorate itself and attempt to break free of its formulaic trappings. This postmodern reading will help us to rethink and expand our current definitions of Bollywood, as well as understand how postmodern techniques can enable a seemingly monolithic and nationalistic cinema to become more fragmented and experimental.

POSTMODERNISM AND ITS SCEPTICS

As with most scholarship on postmodernism, this study will naturally prompt certain reservations and scepticism from those who argue that the 'postmodern' is a much too contested, incoherent and problematic concept to work with, let alone apply to non-Western cinema. It is therefore important to assert here that the purpose of this book is not to affirm postmodernism as an unproblematic, self-evident and self-fulfilling category, but instead to raise further questions about its historical and geographical emergence, whilst examining its usefulness as a hermeneutic tool for studying non-Western popular art forms. Indeed, the entire 'postmodern conundrum' is far from solved here, but as with other seminal works on this subject, the very goal here is to stimulate a new discussion about the value of postmodern theory in film studies and to foster new methods of analysing contemporary Indian cinema. This book *introduces* the concept of a postmodern Bollywood cinema, and this concept deserves (like other new theories and methodologies) to be tested, refined and developed by others before it can be as straightforward and unproblematic as some may urge it to be. Nevertheless, rather than taking the term for granted and overlooking its polysemy, or discussing it too abstractly, I make definitions of key postmodern concepts clear by firstly breaking them down into a series of identifiable aesthetic conventions and then exploring them further through detailed case studies offering close textual analysis of a select range of contemporary Bollywood texts.

Undeniably, postmodernism has traditionally been viewed as a specifically *Western* phenomenon. Key postmodern theorists have spoken of it as 'the West's "modern neurosis"' (Lyotard, 1992: 79–80), as a 'global, yet American postmodern culture . . . a whole new wave of American military and economic domination throughout the world (Jameson, 1991: 57), and have explicitly argued that 'postmodernism cannot simply be used as a synonym for the contemporary . . . [and] does not really describe an international cultural phenomenon, for it is primarily European and American' (Hutcheon, 1988: 4). However, some scholars have since reviewed and withdrawn this opinion (in her 2002 revised edition of *The Politics of the Postmodern*, Hutcheon changes her perspective on postmodernism's global reach and addresses the concept's subsequent internationalisation[14]) whilst others have explored the idea of alternative modernities that may be more culturally specific (see Chapter 4). What is more, Ajay Gehlawat (2010) has reminded us that despite the dangers posed by the application of a Eurocentric hermeneutics, 'indigenous frames of reference can also be a trap' (xvii).

Admittedly, it is still somewhat a challenging task to find explicit examples of (let alone discourses on) postmodern cultural art in India – even after considering the well-publicised novels of British Indian literary author Salman Rushdie (see Das, 2007), the work of artists such as Annu Palakunnathu Matthew (whose portfolio entitled 'Bollywood Satirized' in a 2001 exhibition mocked commercial films for reinforcing Indian traditional socio-cultural prejudices by manipulating and subverting images from existing film posters[15]), or the post-1990s *Adhunantika* movement in Bengali literature, with its poetry and short stories sharing many characteristics with the postmodern including plurality, de-territorialisation, eclecticism, multi-linearity, pastiche, irony and de-centredness.[16] The renowned Indian art critic and curator Geeta Kapur has perhaps been most influential in demonstrating that both modern and postmodern art exist in contemporary India. In her book *When Was Modernism* (2000), Kapur traces both modernism and the postmodern in contemporary Indian art, periodising it from the 1930s onwards. Among India's postmodern pioneers, she notes artists such as K. G. Subramanyan, Bhupen Khakhar and Gulam Mohammed Sheikh, whose work exhibits a self-conscious eclecticism, parodic force (particularly towards high modernism), intertextuality, pop art aesthetics, excess of signs, and a 'pictorial vocabulary' (313–14), often engaging in 'instrumental pastiche' and a play with simulacra, and ultimately exploiting cultural codes (319). From the 1980s onwards, such artists are seen to 'disrupt' and 'provide a relief' from Indian modernism (319), although Kapur explicitly cites cinema as the place from which postmodernism can most effectively emerge (320).[17] Thus Kapur asserts that 'before the west periodizes the postmodern entirely in its own terms and in that process also characterises it, we have to introduce from the vantage-point of the periphery the transgressions of uncategorized practice' (297).

A small handful of scholars, in particular Vijay Mishra (2008), Gehlawat (2010) and Rajinder Dudrah (2012), have recently begun to register and tackle the concept of a 'Postmodern Bollywood' cinema. Gehlawat, who has advocated a study of Bollywood through applying what Arjun Appadurai has termed a 'postmodern praxis' (Appadurai [1996], cited in Gehlawat: 118), acknowledges that a postmodern reading assumes intent on the part of the filmmaker, and arguably requires a certain level of sophistication, literacy and self-consciousness on the part of the viewer, which could be seen as problematic when considering the lesser-privileged and under-educated members of the Indian film audience. However, Gehlawat challenges prevailing scholarly emphasis on passive spectatorship by emphasising the difference between *intentionality* and *consciousness*, highlighting Indian cinema's fundamentally 'transgressive disruptive semiotics' (57) which provide a distancing effect, and arguing that Bollywood in fact serves as a 'teaching machine' for subaltern audiences (79). My own study of New Bollywood, which reveals a dramatic increase in remaking (as homage) and referencing of other canonical film texts, suggests that the cinema explicitly offers a unique kind of pleasure through cinephilia and that audiences are already able to pick up on these playful references. The rise of multiplex cinemas (targeting urban middle classes) and a greater investment in diasporic and broader global audiences also further complicate the argument that the Bollywood audience is too illiterate and passive to pick up on complex postmodern references.

Another issue that could be raised against this application of the postmodern concerns how we account for the appearance of seemingly postmodern processes, such as self-consciousness, in earlier periods of Hindi cinema. This matter is addressed in several ways: (1) by distinguishing the idiosyncrasies of New Bollywood's pastiche/parody/self-reflexivity from other forms of textual referencing; (2) by my identifying a 'postmodern politics' (Hutcheon, 1988, 1989) within recent films; and (3) by exploring the difference between cultural mimicry, which is intrinsic to Indian cinematic tradition, and postmodern blank pastiche or parody in recent Bollywood cinema. However, the very fact that I draw connections between postmodern devices and traditional Indian artistic traditions (for example, Chapter 7 looks at hyperrealism and figural aesthetics in ancient Indian miniature paintings) demonstrates my intention to question also whether postmodernism is purely a contemporary phenomenon, or whether other versions of it have existed in the past. Further distinctions are made with regard to New Bollywood's innovative remaking processes. After considering how repetition has historically functioned as a fundamental process in Indian artistic culture (through a brief historical account of remaking in classical Hindi cinema), I go on to explain how remaking in New Bollywood operates differently. Here, remaking is used to convey postmodern concerns such as the prevalence of stylistic excess over discourse (figural aestheticism), self-referential critique, identity fragmentation, and a questioning or crisis of representation.

THE POSTMODERN TERRAIN

In his attempt to critique various theorisations of the postmodern, Norman K. Denzin (1991) has distinguished how key theorists such as Fredric Jameson (1991), Jean-François Lyotard (1992) and Jean Baudrillard (1983) share a common nostalgic desire for an aesthetics of the past (Denzin: 48). Postmodernism's relationship to the past is multifaceted, but can generally be divided into two perspectives, the first consisting of the postmodern text having an inferior relationship to that of the past/history, with negative, unproductive and often destructive consequences, and the second a perspective that diversely suggests how new postmodern art has the potential for a critical *revaluation* of the past, resulting in a 'freeing up' of the text and its meaning. Jameson, Baudrillard and Terry Eagleton (1986) can be seen to fall into the first category. Jameson in particular, in his essay 'Postmodernism or the logic of late capitalism', warns of the destructive postmodern text, which achieves nothing but a plagiarised copy of an original work of art, stripped of authenticity and aura, which he describes as resulting in a 'waning of affect' (1984: 69). Jameson situates himself as a Marxist, using the concept of postmodernism to tie in with and account for the damage caused by the capitalisation of art. The postmodern text, with its 'depthlessness' (60), its 'blank parodying' (65) of authentic works, and its commercially driven existence, becomes an ideal target as a flagship for capitalism. Eagleton likewise echoes Jameson's argument, complaining of postmodernism as a 'sick joke' (1986: 131), an empty pastiche which 'mimes the formal resolution of art and life ... while remorselessly emptying it of its political content' (132). This pessimism is further added to by Baudrillard, who introduces the notion of the postmodern simulacra – a textual reproduction of an authentic work which aims to subvert and pervert notions of reality, truth and hence history. For Baudrillard, the modern image as simulation 'does no more than resemble itself and escape in its own logic' (195) and thus becomes a 'death sentence' for all possible reference and meaning (196). Baudrillard's preoccupations lie predominantly with the abduction, mutilation and 'terrorism' of the real (196) by the postmodern text. Reality, once it has been swallowed up by the postmodern simulacra, has become unreachable and replaced by empty recycled images of hypersimulation and hyperrealism (197).

For all three theorists, the mass production and recycling of previous works of art has led to current aesthetics being intellectually frowned upon and enjoyed at a purely sensationalist level – resulting in an increased 'painful nostalgia' (Friedberg, 1994: 188) or hopeless mourning for the past. In the case of cinema, mainstream American filmmakers have for a long time, if not always, been guilty of mass profit-based production and the parodying or remaking of previous films. Therefore, in the light of the consequences of these postmodern traits indicated by Jameson and Baudrillard, it would appear that mainstream cinema is doomed:

> A whole generation of films is appearing which . . . lack only an imaginary and that particular hallucination which makes cinema what it is [. . .] cinema increasingly approaches . . . in its banality, in its veracity, in its starkness, in its tedium . . . in its pretension to be the real, the immediate, the unsignified, which is the maddest of enterprises. (Baudrillard: 195)

The constant memory and loss of authenticity of the past are perhaps unavoidable. However, not all postmodern critics have declared this cultural phase a catastrophe. While similarly attempting to uncover the relationship between the postmodern and the past, Jean-François Lyotard has also credited the postmodern movement with helping to liberate texts by questioning the importance and prioritisation of textual meaning (an effort he no longer sees as essential in the pursuit of aesthetic appreciation). Lyotard commends the postmodern for its abstraction of truth and realism, which has resulted in a breaking down of grand narratives such as history, religion, science, and existing art institutions which presume to dictate what is and is not to be classified as a work of art. Postmodernism embraces the popular text, with all its banalities, trivialities and commercialism, merging it with and presenting it alongside established works of 'high art'. This celebratory destabilisation of such totalising social institutions is also, according to Lyotard, accompanied by another liberating postmodern trait – the loss of meaning. To reject the need for a work to mean something is to again defy and break down the rules by which established art institutions operate: 'Such rules and categories are what the work or text is investigating. The artist and writer therefore work without rules . . . in order to establish the rules of what *will have been made*' (Lyotard: 15).

The notion of freedom of interpretation and the breaking of boundaries is further explored by Scott Lash (1988). Lash stresses how postmodern texts fundamentally break down the rules and boundaries of difference (for example, between good and bad art, or high and low culture), resulting in an elimination of difference altogether. This process of 'de-differentiation' (312) can also be seen to free the text and its reader. The indulgence in pure sensation and spectacle renders both textual meaning and interpretation unnecessary. The instability of the boundaries and conventions constructing art and realism are exposed (329), allowing several conflicting styles to coexist within a single text. However, although these theorisations work well in developing an appreciation of the postmodern text, they still do not account for how we are to resolve the problem of that which has been *lost* from past forms of classical and modernist art.

Perhaps the most useful attempt at resolving the conflict between the nostalgic past and present postmodernist age is that of Linda Hutcheon. Rather than perceiving the two as separate, Hutcheon argues that this 'mere' nostalgic return and constant referencing of the past is not simply postmodernism scraping together the remains of what went before, but rather a 'critical reworking' of the past (1988: 4). This method of critiquing previous works is unique to postmodernism as a result of its ability to simultaneously conform to and resist the past and its conventions:

> ... the increasing uniformization of mass culture is one of the totalising forces that postmodernism exists to challenge. Challenge, but not deny ... Postmodernism ... refuses to posit any ... master narrative ... It argues that such systems are indeed attractive, perhaps even necessary; but this does not make them any less illusory. (Hutcheon, 1988: 13)

Hutcheon's theorisation is valuable not only as an attack on those who outwardly reject postmodernism, but also because it exposes an intellectual link between or progression from the past (history, modernism) to the current state of art. As my own study reveals, New Bollywood texts could be seen to be guilty of both – a seemingly full-scale immersion in Jamesonian postmodern blank pastiche, which in fact at times reveals itself as a playful postmodern critiquing of the past.

A STRUCTURE OF THE BOOK

My investigation begins with a review of Indian film criticism (Chapter 2), Bollywood's circulation at film festivals, and pedagogical practices (Chapter 3). I ascertain how previous published work on Indian cinema and certain teaching trends have shaped our current understanding of (and critical attitudes towards) popular Indian films. Inspired by the postmodern notion of history as *narrative* (which chooses to perceive historical discourse as subjective storytelling rather than something conveying [actual] universal truth or fact), I demonstrate how India's cinematic history has been articulated through particular intellectual discourses cultivated within the discipline of Indian film studies. As I reveal, these discourses tend to focus upon a particular set of themes in order to fulfil specific social and political agendas, thus often neglecting to analyse certain aspects of the text's formal aesthetics. Chapter 2 observes the censuring and disregard for Bollywood in traditional approaches to Indian cinema by reviewing a variety of literary sources. These include historical biographies, textbooks and introductory guidebooks by renowned Indian cinema scholars, and press interviews with industry professionals. Chapter 3 goes on to look at film festival brochures, and pedagogical accounts by those who have taught the subject to a Western audience, as well as incorporating more empirically-based data taken from university syllabuses on Bollywood, formal conversations with film scholars at academic conferences, and my own personal observations of non-Indian undergraduate students' experiences of intellectually engaging with Indian film texts. Using this information, I argue that many of the academic approaches towards, and much critical journalistic writing on, Bollywood have worked *against* Bollywood's interests in securing international appeal. Although valuable and informative, this literature has often failed to adequately address significant aesthetic shifts within the industry over the last decade, instead producing outmoded or woolly definitions of contemporary Bollywood which have hindered its global inauguration in terms both of commercial success and academic interest. In order to motion a change in Indian film scholarship, Chapter 3 also draws attention to more recent published work on contemporary Bollywood, which has begun to address the significance of and offer innovative approaches to analysing this distinctive era of cinema.

Since Chapters 2 and 3 demonstrate a widespread devaluation and marginalisation of Bollywood, my subsequent postmodern reading aptly serves as a means of responding to and countering such attitudes by redefining the cinema in its contemporary form. Chapters 4 and 5 demonstrate how the Indian film industry has taken a postmodern turn after the millennium as a response to Bollywood's increased global exchanges and commercialisation. After a review in Chapter 4 of existing academic attempts to place the concept in a global or international context, Chapter 5 observes how the postmodern, as an aesthetic style and fluid cultural practice, manifests in contemporary Bollywood film texts. To aid my investigation, I draw upon the various concepts and traits identified by postmodern theorists such as Fredric Jameson, Jean Baudrillard, Jean-François Lyotard and Hayden White, as well as postmodern film theorists such as Linda Hutcheon, Peter and Will Brooker, and

M. Keith Brooker. As the field of postmodern Bollywood cinema studies is relatively uncharted, I feel it is important to employ a variety of tools and strategies throughout my research in order to demonstrate the cinema's versatility (hopefully assisting its flexible application in future film studies courses) and to aim for experimentation and exploration rather than an absolute concretisation of the concept. Thus, my methodology here shifts between formalist film theory, semiotics, (post)structuralism, broad cultural politics, and some Marxist poetics.

In Chapter 5, my analysis of postmodern Bollywood cinema crucially includes a close reading of three key films which I consider to be prime examples of this new form of filmmaking. The first of these, *Om Shanti Om*, directed by Farah Khan (perhaps Bollywood's female equivalent of pastiche-*auteur* Quentin Tarantino), provides a complex self-critique by employing a variety of postmodern devices including pastiche and nostalgic recycling, which inhabit everything from its narrative and plot to its visual aesthetics and formal structure. Through these strategies, the film is able simultaneously to celebrate, exploit and dismantle its own cinematic conventions and modes of representation. A second example of postmodern Bollywood is offered through *Koi . . . Mil Gaya* – the film that initiated and signalled the Bombay film industry's yielding to the previously unfamiliar territory of science-fiction. This film usefully demonstrates how Bollywood uses postmodern methods to play and experiment with a long-established theme of post-independence Hindi cinema: the tension between modernity (progress, the future) and tradition (regression, the past). Whereas previously Bombay film narratives would conclude with the rejection of the former and a return to the latter, as I reveal, *Koi . . . Mil Gaya* in fact facilitates the *blurring* of these two binaries in order to ultimately render them both as suspect. The film also reveals how a comparative study of a Bollywood remake of a Hollywood original (in this case, *E.T: The Extra Terrestrial*) can help us to better understand both the interconnectedness and the distinctive differences in film language between these two dominant cinemas. My final case study uses *Abhay* as an example of avant-garde techniques emerging within mainstream Indian cinema. Through its constant interchange between conventional cinematic realism and absurd comic book representation, the film demonstrates how some popular Indian films deconstruct (Western) notions of realism by innovatively dissolving the divide between non-fiction and fantasy. In doing so, the film contests the negative elitist criticism Bollywood has received, instead revealing a cinema that cannot be underestimated and easily categorised, instead sitting comfortably between the posts of mainstream popular entertainment and radical art.

Chapters 6 and 7 continue to provide further examples of postmodern aesthetics in contemporary Bollywood cinema, this time looking more specifically at a particular kind of filmmaking that has emerged prolifically over recent years: the Bollywood remake. On the basis of research that considered 144 Indian film remakes (almost one hundred of which were produced after 2000), I discuss how remaking has become a platform for innovation and creative translation in Bollywood, offering a unique form of cinephilic pleasure for its audiences. Drawing upon various theoretical work on textual adaptation – including issues of textual fidelity that continue to plague the Bollywood remake's critical reception – I look at how the diverse methods of remaking that Bollywood employs (intertextuality, cross-cultural borrowing, aesthetic as well as narrative appropriation, pastiche and parody) allow it to experiment with and innovate in its filmmaking practices. For example, in Chapter 6, I explore how certain film stars are used as intertexts through 'celebrity' or 'genetic' intertextuality, while Chapter 7 looks at how Bollywood uses figural excess to *rework* and distinguish itself aesthetically from previous canonical Indian film texts. I also explore how Bollywood cinema hybridises with Hollywood modes of filmmaking in order to de-authenticate and dismantle both American and its own cinematic codes and conventions.

After looking initially at how repetition has always been a fundamental characteristic of Indian artistic culture, I go on to explain how remaking became a central or signature feature of Bollywood cinema in the first decade of the twenty-first century, embodying postmodern concerns such as the prevalence of stylistic excess over discourse, self-referential critique, identity fragmentation, and a questioning or crisis of representation. The film texts I explore include remakes or 're-imaginings' of films as diverse as Hollywood's critically acclaimed *The Godfather* and the testosterone-driven *Fight Club*, the Indian socio-realist drama *Devdas*, the independent American cult movie *Reservoir Dogs*, the special effects sci-fi film *The Matrix*, New Hollywood's taboo-breaking classic *Bonnie and Clyde*, and South Korea's international award-winning *Oldboy*. My analysis of postmodern remaking in Bollywood further explains how the cinema has changed and evolved since the 1990s, and I argue that such films can help enrich our understanding of Bollywood's current film language and aesthetics, revealing an Indian cinema that is at both its most innovative and its most self-destructive.

Finally, in Chapter 8, I provide a redefinition of contemporary Bollywood cinema, propose the value of postmodernism as a new alternative method for studying, teaching and articulating Bollywood in the West (particularly offering us a means by which to better engage with the visual aesthetics of popular Indian films), and, lastly, push towards a more *global* view of the postmodern, which can help us to expand and update our understanding of the concept as well as emphasise its potential for international application and cultural impact.

Over the past fifteen years, Bollywood film production has beckoned to a significant intervention in popular Indian cinema. There has been a break or interruption in its filmmaking methods, an obscuring or *eclipsing* of previous cinematic processes. I believe that newer Bollywood texts contain culturally, aesthetically and politically subversive qualities which endeavour to overpower previous aesthetic modes and conventions, revealing a postmodern shift that has enabled a darkening of these films' internal agendas.

This study of post-millennial Bollywood cinema concentrates on films produced between 2000 and 2009, although more recent film releases and developments are also considered, particularly in the final chapter. It is also important to note that this study will not explore any of the numerous other regional cinemas within India. While choosing to focus on a particular Indian film industry, I have considered that there may be other varieties of Indian cinema containing similar tropes to those discussed in this book. Therefore I do not at this stage wish to sign off my approach as being exclusively applicable or restricted to the remit of Bombay cinema, nor to assert that this is automatically reflective of *every* kind of contemporary popular Indian film. But I do envisage that my approach may be useful and adaptable when analysing other kinds of commercial Indian cinema, such as Tamil Nadu-based films.[18]

The aim of this book is ultimately to explain what postmodernism means in the context of Bollywood cinema, to demonstrate how to apply the concept when analysing Bollywood films, and, lastly, to understand what postmodernism tells us about the change and function of Bollywood film language after the twenty-first century. This postmodern approach to Bollywood film helps us consider what an (originally) Western theoretical framework can actively do to raise our appreciation and alter our understanding of contemporary popular Indian cinema, and what the Indian cinema in turn can do for our understanding of postmodernism as a *global* concept.[19]

NOTES

1. Even Hollywood's then most popular actress, Julia Roberts, described Rai as the most beautiful woman in the world.
2. Unauthored (2003b).
3. From 2000 to 2005 Bachchan was the host for *Kaun Banega Crorepati*, India's version of the British quiz show *Who Wants to Be a Millionaire?*
4. The Mona Lisa remains one of the most famously appropriated images in postmodern art – for example, see Marcel Duchamp's 1919 ready-made *L.H.O.O.Q.*, Andy Warhol's multiple 1963 screen prints and Subodh Gupta's 2010 three-dimensional sculpture *Et tu, Duchamp?*
5. The prize also included a scholarship to study leadership and politics at Harvard University and Rs 50 lakh for a public-welfare project.
6. Star TV channel in India, America and the UK.
7. Although the Hindi film industry had sporadically produced Indian cinema remakes prior to this time, the solid trend for self-remakes was only realised post-millennium.

8. By announcing the demise of family epics and acknowledging the diversifying tastes of the Indian viewing public, Dinesh Raheja and Jitendra Kothari (2004) have also been eager to assert that Bollywood has superseded its 1990s era and that contemporary Bollywood is 'evolving, morphing and mutating' (146). The authors note how the cinema may be on the cusp of a global breakthrough and query the possibility of a new wave emerging from *within* commercial cinema (141).
9. See Chapter 8 for a more detailed discussion of this type of cinema.
10. Bollywood paradoxically moves forward, yet remains stuck in its ways, and this is something that the cinema has explicitly begun to addresses self-reflexively in its films – see my analysis of *Om Shanti Om* in Chapter 5.
11. BFI 'Long List' for Top Indian Films Poll', <http://www.bfi.org.uk/features/imagineasia/guide/poll/india/long_list.html> (last accessed 20 December 2007).
12. In 2007 Khan was heavily criticised for endorsing 'Fair-and-Handsome', an Indian men's skin-lightening product. The advertising campaign was considered racist towards naturally darker-skin-toned Indians.
13. *Koffee with Karan*, India, Star One, 26 August 2007, episode 24.
14. See 'Epilogue: The Postmodern . . . in Retrospect' in Hutcheon (2002).
15. For a more detailed account of Matthew's work see Bhattacharya (2005).
16. From *Adhunika*, meaning 'new' or 'modern' and *Antika*, meaning 'beyond'. See Choudhury (2001).
17. It is important to clarify that the postmodern Indian cinema Kapur refers to here is not necessarily the contemporary Bollywood variety. For example, in her book she refers to the films of director Kumar Sahani, who is more aligned with India's parallel cinema movement. However, in her other work, Kapur does consider postmodern sentiments in more commercial art films, such as *Gaja Gamini* (see Kapur, 2001: 12).
18. See my section on *Abhay* in Chapter 5, which acknowledges that this postmodern approach may be transferable to other Indian cinematic forms. See also Peter C. Pugsley's discussion of image-centred aesthetics in Tamil cinema (2013).
19. This book is based on my doctoral thesis (see Wright, 2010), and some of the ideas discussed in it have been published in the special edition *Scope* e-book *Cultural Borrowings: Appropriation, Reworking, Transformation* (Wright, 2009).

1910s–20s Mythologicals
(Films like *Raja Harichandra*, based on Hindu texts: *Ramayana*, *Mahabharata*)
↓

1930s–40s Stunt movies
(Star persona: Fearless Nadia)
↓

1950s Socials: the 'Golden Era'
(Directors: Raj Kapoor, Guru Dutt, Bimal Roy)
↓

[1960s: overlap with 1950s]
↓

1970s 'Angry Man' era and Parallel Cinema movement peak
(Social retribution action films; directors Shyam Benegal and Ritwik Ghatak)
↓

[1980s: overlap with 1970s. Dip in cinema-going due to rise of television]
(Doordarshan channel launches successful *Ramayana* TV series)
↓

1990s NRI and Family Movies
(Diaspora-oriented productions; patriotic, traditionalist, family-oriented 'multi-starrers')
↓

[2000s: continuation of 1990s?]

Figure 2.1: A (hi)story of Indian cinema.

trends and biases of Indian cinema scholarship. The decades that tend to skimmed over in Indian cinema timelines are the ones that have produced politically oriented and more populist films. For example, with only a few or passing references to the rise of star comedian Mehmood, legendary en hero Dev Anand or romance movies such as *Guide*, *Jewel Thief*, *An ing in Paris* and *Waqt*, the 1960s decade of Bombay cinema has gener- been seen as non-distinctive in itself, instead overlapping with the 1950s en era of social satires. Similarly, the 1980s decade is often either seen as ked by the fizzling out of the 1970s Angry Man era, or simply skipped entirely, an omission justified through the supposed dip in film produc- due to the rising popularity of Hindu religious television serials in India e time. Eighties Bombay cinema also has the misfortune of being littered low-brow 'masala' entertainment films,[2] which again are given less critical tion. As a child growing up in the 1980s, I remember this as a time when an film watching distinctively moved into the home owing to the rise of

CHAPTER 2

Anti-Bollywood: Traditional Modes of Studying Indian Cinema

POPULAR TRENDS: THE (HI)STORY OF INDIAN CINEMA

Compared to longer-established studies of other popul[ar cinemas like] Hollywood, Bollywood cinema still seems to be in the [early stages] as an area of academic research in the West, and its histo[ry may] equally still be considered a relatively young practice. At [times,] for Indian film scholars to go back to the beginning of its h[istory] seems logical and essential, so that we may chronologically [begin trac]ing Indian cinema's history and explain how it has evolve[d into its contempo]rary form. Mihir Bose's book *Bollywood: A History* (2007)[, offers] a detailed study of the development of cinema in India o[ver time, from] its first introduction in Bombay in 1896 (courtesy of Franc[e's Lumière broth]ers), all the way to rising film star producer Amir Khan's [2006] commercial blockbuster *Rang De Basanti* (2006). Interes[tingly, despite] an extensive and complex history of filmmaking (and a c[omparably short] period of academic research), it seems that we have alread[y developed a] which many writers, commentators and educators feel th[ey can use as a con]densed version of this history, emphasising the Hindi fi[lm industry's] significant aesthetic and thematic shifts, which can be repr[esented as in] Figure 2.1 overleaf.

Such a history of the development of the Bombay fil[m industry, while] useful for its categorisation and emphasis on the dominan[t film trends over] the decades, clearly contains certain gaps. By focusing our [attention on so-]called 'milestones' in the history of Indian cinema in such [a way, we begin] to see how entire decades (presumably considered less i[mportant or aestheti]cally significant) appear to be pushed aside.[1] But while t[hese apparent gaps] in Indian cinema's history, these gaps do tell us a very int[eresting story]

CHAPTER 2

Anti-Bollywood: Traditional Modes of Studying Indian Cinema

POPULAR TRENDS:
THE (HI)STORY OF INDIAN CINEMA

Compared to longer-established studies of other popular cinemas, such as Hollywood, Bollywood cinema still seems to be in the process of emerging as an area of academic research in the West, and its historical excavation can equally still be considered a relatively young practice. At this stage, the need for Indian film scholars to go back to the beginning of its historical emergence seems logical and essential, so that we may chronologically go about constructing Indian cinema's history and explain how it has evolved into its contemporary form. Mihir Bose's book *Bollywood: A History* (2007), for example, offers a detailed study of the development of cinema in India over 110 years, from its first introduction in Bombay in 1896 (courtesy of France's Lumiere brothers), all the way to rising film star producer Amir Khan's critically acclaimed commercial blockbuster *Rang De Basanti* (2006). Interestingly, despite such an extensive and complex history of filmmaking (and a comparatively short period of academic research), it seems that we have already reached a stage at which many writers, commentators and educators feel they can offer a condensed version of this history, emphasising the Hindi film industry's most significant aesthetic and thematic shifts, which can be represented as shown in Figure 2.1 overleaf.

Such a history of the development of the Bombay film industry, though useful for its categorisation and emphasis on the dominant trends throughout the decades, clearly contains certain gaps. By focusing our attention on the so-called 'milestones' in the history of Indian cinema in such a way, we also come to see how entire decades (presumably considered less innovative and critically significant) appear to be pushed aside.[1] But while they may leave holes in Indian cinema's history, these gaps do tell us a very interesting story about

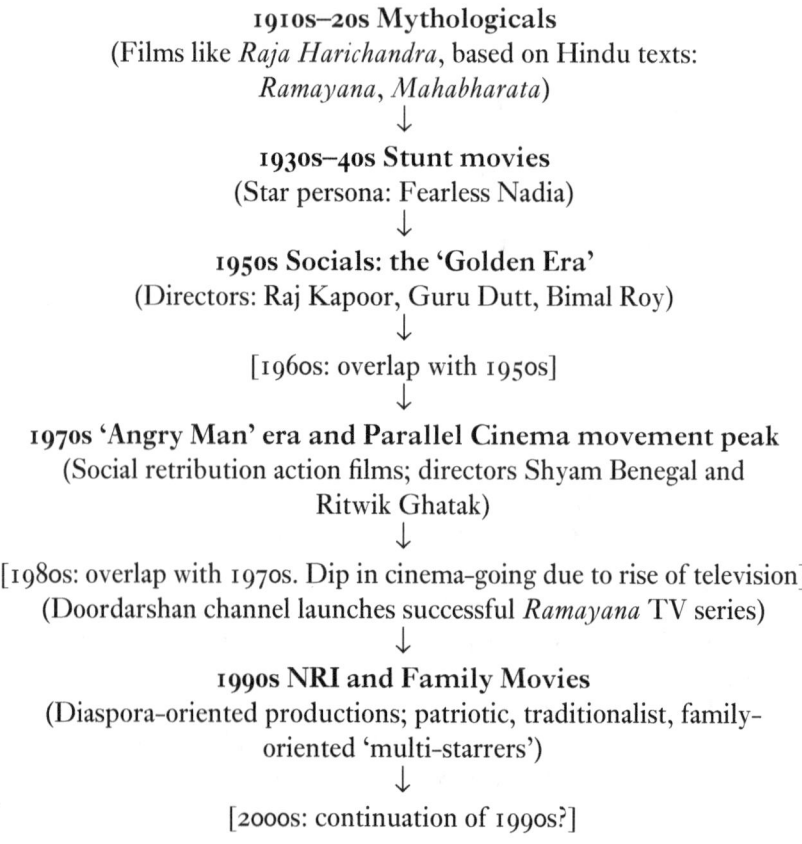

Figure 2.1: A (hi)story of Indian cinema.

the trends and biases of Indian cinema scholarship. The decades that tend to be skimmed over in Indian cinema timelines are the ones that have produced less politically oriented and more populist films. For example, with only a few minor passing references to the rise of star comedian Mehmood, legendary screen hero Dev Anand or romance movies such as *Guide*, *Jewel Thief*, *An Evening in Paris* and *Waqt*, the 1960s decade of Bombay cinema has generally been seen as non-distinctive in itself, instead overlapping with the 1950s golden era of social satires. Similarly, the 1980s decade is often either seen as marked by the fizzling out of the 1970s Angry Man era, or simply skipped over entirely, an omission justified through the supposed dip in film production due to the rising popularity of Hindu religious television serials in India at the time. Eighties Bombay cinema also has the misfortune of being littered with low-brow 'masala' entertainment films,[2] which again are given less critical attention. As a child growing up in the 1980s, I remember this as a time when Indian film watching distinctively moved into the home owing to the rise of home VCRs and VHS piracy, and a time when Amitabh Bachchan (flagship star of the 1970s Angry Man films) still had many people crowding in the film rental section of both India's and the UK's Indian-owned grocery stores. I remember the excitement surrounding Bachchan's new look (a notable departure from the 1970s Angry Man) as gloomy anti-hero *Shahenshah* (1988) or his double role and horse-riding super-heroics in *Toofan* (1989).[3] The same decade saw the emergence of new actors such as college-boy romancer Amir Khan and the on-screen sex symbol and seductress Rekha – both of whom are regarded as icons of the cinema today.

I would argue that the 1960s and 1980s are decades from which we can best study Indian cinema's most popular form of filmmaking – the masala movie – as the genre has prevailed at these points more than over any other ten-year period. Both the 1960s and the 1980s should be considered important phases in Indian cinema's development. They are equally valuable for a study of evolving aesthetics and styles in popular Indian film, even if their films may not always explicitly reveal the national sentiments or socio-political psyche of their audiences at that time. More recently, we can see a similar gap emerging in relation to our understanding of popular Indian cinema in the 2000s. There is a tendency either to view noughties films as a continuance of 1990s NRI[4] films, or simply to focus on a select few texts which posit a political stance or offer up social commentary. Indian films from the 1960s, 1980s and 2000s thus share a lack of direct socio-political engagement and mark an increase in so-called 'run-of-the-mill' populist entertainment. From looking at such a historical narrative of the Bollywood cinema industry, we can begin see how socio-politics and cultural tradition ultimately determine the significance of and scholarly focus on certain periods over others.

The above gaps in Indian cinema's narrative history are apparent in some well-known 'guidebook' essays produced by leading scholars in the field of Indian film criticism. For example, in *The Oxford Guide to Film Studies* (1998) Ashish Rajadhyaksha offers a condensed history, both of Indian cinema – ending with the late 1980s and largely following the structure I described above – and Indian film scholarship (1960s to mid-1990s). He suggests here that Indian films are largely discussed in relation to the following themes and contexts: film policy, government-controlled film production, censorship, New Wave Indian cinema, 1970s 'national emergency' (Angry Man films), Indian modernism, postcolonial theory (nationalism and identity), politics, economics, the India–Pakistan partition (terrorism), and subaltern studies (citizenship, nationalist historiographies). Choosing not to include or address the analysis of textual film form in his account, Rajadhyaksha presents the above research trends as the 'nationalist critical tradition' of Indian film criticism. He explains how orthodox periodisations of Indian cinema serve as 'cinematic equivalents of the 'biography of the nation state' (Rajadhyaksha,

1998: 536), and that India's film history is 'largely written from the stand point of state policy on Indian cinema after 1947', with a critical-theoretical focus on 'realist cinema', 'respectability' and 'political usefulness' (535). Later, in another essay, he affirms that 'film theory has repeatedly demonstrated the crucial role that nationalist-political constructions play in determining narrative and spectatorial practices' (2003: 33).

Many film academics will try to declare that Bollywood films are too culturally specific (requiring a lot of prior cultural knowledge) and suggest these films are perhaps more suitable for sociology-, anthropology-, political-economy- or postcolonialism-based courses. Therefore it is hardly surprising that the majority of prominent Indian cinema scholars tend to have come from a social science rather than a film studies background. These commentators on Indian cinema present themselves (often assertively) as culturologists, historians or cultural philosophers, rather than as film theorists or film analysts. Heidi Pauwels, who has more recently tried to break from the above patterns and traditions of Indian film research and criticism, notes how in such accounts the film text itself is rarely looked on as a work of art. Pauwels comments:

> Ironically, although many of these studies argue for and see themselves as part of a rehabilitation of popular movies as a serious object of study, little sustained attention has been paid to detailed analysis of the films themselves. Sometimes scholars seem mainly interested in the way films may be invoked to address larger debates over theory within specific academic disciplines . . . (Pauwels, 2007: 2)

Social scientists have stated their objective of 'rescuing' Indian cinema scholarship from being limited by over-exhaustive formal analysis and textual parameters. As Rajadhyaksha and Kim Soyoung remark in their essay 'Imagining the cinema anew': 'restricting the investigation to inside the movie theatre and the textual practices we find there is hardly sufficient', and they favour instead looking at the history, spectatorship and distribution of films (Rajadhyaksha and Soyoung, 2003: 7). Furthermore, in her guidebook on Bollywood, Tejaswini Ganti is quick to assert that her work is 'written from the point of view of an anthropologist rather than a film critic' and therefore 'does not undertake qualitative judgements' or much textual analysis of the texts themselves (Ganti, 2004: 4). However, when one actually looks for this supposed excess of formalist study, it is nowhere to be found. On the contrary, there appears to be a fundamental dearth of critical attention paid to Bollywood film form, particularly covering the cinema of the 2000s. One of the few published monographs wholly focusing on popular Hindi film form and style is Rachel Dwyer and Diva Patel's *Cinema India: The Visual Culture of Hindi Film* (2002). But this book's chapters on *mise-en-scène* and visual style are sketchy at best, offering generalised introductory accounts and lacking any in-depth textual analysis. Dwyer and Patel fail to offer any detail or elaborations on Bollywood visual film language (for example, aspects such as tone, pace, cinematography, ornamental framing, image composition, camera work), and they do not account for any of the more recent contemporary aesthetic shifts in Bollywood film style.

This social-science- and history-based scholarship on Indian cinema has indeed helped to draw our attention to and raised our appreciation of a highly populist form of mainstream Indian cinema. But in exploring the cinema within the prism of political, historical and sociological frameworks, the film text itself (in terms of its formal aesthetic and stylistic values) can become peripheral or of secondary importance – simply an accessory to help serve socio-political thoughts and functions. Indian cinema's history is therefore rather exclusively seen as driven or shaped not so much by its aesthetics or technological changes as by, primarily, cultural, political and social factors. This vernacular, although by no means unimportant, can become a great obstacle when we try also to consider and engage with the cinema as an art form in its own right.

TRADITIONAL APPROACHES TO INDIAN FILM: NATIONALISM, DIASPORA, POSTCOLONIALISM AND CULTURAL IDENTITY

As was revealed earlier in Rajadhyaksha's account of Indian film criticism, nationalism prevails as the most common and popular theme in Indian film studies. The idea of popular Bombay cinema as India's 'national cinema' is often justified through its history of governmental control and financing, its entanglement in state policies, its trans-regional appeal and thematic versatility, its ethnic neutrality,[5] and its unique application of mixed Indo languages.[6] But despite Bollywood's mass popularity, a large majority of the total film output in India still comes from the South, and claiming Bollywood as the nation's official film producer leads to many other productive regional cinemas being ignored. There are also problems with the fact that industry and state do not necessarily work to support each other's interests (for an interesting discussion of the lack of co-operation between the industry and state, see Ganti, 2008).

In recent years, the rise of globalisation and the film industry's economic liberalisation have also put this label under some strain. Notions of 'national cinema' are now being broken down and replaced by newer labels such as 'transnational', 'Asian' and 'global' cinema. In fact, determining the national cinema of India has never quite been so straightforward. Previously, Bengali director Satyajit Ray's socio-realist films frequently stood as fitting flagship examples of national Indian cinema, yet his specific regional focus and lack of appeal for mass Indian audiences suggested otherwise. Popular Indian films rarely directly address the nation, and the fact that American cinema is continually adopted as Bollywood's 'blueprint' also makes the study of both pre- and postcolonial Indian cinema problematic (Vitali, 2006).

The nationalist focus of Indian film scholarship has naturally led to certain film texts being studied on film courses and written about more than others. For example, *Mother India* (1957), as national allegory, is perhaps the most written-about Indian film and regularly tops the lists of core texts of most Indian film studies courses. Another popular pair of topics which have been increasingly drawn upon in recent years and are tied up with issues of nation are terrorism and border-crossing – both relating to India's ongoing conflict concerning the Indo-Pak partition. But focusing solely on the national-ness or political function of Hindi films is not only problematic for the mass of commercially successful films produced by Bollywood that do not engage with these issues, but also reductive for the way it can assume the homogenisation and fixing down of Indian identity. On the contrary, the Bollywood cinema of recent years aims not for a straightforward binding of Indian identity and nation, but rather for a fragmentation, confusion or disassembling of identity.

Another popular area of study, branching off from national cinema, is diasporic representation and film viewing. Since the mid-1990s, contemporary Indian cinema has been described chiefly in relation to how it engages with Indian diasporic communities around the world and particularly the UK and USA. Nineties Bollywood saw the emergence of a new so-called 'brat-pack' generation of young filmmakers, including Aditya Chopra and Karan Johar. Johar is perhaps the most illustrious of the group, having been responsible for producing, if not directing, some of the most famous films in the NRI film canon: *Dilwale Dulhaniya Le Jayenge* [aka *DDLJ*] (assistant director), *Kuch Kuch Hota Hai* [aka *K2H2*] (director), and *Kabhi Kushi Kabhie Gham* [aka *K3G*] (director).[7] The early films of these filmmakers usually portray NRIs as either corrupted by their Western cultural lifestyle (in the film *Pardes* [1997] the heroine's US-residing Indian groom is depicted as an amoral, alcoholic, misogynistic rapist) or, in a moment of self-realisation and self-reformation, yearning to return to their true cultural origins (in *DDLJ* characters repeatedly express a desire for the preservation of their culture and Indian identity – most directly seen in the film's opening sequence, where the heroine's father expresses a wish to leave a cold and grey London and go back to the luscious fields of an unspoilt colourful Punjab). Such depictions are largely based on stereotypes and caricatures, forcing the identity of the non-resident Indian into homogenised representations. As Sanjay Srivastava (1998) has pointed out, these films create 'a Westernised Indian-ness, a 'real' identity which is fabricated and contradictory to actual identity' (Srivastava: 196). Nevertheless, film sociologists have demonstrated how these texts correspond to and serve NRI spectators' supposed own desire to reattach themselves to an imaginary India – the 'Desi' homeland:

> ... there has been a re-mapping of the 'Indian' subject ... located not just within the confines of India but also outside the nation-state where countries of actual residence appear to matter little next to the diasporic character's 'essential' identity premised upon origins. (Kaur, 2005: 310)

Pleasure in film viewing for NRI audiences is equated to the text's open patriotism and securing of Indian cultural identity, although some empirical work on audiences suggests that this is not the case and that the pleasure received from such films is based more on aesthetic grounds: the originality of the script, the performance and star power of the actors, and the look of the film in terms of its musical picturisations[8] and fashionable costumes (ibid.). Furthermore, as Kaur tries to prove through her interviews with diasporic viewers, these misrepresentations can at times backfire and actually be rejected by the NRI audience as inaccurate and somewhat cringeworthy.

Although NRI characters are not unfamiliar to Indian cinema (having regularly served as negative stereotypes even before the nineties), the release of *DDLJ* is often seen as the milestone that signalled a shift of agenda in the Indian film industry. *DDLJ* is regarded as a flagship example for the Bollywood NRI film. The film has famously broken records for being the longest consecutively running Hindi movie (by January 2013 it had sustained 900 weeks in a Mumbai theatre[9]), and is a core text used on Indian cinema courses to explore notions of national identity in Hindi cinema. The film broke international records for Bollywood, and was one of the first films to set the majority of its story on location abroad, in Switzerland (although in reality this was achieved much earlier, such as in the 1960s with films like *An Evening in Paris*). *DDLJ* was seen to signal a switch in Bollywood's targeted audience, from local Indians to global NRIs. It perhaps marked the beginning of Bollywood's international profile, although the first Bollywood film to reach the top ten UK box-office charts was *Dil Se* (1998). The NRI-centred plots of films like *DDLJ* transformed the style and form of Hindi films, providing more opportunities for foreign location shoots (outdoor song sequences), an increased use of English, a greater engagement with modernity and displays of extreme wealth, and raising issues surrounding family separation and detachment.

Studies of diasporic cinema have considered splitting it into two different stages: firstly, the 1990s patriotic Bollywood nostalgia film, and secondly, the rise of films from NRI diasporic filmmakers such as Mira Nair, Gurinder Chadha, Deepa Mehta and Srinivas Krishna (Desai, 2004). However, the fact that the Bollywood NRI genre has evolved in recent years requires us to now consider adding a third kind of cinema to this category. The films of directors such as Karan Johar are held to be prime examples of the first stage of the Bollywood NRI genre, yet it is interesting how Johar's later films such as *Kabhi Alvida Naa Kehna* (aka *KANK*, 2006), *Kal Ho Naa Ho* (aka *KHNH*, 2003) and *My Name is Khan* (aka *MNIK*, 2010) do not quite fit this model and complicate the supposed NRI pursuit of soulful Indian-ness. For example, we can read *K3G* as a highly ironic critique of Indian values (see Hogan, 2008: 160–93), while Johar's subsequent three films can be seen to embrace a fragmented Indian identity that does not wish to return to its roots. Characters in *KHNH* now celebrate the split or diffusion of Indian and Western identity and are happy to remain in New York, and in the case of *KANK* there is no mention of India at all. On a more general level, there seems to be a more Western-friendly outlook and positive view of Western cultural consumption in these films. Even in *MNIK*, which describes how terrorism has disrupted the lives of the US-residing diaspora, there is a strong desire for assimilation and the focus shifts towards the need to act out one's rights as a diasporic US citizen.

Discussions surrounding NRI representation in Hindi films can tend to lead us to the assumption that these films work on the level of patriotism and cultural preservation, but I think there is also room here for self-critique, as I will reveal later when I discuss the fragmentation of Indian identity (of both NRI and resident Indians) in recent Bollywood films. Some scholars are more cynical and warn of how far this diaspora argument can be taken. For example, Kaur states that many commercial Hindi NRI films often fail on the level of misrepresentation, and therefore

> it is too glib and cursory to say that Bollywood enables a religion-like nostalgia for people of the Indian diaspora ... It is also specious to presume that Indian popular films provide a 'shared culture' that links everyone who is ethnically Indian as a general rule. (Kaur, 2005: 313–14)

The diaspora approach, for all its revelations about Bollywood's internationalisation, has been complicated, if not superseded, by new agendas and modes of representation. Contemporary Bollywood mediates and celebrates more significantly the experience of the (post)modern Indian and his or her fragmentation. Instead of simply aspiring towards caricaturing and capitalising on the diasporic experience, newer Bollywood films are now invested in the questioning and blurring of identity, rendering the previous separation of 'foreigner' and 'desi' problematic. Owing to the somewhat exhaustive output of diaspora-related work on post-1990s Hindi cinema, I have chosen to shift the focus away from the NRI. Instead, I draw attention to aspects of the film text that operate outside issues of migration, for not everything in Bollywood these days is determined and shaped by the diaspora. I aim to bring attention back to Bollywood's textuality and, in doing so, also consider its effect on other emerging targeted audiences within modern developing India and the non-Indian global market.

Postcolonial theory has also provided a fairly solid backbone to much Indian film scholarship. Postcolonial approaches to Indian cinema have helped to trace and explain the industry's shifts during India's pre-colonial, colonial and post-independence eras. As my own study engages with postmodern approaches, it overlaps with and shares similar interests to postcolonialism (such as the desire to rewrite or reconstruct past histories and the use of textual hybridity), but it also seeks to offer something beyond the postcolonial perspective. The application of postcolonial criticism can present problems for the study of contemporary Bollywood cinema, particularly when it calls for a righteous return to cultural autonomy and tradition instead of addressing the more complex emerging modes of resistance to cultural authenticity accounted for in my own research. Postcolonial issues are further addressed in Chapters 4 and 5 in relation to postmodernism and postmodern Bollywood.

Cultural studies approaches have also been prevalent in Indian film studies and have also tended to help tie Bollywood films to issues of national identity. However, in contrast to the nationalism-focused discussions mentioned above, cultural studies of Bollywood films differ by placing a greater emphasis on and investing more in religious thematics as opposed to state politics by drawing attention to mythology, ritual customs, and particular culturally-driven signifying and belief systems (Dissanayake, 1988: 1). The cultural studies approach is important in helping explain how Indians construct, maintain, and respond to certain meaning systems that operate through the medium of film. However, by introducing postmodernism into the equation, I take this a step further and examine how Indians also *deconstruct* their own cinematic culture and meaning systems, as well as those of others (such as the West and Hollywood). My own investigation reveals an increased playfulness, inversion, subversion and questioning of such systems. For example, the tension between tradition and modernity is often considered a central theme in contemporary Asian cinema within cultural studies. But rather than seeing these two themes as polarised within Indian films (where modernity often represents the threat), my postmodern reading reveals how the lines between them have become erased or blurred. This is best seen in Bollywood's recent blending of traditional mythological and science-fiction codes to convey an ambiguous, if not pessimistic, outlook on traditional Indian values (as explored in Chapter 5 through my reading of *Koi . . . Mil Gaya*).

Some cultural sociologists have even equated Bollywood's recent internationalisation with Hollywood hegemony, viewing the cinema's global move as a threat to its cultural authenticity (see Dissanayake, 1988). Bollywood's more recent globalised texts often fail to feature in cultural studies readings, perhaps because they do not present themselves as straightforward cultural political tools or 'indigenous instruments of communication' (ibid.: 3). They are too explicitly and self-consciously steeped in their desire to make money as commercial hybridised products, and as Wimal Dissanayake has confirmed, Indian films are deemed valuable only as windows to Asian culture and not for their artistic merit, unlike the 'good artistic films' of Satyajit Ray or Yasujirō Ozu (ibid.: 7). I would argue that as Bollywood has become increasingly conscious of its capacity for cultural hybridity, it has used this to its advantage. Through my own analysis, I determine how the recent cross-cultural 'inauthentic' influences in Bollywood films do not simply set out to sabotage Indian cinematic culture, but instead also enrich and affirm it. These postmodern-esque film texts, particularly in the form of remakes, allow Bollywood to shift between Hollywood universality and cultural specificity, maintaining a unique film language as *original plagiarisms*.

POPULAR DEFINITIONS: GUIDES TO BOLLYWOOD CINEMA

The publication of several introductory guidebooks on Bollywood since 2000 has paved the way for many further and higher education courses on popular Indian cinema in the West. These first-hand resources prove ideal for new audiences and novices seeking to grasp the (once daunting) general mechanics and peculiarities of the Bombay film industry. But some of these comprehensive guides have misled readers towards restrictive (if not outmoded and derogatory) definitions of the cinema they seek to understand. Wimal Dissanayake and K. Moti Gokulsing's *Indian Popular Cinema: A Narrative of Cultural Change* (1998) is one such text, which, in its opening chapter, promotes its use as an introductory reading of Indian cinema for future Western media and film studies courses. Unfortunately, the book pays poor attention to styles and techniques in popular films beyond their musical dimensions and a handful of outmoded genres, here labelled as the mythological, the devotional, the social drama, and the erotic or romantic drama. The authors fail to unpick the 'emotional excess', 'flashy' (32) and 'obtrusive' editing (92) and 'melodrama' of popular films, or explain the possible intentions behind and desired effect of their 'lack of realism', 'extravagant use of colour' and 'self-conscious use of sound' (32). Instead, the authors' focus on style and form is reserved for artistic films outside the remit of popular Indian filmmaking, which are explored in more detail and celebrated for their sequential editing, balanced framing, centred shots and image continuity. In separating the two, Dissanayake and Gokulsing suggest that art cinema's purpose is to innovate and provoke, while the popular cinema's is to conform. As pure escapism, Bollywood is not associated with any kind of aesthetic politics. Themes such as selfhood, tradition versus modernity, alienation, and the impact of Westernisation are deemed to only find expression in the artistic cinema of Ray et al. (32). While the work of art film *auteurs* such as Ray (who is described by the authors as India's greatest filmmaker) is discussed, the directors of Bollywood are presented as more homogeneous and therefore not distinctive enough in their technique to deserve individual attention – with the exception of Mani Ratnam, whose broad directorial work is only explored through a narrow selection of his most controversial and politically edgy films. Thus, despite their book's title and opening promise to present and promote popular Indian cinema, Dissanayake and Gokulsing's reading is driven by a partiality for 'serious' cinema. In their conclusion, the authors assert that popular cinema is best understood in relation to artistic cinema (136), which does nothing to assist the West's already fuzzy definitions of Bollywood. The authors' discussion of new popular Indian cinema, while hinting at its frenetic MTV and hybridised Hollywood visual style, also has a rather negative outlook. Contemporary Bollywood is pessimistically described as the 'cardboard age' – an error which is later corrected in the 2004 revision of the book. The second edition (Dissanayake and Gokulsing, 2004) includes an additional chapter noting the 'broad concerns and technical attributes . . . [and] the narrative grammar of Hindi mainstream cinema [which] has metamorphosed significantly' over the last decade (142). Here the authors note and begin to appreciate contemporary Bollywood cinema's inherent contradictions and polysemic nature, its complex blending of Hollywood-style gloss and indigenous narrative ethos, its sexual openness, its potential for creative innovation via a fresh breed of directors,[10] and its conflict between serving Western or modern material needs and negotiating cultural identity (143-4).

Tejaswini Ganti's *Bollywood: A Guidebook to Popular Hindi Cinema* provides a little more emphasis on recent changes in Bollywood, although her account still paints a fairly grey picture of contemporary popular Indian cinema. Discussing contemporary Bollywood through its corporatisation since the year 2000, Ganti (2004: 88) presents the cinema as the antithesis of the industry's nostalgically mourned-for 1950s golden era, which is conversely seen as embodying creativity, originality, talent, quality and sincerity (28). She typifies newer Bollywood films through their 'matter-of-factness', their 'essentially conservative outlook . . . regardless of their cosmopolitan and MTV inspired style' (41), and their continuation of nationalist trends (emphasising their thematic focus on terrorism and Pro-Hindu politics). But Ganti does highlight important changes in the cinema's stylistic presentation: fluid camera movements and rapid editing are mixed with more traditional frontal encounter or frontal aesthetics[11] to create a unique hybrid style (144).

However, ultimately the author's aesthetic account falls short owing to the socio-anthropological perspective she chooses to apply to her analysis. For example, her explanation for Bollywood cinema's distinctively rich saturation of colours sees this not as a matter of aesthetic choice, but rather as a practical requirement to overcome the poor projection conditions at screenings in Indian villages (143). As other film researchers have discovered, colour plays an important part in the coding of Hindi films, guiding viewer pleasure and shaping the aesthetic agenda of the films (see Patrick Colm Hogan's cognitive study of colour in Hindi films [2008: 194–249]). It can even serve as a filmmaker's stylistic trademark, as in the case of Sanjay Leela Bhansali (see my analysis of Bhansali's *Devdas* in Chapter 7).

'BOLLYWOOD': THE DOUBLE-EDGED WORD

> Bollywood, n. Brit./blwd/US/bliwd/[Humorous blend of the name of *Bombay* (see BOMBAY n.) and HOLLYWOOD n.] The Indian film industry, based in Bombay; Bombay regarded as the base of this industry. (*The Oxford English Dictionary Online* [dictionary.oed.com])

Indian cinema guidebooks will often begin with a proclamation that the Western world has finally 'discovered' popular Indian cinema through its global marketing under the guise of 'Bollywood' (Ganti, 2004: 2). But these commentaries reveal an ambiguous relationship with the term, which has been both exploited and sneered at by industry professionals and film scholars alike. The word 'Bollywood' can still be a taboo term which many writers on Indian cinema (such as Dissanayake and Gokulsing) have, with good intentions, tried wholeheartedly to reject or shake off in haste. Until more recently, much of the published work on Bollywood cinema has capitalised on the word by using it in book titles and on cover faces, while the authors of these texts have, within the opening pages, felt the need to offer justifications for its use through lengthy footnotes (see Pauwels, 2007: 43) or to frequently replace it with substitutes such as 'Bombay', 'Hindi' or 'popular Indian' cinema (see Ganti, 2004). But these alternative terms can be equally problematic: 'popular Indian cinema' is too vague and nation-centric, failing to emphasise the industry's global, transnational and diasporic ventures; 'hi-fi' or 'popular Hindi film' misleadingly associates all films with Hindi-centred dialogue, ignoring the fact that many of the films (especially their song sequences) include Urdu and Islamic metaphors and English dialogue; and 'Bombay film' is problematic again owing to the industry's numerous transnational and trans-regional productions. Of course, 'Bollywood' also brings its own complications by conversely trying to be all-encompassing. As Madhava Prasad (2003) notes, the phrase becomes an 'empty signifier', collapsing together and thus suppressing the individuality and variety of films produced in India:

> ... those who have invested in earlier models of the Indian popular cinema – the 'so many cinemas' model, the folk culture model, the 'yeh-to-public-hai-yeh-sab-janti-hai'[12] model, the regressive 'pulse of the people' model, the ideological model, art versus popular, and so on, should feel slightly resentful of this development which threatens to absorb their own special areas into its commodious (because ill-defined) purview. (Prasad, 2003: 1)

Quietly avoiding use of the term in his *Encyclopaedia of Indian cinema* (co-authored with Paul Willemen, 1999), Ashish Rajadhyaksha later outwardly rejects it in his article 'The "Bollywoodization" of the Indian Cinema' (2003), suggesting that the word has little to do with the actual film industry and instead signals a rather separate cultural phenomenon created by surrounding ancillary paraphernalia (theatre shows, art exhibitions, fashion culture). Rajadhyaksha argues that 'Bollywood' in fact signals the demise of the Bombay film industry, where marketing and product placement reduce cinema to 'only to a memory, a part of the nostalgia industry' (38). It therefore seems that the phrase 'Bollywood', despite all its commercial appeal and lure, has become a subject of shame and denial within film academia, and I believe that this ambivalence has in turn served to suppress our understanding of the cinema that the term alludes to. While the word may indeed stand for a cultural trend, fad or fashion, I believe it also serves as an artistic term: a marker of a particular kind of visual aesthetic phenomenon that is representative of a contemporised Indian film style. Rajadhyaksha's call to 'drive a wedge' (31) between Bollywood and the Indian cinema is, I think, in itself damaging and unhelpful as the word offers us great insight into the cinema in its contemporary form.

The term's origins are disputable. Some believe it was phonetically transposed from 'Tollywood' in the late thirties (Prasad, 2003). Others argue it was self-created by the Bombay industry (Bhaumik, 2007) or India's English-language press (Ganti, 2004). Actors within the industry have dismissed and resented it as a Western term created for kitsch value (Malcolm, 2002) or for referring to Indian films as simply rip-offs of Hollywood texts (see director Subhash Ghai in Hardy [2002] and actor Ajay Devgan in Prasad [2003]). However, it is important to note that many of the actors and directors who once rejected the term, including megastars Shah Rukh Khan and Amitabh Bachchan, have since accepted it, adopting it during the international marketing and promotion of their own films.

The *Oxford English Dictionary* has cited the first publication of the term 'Bollywood' as occurring in a British crime writer's mystery novel, *Filmi, Filmi,*

Inspector Ghote (Keating, 1976), although a handful of Indian film journalists have also tried to claim they coined it. Whatever the case, these mysterious and disputable origins of the term confirm it as something that crept up behind the backs of industry professionals and academics without invitation, and emphasise the cinema's refusal to be pinned down and categorised. The word's loose application and somewhat inappropriate nature (the 'B' in the word becomes ever more problematic with the city's name-change from Bombay to Mumbai) can also be seen to reflect the informality and displacement associated with the cinema. The fact that 'Bollywood', unlike its Western American counterpart, does not refer to an actual geographical location set in wooded hills indicates the homelessness of the cinema. Bollywood's transferral to the global international market means that it does not necessarily exist in any physical space as a studio-based industry. The word therefore indicates both the cinema's fragmented production and the trans-locational experiences of the characters within its more recent films. Some have therefore chosen to specifically use 'Bollywood' to refer to a transnational cinema 'at once located in the nation, but also out of the nation in its provenance, orientation and outreach' (Kaur and Sinha, 2005: 16).

As a portmanteau term, 'Bollywood' indicates an important dialogue between two of the world's biggest cinemas and, in fact, hints at their inseparability. It expresses the recent concrete indigenisation of Hollywood aesthetic modes in Indian films and the cinema's tendency towards cultural fusion or blending. As such, the term also alerts us to the cinema's problematic relationship with cultural authenticity, indicating the loss of identity and nationally or culturally distinctive boundaries within its films. 'Bollywood' is often blamed for wrongly drawing associations between Indian cinema and Hollywood and for implying that popular Indian films simply produce inferior copies of popular American cinema. Interestingly, Kaushik Bhaumik (2007) has revealed how the appropriation of Western cinematic modes in Indian cinema in fact precedes the creation of the word 'Bollywood', tracing Hollywood influences as far back as the early 1900s (although I later argue that this kind of appropriation differs from that of newer Bollywood texts, particularly with regard to narrative remaking and the adoption of certain stylistic codes). Nevertheless, Bollywood is continually perceived as a pejorative term placing Indian cinema forever in the American film industry's shadow. Its hijacking of an essentially Western term also hints at the Indian cinema's 'indulgent lampooning' of English dialogue in order to assist its integration into a Eurocentric world and its desire to appeal to its growing middle-class audience (Prasad, 2008: 43). But what may at first appear to simply be Indian cinema apeing the West can in fact conversely be a strategy for the 'reproduction of difference . . . which the industry itself, in its current reflexive moment, is responding to' (Prasad, 2003). 'Bollywood' simultaneously presents Indian cinema as imitative and derivative of *and* alternative to the dominant Hollywood idiom – something which I explore in more detail later in my analysis of Bollywood-Hollywood remakes. As Bhaumik comments, 'Bombay films are [also] a subversion of Western cultural and political expectations, carving out their own autonomous history outside Hollywood' (2007: 202).

To use the word 'Bollywood' is to continually be conscious of the shadow of Western cinema, which forever looms over popular Indian cinema as a constant source of comparison and value-marking by film critics and academics across the world. It connotes the Indian film industry's current obsession with capitalism, mass production and celebrity populism. Furthermore, the hybrid nature of the term conveys Indian cinema's own inherent hybridity, particularly in recent years when its films have outwardly meshed together multiple cultures and identities and negotiated between traditional Indian-ness and Western modernity. The linguistic similarity between the two film industries also indicates a hidden imperialist agenda: Indian cinema's (perhaps naive) desire for super-power and aspirations to replace Hollywood as the dominant global cinema.

At its most basic level as a humorous blend of terms, 'Bollywood' refers to the jest and ridicule which the cinema both embodies and is subjected to by its harshest critics. It refers to a cinema that is not taken seriously and is often mocked – it 'denotes the user's distance from the object, a non-participatory passion for description' (Prasad, 2003). Most importantly, as word-pastiche, it is an indicator of intertextual playfulness, unabashed plagiarism, cultural appropriation and parody. As Madhava Prasad has wisely pointed out in 'This Thing Called Bollywood' – a more optimistic account of the word's appearance and usage – the change of name might indicate a change in reality too:

> . . . we do find, do we not, that this cinema has given us, in the last decade or so, a large number of films which may be said to constitute a new genre of sorts, which has been, moreover, the staple of the new global Bollywood presence. (Prasad, 2003: 2)

As Prasad later argues in extending his previous discussion in 'Surviving Bollywood' (2008), 'Bollywood' is an important indicator of *change* within the Indian film industry, specifically in terms of contemporary Indian cinema's increased bilingualism, its internationally educated directors, its shifting notions of Indian identity via globalisation, its textual struggles and contradictions on the level of representation, its increased commoditisation as a 'fetish object' (50), and, most importantly of all, its now inherent self-referential exploitation as a global brand:

> 'Bollywood' also signals the advent of a certain reflexivity, becoming a cinema for itself as it were, recognizing its own unique position in the

world, the contrastive pleasures and values that it represents vis-à-vis Hollywood. This reflexivity is as much a form of self-awareness as it is a know-how that enables the Hindi film to reproduce itself for a market that demands its perpetuation as a source of cultural identity. (ibid.: 50)

NATIONAL, THIRD, WORLD, ASIAN, GLOBAL OR TRANSNATIONAL CINEMA?

Our perceptions, understanding of and critical approaches towards popular Indian cinema will be shaped by how it is categorised. Particularly with its recent move into global territory, the concept of Bollywood cinema as 'national', 'third' or 'world' cinema has been complicated if not compromised, inviting newer and more elusive labels such as 'Asian', 'global' and 'transnational'. These latter labels, although arriving with their own set of problems, have helped broaden our understanding of the changes that have taken place within the industry in recent years.

When perceived as 'third cinema', Indian films are predominantly analysed as instruments of social change and 'nation-bound' national allegories (Virdi, 2003: 4), with a focus on political themes drawn from a narrow selection of exemplary canonised classical texts. Anne Tereska Ciecko (2006) has criticised this category for homogenising all non-Western cinema, arguing that it does not suit Bollywood's levels of production. This includes its textual diversity, its obsession with luxurious wealth, happy endings and big budgets, and its investment in modernity, capitalism and multinationalism (Ciecko, 21–2). Furthermore, as James Chapman (2003) also suggests, it becomes very difficult to present Indian cinema as an 'alternative' to Hollywood, owing to the cinema's own governance, dominance and mass popularity within India. Thus, some argue that Bollywood is much better suited to the category of 'first cinema' owing to its commercial studio base and Hollywood-style production model (Chaudhuri, 2005), and that it is no longer humble enough to fit the 'world of the disadvantaged' model of world cinema (Bhaumik, 2006: 196), unlike the past works of Guru Dutt, Raj Kapoor or Ray.

The category 'world cinema' has also faced much scrutiny recently as an outdated film concept, particularly with the increase in transnational film production. As Chapman notes, world cinema has traditionally given privilege and preference to texts that visibly differentiate themselves from Hollywood, while those cinemas (like contemporary Bollywood) which share common traits or model themselves on Hollywood fall into a trap of being marginalised (Chapman: 35). Similarly, Bhaumik has commented that 'any popular cinema without art-house, realist or genre credentials on the West's terms stands condemned to a marginal position in the mainstream' (Bhaumik, 2006:

195). Following Rajadhyaksha's concept of 'Bollywoodization', he argues that Bollywood's world profile is suspect as its impact and presence in the West has been non-cinematic, or rather *extra*-cinematic. Bollywood's marginal success as a recognisable world cinema is therefore regarded as purely a by-product of marketing and political multiculturalism (194), as the cinema fails to satisfy world cinema's taste for high modernism, realism, genre, serious subjects and political edginess. Bhaumik suggests that Bollywood can only be accommodated if the West expands its rather restrictive criteria of 'good' world cinema.

Unlike world cinema, the 'Asian cinema' model has more explicitly accommodated both popular and niche (artistic or cult) texts and brought into play a larger variety of identities and subject positions (Ciecko, 2006). But some commentators have also warned how the use of the prefix 'Asian' can be accused of ghettoisation and of 'Otherising' Eastern cinema. It is often posited away from or against Hollywood, thus reinforcing the centrality or 'false universalism' of American cinema in film studies (Yoshimoto, 2006). Such arguments fail to account for the fact that the mainstream cinema under the umbrella of 'Asian' (including Hong Kong and Bollywood blockbusters) also often engages in a complex dialogue-exchange with Hollywood on the level of textual style and form, which cannot be ignored.

There has recently been a boom in published criticism on 'global' contemporary Indian cinema, seen most notably in recurring titles such as *Brand Bollywood: A New Global Entertainment Order* (Bose, 2006), *Once upon a time in Bollywood: The Global Swing of Hindi Cinema* (Jolly, Wahwani and Barretto, 2007), *Global Bollywood* (Kavoori and Punathambekar, 2008), *Global Bollywood: Travels of Hindi Song and Dance* (Gopal and Moorti, 2008), *Untimely Bollywood: Globalization and India's New Media Assemblage* (Rai, 2009), *Bollywood and Globalization: Indian Popular Cinema, Nation, and Diaspora* (Mehta and Pandharipande, 2010) and *Bollywood and Globalization: The Global Power of Popular Hindi Cinema* (Karan and Schaefer, 2013). For the most part, these texts tend to focus on diasporic filmmaking and crossover films produced outside of the Bollywood film industry, but a number of these global studies have also helped elevate the analysis of Bollywood's dialogue-exchanges with and influences from other cinemas. For example, Gurbir Jolly sees globalisation as India's 'invitation to the Anglosphere' and its opportunity to both generate wealth and 'civilize India' (Jolly, 2007: xiv). Other scholars see this global move as an opportunity to learn how the cinema negotiates, fixes and unfixes national narratives in a global context (Kaur and Sinha, 2005). But the national is no longer Bollywood's only concern, with many of its seemingly nation-centred films now additionally seeking 'international authentication' (see for example Susan Dewey on the Oscar expectations surrounding *Lagaan* [Dewey, 2007: 11]). The 'global cinema' approach may be one of the latest developments in Bollywood studies, but scepticism towards this newer form of cinema is still abundant. For example, Ashok Raj perceives Indian cinema's global move as a 'curse' and calls for a nostalgic return to a previous cinematic era:

> The macho heroes and sensuous heroines are . . . worshipped for their . . . ad-model looks. And as these third-generation actors are part of the new materialism and representatives of the prevailing yuppie culture – they are simply not equipped to evoke the awe, the dignity and the grandeur of the era of our cinema's earlier legendary artists [. . .] the future Indian film will continue to be a reflection of the profound crisis of values being faced by society, which will only grow more complex in the future. (Raj, 2004: 802, 804)

Similarly, Monika Mehta (2007) pessimistically sees the global as the national in sheep's clothing. She argues that the film industry's recent economic liberalisation is simply a way of the state reinscribing its authority and values. But Mehta's argument is largely directed towards the diaspora and family films of the late 1990s and does not account for the noticeable apathy towards social and political discourse that follows in later films (Mehta: 22–3).[13]

The most recent (and arguably the most appropriate) category used to explore Bollywood's current manifestation is that of 'transnational' cinema. Popular Indian cinema has become infused with different cultures through a variety of means. Not only has it appropriated other cultures in its formal aesthetics and subject matter – setting its entire film story abroad in foreign locations such as South Africa (*Race*), Australia (*Salaam Namaste*) and Miami (*Dostana*), but it has also invested in loaning its talents to produce films for other countries (for example, Farah Khan's choreography work in Chinese musical *Perhaps Love*) and, conversely, employing Hong Kong martial arts experts for its own action films (*Krrish*). Bollywood is also becoming increasingly transnational through having its films co-financed by Hollywood conglomerates such as Sony Pictures, (*Saawariya*), Walt Disney (*Roadside Romeo*), Warner Brothers (*Chandni Chowk to China*) and most significantly, Twentieth Century Fox (*My Name Is Khan, Dum Maaro Dum, Bol Bachchan, Raaz 3*).[14] Despite initial fears of possible ethnocentrism, film scholars have slowly begun to investigate cross-cultural and inter-cultural play within these transnational films (see Mitra [1999]; Desai [2004]; Govil et al. [2005]; Bhaumik [2007]).

Transnational cinema has particularly been considered an important object of investigation for the way in which it self-orientalises through an 'autoethnographic gaze' (Rey Chow, cited in Chaudhuri: 97) – consciously exploiting, exoticising, parodying and critiquing both home and foreign cultural conventions (as demonstrated in my later analysis of *Om Shanti Om* and *Kaante*). It has enabled Bollywood cinema not only to negotiate Indian identity among multiple identities, but also to dismantle and *remystify* Indian-ness. Most importantly for my own investigation, transnational cinemas have been identified as operating through, occupying and serving postmodern principles. Shohini Chaudhuri has noted the widespread influence of postmodern aesthetics in various contemporary world cinemas (particularly MTV-style filmmaking practices), which in China, for instance, have signalled 'the full-blown arrival of postmodern culture . . . hand-in-hand with its cities' consumer lifestyles boom' (100) and, paradoxically, in conjunction with the rise of modernity (10). In her discussion of recent commercial Chinese transnational cinema which has tried to resist the realist conventions of sixth-generation Chinese films, Chaudhuri notes several markedly postmodern cultural traits, such as the rejection of excessive politics and the blurring of (American) popular and (European) artistic styles (99). She also refers to the postmodern pastiche present in contemporary Thai cinema, best exemplified through its recent Westerns. We can find similar postmodern traits within contemporary Bollywood films and, whereas national cinema approaches to popular Indian cinema looked at the filmic construction of nation, such a postmodern reading helps us consider the way in which transnational Bollywood films *dissolve* nation and Indian identity.

Whilst 'Asian cinema' may be oversimplified and 'third' and 'world' cinema have become outmoded, it seems that 'global' and 'transnational' are the categories that are being adopted in haste owing to the indisputable impact of globalisation upon Bollywood filmmaking processes. But while the 'global' is still a fuzzy term, the 'transnational' draws a convenient line from the national to the global in specifically addressing co-production. The transnational also refers to cross-cultural exchange on the level of textuality. Whilst a film like *Chandni Chowk to China* is a transnational film on all levels – transcending geographical boundaries in its production (produced by a Hollywood studio and filmed in Chinese studios and locations) as well as incorporating conventions from Hong Kong martial arts films and Bollywood musicals – a film like *Koi . . . Mil Gaya* may initially only be seen as a nationalist film, having being made in India and backed by the Hindu Bharatiya Janata political party. However, as I later reveal in my analysis of the film, *Koi . . . Mil Gaya*'s adoption of Hollywood narrative and generic codes still suggests some sort of transnational exchange in operation. New perspectives on Indian cinema in its global form are further explored in the next chapter.

DISPLEASURE AND UNPOPULARITY IN THE WEST

Popular Indian cinema had been subject to marginalisation well before its kitsch Bollywood status. In a 1949 *UNESCO Courier* article reviewing India's various artistic practices, Kwaja Ahmad Abbas contemplates how the cinema's intelligibility and success with Euro-American international audiences was 'doubtful', and that a specialised audience could only be secured with the 'right kind' of 'good Indian films'. While claiming to offer a list of such films, which represented a 'complete cross-section of . . . Indian cinema', Abbas places a firm emphasis on historicals, non-commercial realistic feature documentaries, 'dignified' mythologicals (that had 'none of the tinselly gaudiness' associated with some of the more typical films of that genre) and artistic 'masterpieces' depicting social themes in feudal society – offering 'simplicity', 'fidelity' and a 'humanistic approach'. Many of the films in Abbas's recommendation are valued for their 'utter realism' and their holding up a 'mirror to Indian life'. They are 'daring and progressive', with a 'dignified restraint'. The few popular texts that are considered worthy of merit are specifically 'Hollywood-style melodramas', whose 'colourful pageantry would appeal to the Western audiences . . . notions of the exotic [East]'. No recognition is given here of Indian cinema having its own popular dominant alternative to the Hollywood melodrama. Abbas warns his Western readers that they should not approach Indian films with the same expectation as that of Hollywood products, and should instead expect a certain level of frustration at the over-lengthiness, exasperating musical basis and slow tempo of the films. Interestingly, Abbas suggests how these films 'will acquire the nervous tension and mounting tempo of a Hollywood thriller when the impact of industrialism has created the same psychological atmosphere in India as in England and America' (Abbas, 1949: 8). Abbas was certainly onto something here. Global capitalism has indeed led to a shift in tempo within Bollywood films, although not necessarily matching that of Hollywood films. Abbas's review indicates early on how Western pursuits of realism, logic and seriousness have served to marginalise popular forms of Indian cinema. Not all Western responses to commercial Indian films have been negative, but I would argue that even the positive discourse can be vague, non-specific and kitschy. It is celebratory, yet fails to critically explore the films beyond their bizarre novelty value. For example, as writer Justine Hardy describes almost fetishistically in *Vanity Fair*'s 2002 special-edition 'salute' to popular Indian cinema,[15] Bollywood offers 'dreams where everything is over-lit, over-fed and neo-nausea bright. This sweaty technicolour hallucination, this spinning core of Hindi film, is forever in your face here at flesh-on-Arabia sea' (Hardy, 2002: 12).

Western film reviewers seem to be the usual suspects contributing to the wave of negative censure Bollywood has received over the years, and this is something that has already been explored by Rosie Thomas in her landmark 1985 *Screen* article 'Indian cinema: Pleasures and Popularity', and later in a more contemporary context by Kaushik Bhaumik (2006). Thomas's article is possibly the most widely cited piece of academic critical writing on popular

Hindi film today. Despite being written three decades ago, it still finds its way into almost every introductory university course and guidebook on Indian cinema, so much so that it could be described as Indian film studies' (somewhat less contested) answer to 'Visual Pleasure and Narrative Cinema' (Mulvey, 1975). Thomas's essay is essentially an introduction to Indian cinema's place in the Western context. It candidly conveys the fact that mainstream Bombay cinema had, up until the mid-1980s, remained generally ignored, ridiculed or misunderstood by Western critics, and that such a condescending reception was ultimately facilitated by upper-middle-class intellectuals, critics, and governing bodies within India who 'shamefacedly disavow[ed]' and made 'defensive apologies' on behalf of the cinema (118). As a consequence, Indian cinema's recognition in the First World leaves something to be desired. Popular Hindi films are Otherised (more so than some other Asian cinemas) and are defined by extreme difference as a markedly 'alternative' marginal mode of cinema. Indian films are generally 'unseen' and 'unspoken' of. They are met with 'arrogant silence' and 'complacent ignorance'. Those who do take the opportunity to watch the films dismiss them with 'patronising amusement' or 'facetious quips' accompanied by an assortment of excuses and complaints (as noted below), attacking various aspects of the films' stylistic and formal construction (117). Throughout her article, Thomas offers us a wide vocabulary of terms that have been used (by different people, at different times, in different contexts) to describe popular Indian films. Together, these descriptions can offer us a deeper understanding of what it is exactly about Indian cinema that repels the Westerner (both critic and spectator). In an attempt to explore this displeasure with more clarity, these critical comments and phrases collated by Thomas have been presented in the table below and grouped under the key aspects of a film to which they refer.

As the above collected comments (which Thomas largely extracts from various Western film review magazines) reveal, Indian cinema unashamedly stands in opposition to the very things Western critics tend to value in cinematic works of art: a concrete and carefully paced narrative; textual depth of meaning, preferably with socio-political undertones; a commitment to authenticity and originality; a gracefulness and gentility in execution; characters with robust psychological profiles and clear agendas or functions; a genuine, metered display of emotion; a sense of realism conveyed through plausible scenarios and lucid distinctions between the real and the fantastical (something *perceivably* real); and a certain obligation towards historical, geographical and spatial accuracy. More importantly, these traits relate to those often attributed to criticisms of postmodern art – depthlessness, meaninglessness, fragmentation, unoriginality and recycling, stylistic excess, presentation of the sublime, anti-politics, unconventional representations of reality, and anti-intellectualism (each is explored in more detail in Chapter 5).

Narrative content: *Style/image over narrative; depthless*

- Emphasis on spectacular events and songs at expense of narrative
- Lack of story

Story comprehension: *Meaninglessness*

- Mystification
- Nonsensical plots
- Senselessness
- Convoluted plot

Structure and pacing: *Fragmentation*

- Elephantine capers (slow movement of narrative)
- Lengthy duration

Originality and quality: *Recycling; repetition; inauthenticity*

- Poor imitations of Hollywood film conventions and texts
- Mediocre
- Sub-standard
- Formulaic

Tone and performance: *Sublime; exhibitionism; disclosure*

- Over-enthusiasm
- Lack of gentility
- Manufactured emotions
- Enthusiastic quality
- Brutalism (in talk and acting)
- Exaggerated stylised acting
- Overblown dialogue

Western spectator's experience of watching: *Shame*

- Disarming
- Charming
- Embarrassing (cringeworthy)
- Resistance to admitting finding pleasure in viewing

Levels of realism: *Unrealism; reality and fantasy blurred*

- Absurd elements mistaken for reality
- Lack of truthfulness
- Unregulated, uncontained spectacle
- Overt fantasy
- Preposterous narrative
- Disregarding of character psychology
- Lack of historical, geographical and spatial accuracy
- Unreal
- Ridiculous

Intellectual value: *Anti-intellectualist*

- Mindless *mélange*
- Non-serious themes
- Immature, naive
- Stupendous
- Inane
- Lacking in 'sensible themes'
- Gauche

Political content: *Confusion or lack of social politics*

- Capitalist
- Sexist (insensitive)
- Exploitative
- Politically reactionary
- Purely escapist intentions

Aesthetic mode: *Figural excess*

- Visually garish (overt spectacle)
- Exotic
- Artificial
- Vulgar
- Aesthetically reactionary
- Spectacle
- Stylised

Figure 2.1: Critical comments on Indian cinema, sourced from Thomas (1985).

If Indian cinema does indulge in extreme, extrovert emotional displays and 'vulgar' excess, one can instantly see why the intellectuals of whom Rosie Thomas speaks have a problem engaging with and admitting to enjoying the 'guilty-pleasures' it offers. Perhaps the 'intellectual and emotionally cold' (121) Western critic cannot handle the Hindi popular film because, in requiring identification while viewing, it assaults his or her Ego and ideas of respectability and sensibility. The cinema asks the grown-up adult to engage (through identification) in infantile displays of emotion, to return to a naive sense of the world and to forgo the real, logical or rational in favour of fantasy, play and imagination. It asks the spectator to externalise repressed emotions until he or she is emptied out, and as such, it takes away one's privacy, depth, individuality and all that is secret. What happens to Western standards of taste, quality and self-respect in such a context? Indian cinema is fundamentally and essentially undignified. It assaults the composed, noble image that the Western critic has worked so hard to maintain, by threatening to take it away. If Western audiences do indeed identify with on-screen images as mirrors of their more perfect selves, then perhaps it is their discontent with the shamed, naked emotions of the Indian film protagonist that repels them – coupled with their inability to transfer or surrender to the imaginary realm to the extent that the Indian spectator does with remarkable ease.[16]

Thirty years after Thomas's article was published it seems that these same negative attitudes are still festering, and other scholars have tried to bring the same discussion to a more contemporary context. In discussing its place in the global age, Kaushik Bhaumik explains how the concept of world cinema is problematic for contemporary Bollywood, which he describes as an 'unfine' cinema, particularly when considered from a Western critical perspective (Bhaumik, 2006). Bhaumik concludes that Bollywood's failure in the West is a result of its generic impurity. It lacks the kind of defined genre conventions which assist filmic comprehension and typically help Western audiences to digest foreign films. Another reason for its unpopularity is its continued musical elements, and Bhaumik suggests that a revival in Hollywood musicals may be its only saving grace. However, even with the rise of genre-based films in Bollywood (particularly horror and science-fiction films) and the recent success of Hollywood musicals such as *Mamma Mia!* (2008), we see very little increase in the West's taste for Bollywood song and dance – implying that the problem lies in something else inherent in the design of Bollywood films. Bhaumik warns against the overemphasising of song and dance elements in Bollywood films, which leads to the assumption that the cinema is restricted to its musical dimensions. Many Western audiences fail to realise that this element is a naturalised feature of Bollywood films that one becomes more accustomed to when watching such films, and Bhaumik asserts that the West needs to learn to look beyond the music, just as it has done with films such as *The Wizard of Oz* (1939) as road movie and *Sweeney Todd: The Demon Barber of Fleet Street* (2007), with its elements of horror.

From some perspectives, the situation and the damage could be worse now, as popular Indian cinema has achieved a more permanent public awareness and has a rapidly growing international profile. In February 2009, BBC Radio 4 broadcast a news feature about the critical success of *Slumdog Millionaire* (2008), which asked if the Mumbai film industry 'could ever produce a film like it'. After mentioning how Bollywood has previously failed to attract Western audiences, the report suggested that the Indian film industry may need to consider abandoning its fantasy-based style for a more realist aesthetic, firstly by showing the grittier side of India – as seen in Danny Boyle's film. This argument concerning Bollywood's problematic 'unrealism' is longstanding. But is it really a solution to insist that Bollywood drops its fundamental characteristics for what some have crudely described as 'poverty porn' (Miles, 2009)? And what about the other fantasy- and spectacle-based movies that drew in Western audiences and award nominations in the same year (*The Curious Case of Benjamin Button*, *The Dark Knight*)?

This chapter has observed how commercial Indian cinema has often been inadequately represented and unfairly censured, and has become the subject of ridicule or shame in film criticism and traditional scholarship. I have explained how and why the cinema's fundamental characteristics are frequently devalued and evoke displeasure, particularly in the West. By acknowledging these internal prejudices, we may be able to overcome them. It is necessary to dismantle such value judgements in order to better access and comprehend Bollywood, particularly in its newer (postmodern) form. Having addressed the limitations of traditional and popular approaches to critiquing and theorising commercial Indian cinema, we can now develop the discussion and reflect on Bollywood studies in the contemporary context, observing how the cinema has been circulating in film institutions, and how it is being accounted for in film academia/education. It is also important to acknowledge more recent (and innovative) scholarship on contemporary Bollywood, which aims to reframe the cinema and take Indian film studies into new territory.

NOTES

1. This is common among many academic accounts of Indian film history. For example, Tejaswini Ganti's guidebook on Bollywood emphasises the 'three eras of filmmaking' in Indian cinema history – the 1950s, 1970s and 1990s (Ganti, 2004: 24).
2. A sometimes derogatory term referring to all-round entertainers who explicitly seek to provide audience value for money by including a mixture or blend of different generic ingredients within a single film (action, romance, comedy, music, tragedy and drama). Masala films are often stigmatised as mindless, formulaic, predictable and unoriginal in their execution, although it should be noted that the term is also sometimes used more broadly to represent all films under the popular Indian cinema banner.
3. Although films such as *Shahenshah* and *Toofan* may not have been cinema box-office hits,

the rise of VHS piracy and home video rentals needs to be acknowledged, as they significantly call Bollywood cinema's assumed unpopularity during this decade into question.
4. A common term used to refer to the Non Resident Indian diaspora, who form part of the 1990s Bollywood films' subject matter. These films used the figure of the NRI to target a more international audience.
5. Bollywood has a long track record of employing successful Muslim artists, although some will still insist on the industry's Hindu-fascist base, particularly through its publicised backing by the Bharatiya Janata Party (BJP) and Shiv Sena (the far-right Hindu nationalist political party): see Ganti (2002, 2004).
6. Unlike other Indian cinemas, Bollywood's films are more widely viewed across different Indian states and use a self-invented and self-serving language combining Hindi and Urdu vocabulary.
7. Most of the films associated with Johar are known in India by their standard abbreviations, which I have referred to and used hereafter.
8. This is a term widely used by the Indian press and Indian filmmakers and film scholars to refer to the song sequences in Indian films (see Jha, 2003).
9. See Mehta (2013).
10. In addition to Mani Ratnam, Ram Gopal Varma is now put forward as a Bollywood *auteur* with a unique signature style.
11. Frontal aesthetics are explained here as the films' use of flat planes, their elimination of middle distances, and their lack of points of entry into the frame, as if performing to a live audience.
12. Roughly translates as: 'this-is-the-public-they-know-everything'.
13. Although this new era certainly assists the dehistoricising and depoliticising agendas of transnational capital (Yoshimoto, 2006), through my research I will demonstrate that New Bollywood is in fact remarkably conscious and critical of its methods of representation and political in its anti-political stance.
14. These films are a small selection of a rapidly growing list of productions following Fox's merger with the Indian media company STAR, forming Fox Star Studios. In a similar venture, the Walt Disney Company acquired the Indian media company UTV and now owns UTV Motion Pictures.
15. This supplement was produced in association with the UK departmental store Selfridges' high-profile promotional event paying homage to Bollywood in 2002.
16. Psychoanalytical approaches, although rare in studies of Hindi film, are worth investigating in order to identify such discrepancies. Although this is not the focus of my own investigation, I refer to the work of Jacques Lacan (1977) here to demonstrate this interesting hypothesis, which supports further study into issues of displeasure. According to Lacanian film theory, the film text satisfies the desire to connect with one's on-screen ideal-ego (our identifiable better self or Other), who will be suitably composed on-screen. If the ideal-ego (the film protagonist) is shamed or embarrasses itself, this could in turn cause the spectator to experience a sense of disgust and lead to dis-identification.

CHAPTER 3

Pedagogic Practices and Newer Approaches to Contemporary Bollywood Cinema

FILM INSTITUTIONS AND REPRESENTATIVES

The supposed Western appetite for sophisticated and realistic Indian films seems to trickle down into the film festivals, which ironically claim to celebrate and raise the international profile of popular Indian cinema. For example, the official press release for the British Film Institute's 2007 *Indian cinema now* film showcase included an opening paragraph which openly rejected the 'frivolity and glitz of Bollywood'. Even in the programme's synopses for the few contemporary Bollywood films that were selected for the festival, there was a need to include justifications for the film's unintegrated song sequences and historical inaccuracies.[1] Furthermore, unusual choices behind the appointment of Western ambassadors for popular Indian cinema also add to the problem. In 2004, the independent Hollywood producer Ismail Merchant wrote a foreword to Dinesh Raheja and Jitendra Kothari's *The Bollywood Saga*, a book which aimed to celebrate and promote popular Indian cinema. But Merchant's firm Western base and history of producing elegant Western period dramas made him an unusual spokesperson for Bollywood cinema, and in his foreword he in fact criticises 'the glut of such formalised entertainment without variation in style or substance [which] may soon alienate all but the most jaded of cinema-goers' (Merchant, cited in Raheja and Kothari: 10–11). Merchant goes on to warn against Bollywood's dangerous over-production and its over-hyped films, and he suggests that instead of copying from the West, it is 'imperative' that Bollywood filmmakers instead learn from world cinema.

Correspondingly, *auteur* Satyajit Ray has been a long-standing representative of Indian cinema in the West, despite his distinctively European film style and lack of popularity with the mass Indian audience. Ray's high international profile has proved an obstacle for Indian popular cinema, particularly given his condemnation of popular Hindi films. In his 1976 essay 'What is wrong with Hindi films?' Ray suggested that popular Indian films had in some ways become a source of shame. He blamed the negative influence of American cinema, which depicted a way of life 'so utterly at variance' (22) with that of Indians, and instead presented Italian neo-realism as a positive role model, arguing that it would be impossible for India ever to achieve Hollywood's high-tech polish. Ray insisted that what Indian cinema needed was not more gloss, but integrity and a more intelligent appreciation of the limitations of the medium, and that it needed to adopt unique, recognisably Indian iconography. Almost forty years on, it seems that Bollywood has partly invalidated Ray's statement, at least in terms of its technical proficiency. Such calls for culturally authentic Indian films also become increasingly problematic in view of the abundance of remaking and textual appropriation in Bollywood cinema in recent years (something I will return to more explicitly in Chapters 6 and 7).

ACADEMIA

Despite the proliferation of Indian film research from the mid-1980s onwards, Indian cinema's appearance in film studies courses remains somewhat cursory. Some of the Western film academics I have spoken to over the course of my research for this book have offered very straightforward and practical reasons for this, such as the films previously being hard to get hold of, badly subtitled, and too long in duration to fit lecture booking slots, or the cinema seeming too large in scale for it to be done justice in the time allocated. A few UK film scholars were honest enough to admit that they also had an aversion to Bollywood and instead felt more drawn to other Eastern world cinemas (Iranian and Japanese in particular), which they found to be much more approachable. Many argued that Bollywood films were less accessible, or 'hermeneutically sealed' (Bhaumik, 2006: 188), and required an entirely different set of analytical tools. As a film academic from the University of Bristol explained to me, 'the frustration comes when one watches and enjoys a film like Sanjay Leela Bhansali's *Devdas*, and yet does not know what to *do* with it'. A further reason for this avoidance, this time given by a Media and Cultural Studies academic at the University of Sussex, concerned the issue of Western film academics and their 'white liberal guilt'. Bollywood films were perhaps too culturally alien or intimidating owing to their ethnicity-centred form and style, which made non-Indian academics feel it was inappropriate for them to comment on the texts, or feel fearful that this would shamefully expose their lack of understanding of Indian culture. Although controversial, this reason may go some way to explaining why the few Western academic film courses that do incorporate Indian cinema will emphasise the cinema's cultural or social attributes rather than expose it to more straightforward aesthetic criticism akin to that found in studies of American popular cinema.

Another related contextual problem concerns the difficulty of getting some Western students to take Indian film material seriously in the first place, as they can often turn to ridicule or become confused at the lack of familiar visual cues, not knowing whether to read the films as serious works or highly ironic comedies ('Am I *supposed* to laugh at this?'). From my own observations of teaching this cinema to students, the Indian-accented use of English (or 'Hinglish', as its now termed) is a source of some irritation (students described hearing phrases such as 'bloody hell' and 'bloody shit' in Hindi films as 'annoying'). Certain English or American expressions may be read as poor cultural mimicry rather than being understood as phrases genuinely used by modern-day Indians (interestingly, one student described scenes with English dialogue as specifically 'non-Bollywood moments'). The paradiegetic nature of Bollywood song sequences also proved a confusing and surreal viewing experience, as sometimes it was unclear whether the sequence represented the course of a character's dream-fantasy or some sort of revived memory of an actual past event.

IN THE CLASSROOM: STUDENT RESPONSES TO STUDYING POPULAR INDIAN FILMS

Whilst auditing an Indian cinema class for a group of non-Indian film studies undergraduates,[2] I observed student responses to *Kabhi Kabhie* (1976), which represented, for many, their first encounter with popular Indian cinema. Almost instinctively, students mocked the film for its amateur special effects and historical inaccuracies, as well as certain cliché-ridden gestures and peculiar dress codes (the throwing of a scarf in the wind or a man wearing a thin white polyester pant-suit in the pouring rain). Changes of characters' outfits during song sequences were read as continuity mistakes due to the lack of production experience of filmmakers, rather than understood as conscious stylistic decisions made to enhance visual pleasure. The fashioning of flared trousers and skirts instead of traditional Indian attire was seen not as 'normal', but as a naive attempt on India's part to keep up with Western culture. Tilted-angle camera shots were not artistic, but 'bizarre'. Students felt jolted by the compactness of narrative events, complaining that the story-time moved too quickly: 'it was like watching the middle section of a story. There was not a beginning or an end and no establishing of character relationships . . . [it was as if they had] already fallen into the story.' While the students followed the film's longer developing stories, they often failed to remember or follow incidences compressed and represented by montage sequences, insisting that they 'needed more time' or information to process the action. Acting styles were regarded as oddly inconsistent – switching from realist and serious to performative and parodic. Likewise, certain stars' acting styles were regarded as 'cringeworthy', presenting insincere emotions which seemed unnaturalistically magnified. Furthermore, the surface nature and artificiality of fight sequences caused them to be compared to the 'stupid overacting' of TV shows such as *Power Rangers*.[3] The film's narrative conclusions were considered unsatisfying as they were either illogical or did not meet the students' expectations and taste for controversy. For example, one student said she expected the film to end with an adulterous relationship as opposed to a faithful return to marriage: 'I wanted the predictability of controversy and found the traditional balanced happy ending quite jarring.' The students felt unsatisfied by the way a family conflict was resolved by a simple apology or family hug. They also lacked the willing suspension of disbelief required to fill in gaps to explain certain 'implausible' scenarios, such as a horse suddenly appearing from nowhere to rescue the hero. Such coincidences were considered unbelievable and distracting, as they were 'not like real life'. Character motives were also discussed at length for their lack of logical justification, and some on-screen relationships were described as 'uncomfortable' and 'weird', particularly interactions and affections between mothers and sons, which were 'too intense' and confusingly appeared to suggest romantic undertones. Politically conscious students found the films' reinforcement of clichés and racist stereotypes shocking and problematic, whilst at the level of presentation, students were generally surprised by the amount of explicit metaphors, particularly the text's dependence on visual representations where dialogue did not work independently and was often backed up by non-diegetic imagery ('they [the films] are so in your face ... we *hear* the dialogue about the waves, so we don't need to actually *see* the waves').

The majority of the students' reasons for initially choosing to take the Indian cinema course were related to tourism, exoticism or cultural capital. Some students appreciated Bollywood's novelty and kitsch cult value – citing Western popular cultural references (the opening sequence to Terry Zwigoff's *Ghost World* [2001] and various novelty Bollywood music compilation CDs) as a source of inspiration – or its culture-shock value. However, many students also admitted that although they had not been exposed to Indian popular cinema before, they were familiar with the stigma attached to more commercial Bollywood films, which they thus expected to enjoy less. Some outwardly rejected the term 'Bollywood', instead emphasising their interest in more 'authentic' and 'traditional' modes of Indian cinema, which were 'gritty' and dealt with serious issues such as poverty. The co-British-funded film *Monsoon Wedding* was cited as one such film which, unlike Bombay-produced films, seemed to fulfil their ideas of 'what *real* India is *really* like'. Interestingly, at the end of the course, the few students who had previously discovered Indian cinema through Satyajit Ray (via previous world cinema courses they had taken) said that this might have misled them into automatically associating 'real Indian-ness' with social deprivation, poverty and realism. They agreed that Bollywood films had instead allowed them to rethink, redefine and broaden their understanding of genuine Indian experiences in a more contemporary and modern context. However, this exposure to newer Bollywood texts still did not necessarily lead to positive viewing pleasures. One student, who originally expressed a wish to overcome negative attitudes towards Bollywood cinema ('I want to understand it, to be able to take it seriously . . . not to laugh *at* it but to be laughing *with* it'), noted her constant frustration at the popular films' persistent lack of realism, eventually finding herself unable to adjust to this, and in the end largely preferring the socially realist and 'polished' earlier films on the course (specifically, those directed by Guru Dutt). Interestingly, despite all the above issues, at the end of the course all the students cited 1990s Bollywood archetype *DDLJ* as one of their favourite films on the course, although they struggled to articulate how and why this was the case. Particularly when writing their essays about these Indian films, the students said that they struggled to find the means to describe or articulate the films in terms of their form and style – perhaps largely owing to the general absence of formal analysis in their critical readings.

Of course, the above observation does not reflect the experience of every student. But it does identify an initial response to popular Indian films that is familiar, if not commonplace, and worthy of further investigation. Contemporary Bollywood does have the potential to attract wider non-Indian audiences (see for example Adrian M. Athique's [2008] Australian audience survey and Sunitha Chitrapu's [2012] summary of non-Indian global viewing practices which substantiate this). The argument made about displeasure here does not intend to assume or suggest that *all* Western or non-Indian viewers have a steadfastly negative or derogatory attitude towards Hindi cinema (the aforementioned Indian film students all actively chose to study the subject and reported in their end-of-course feedback that they had gained respect and admiration for Hindi films). But while negative stereotypes need to be avoided here, positively stereotyping Indian cinema as a subject which is generally embraced by Western audiences and academia would not account for the reaction that Bollywood films elicit in their foreign viewers and critics and the long-standing censure to which this cinema has been subjected.

Although the cinema's lack of global success or wider appeal can in part be put down to issues of cultural proximity (audiences preferring products which are localised or culturally similar [Straubhaar, 1991]) or poor overseas marketing, this does not remedy the fact that, in the West, Bollywood is generally understood as a more niche film preference and is coveted far less by Western audiences than some other Asian cinemas. There is to some extent an established culture of viewing Hong Kong martial arts films, or Korean extreme cinema, or Japanese horror films, but not necessarily a Bollywood musical. It is equally important to address the fact that there are a substantial number of film students and academics who feel more suited to viewing, or comfortable approaching East Asian films (which are still culturally different) – and to investigate whether Bollywood's unique film language, aesthetics or methods of cultural appropriation play some part in this.

INDIAN FILM EDUCATION

Looking at a sample selection of Indian cinema course outlines collected from several UK, US and Indian universities, it is noticeable how historical or biographical accounts of Indian cinema tend to skim over less politically focused periods – often dissolving them into decades which have a more socio-political premise (as discussed in Chapter 2). More often than not these biographies stop at the 1990s, and, as a consequence, this decade's family-based diaspora-themed films are often mistakenly represented as the current phase of Bollywood filmmaking. When Indian film courses have included films produced after the year 2000 Bollywood texts tend to be sidelined, and instead, contemporary Indian cinema is often explored through crossover films of diaspora directors like Mira Nair or Canadian filmmaker Deepa Mehta.[4] Of course, those compiling Indian film courses have to make do with whatever accompanying critical literature is published and readily available to them. There is still not enough substantial published work on how Bollywood has formally changed since 2000, other than minor points made within broader discussions around the industry's global-economic shifts.[5]

A few Indian cinema educators have attempted to discuss their experiences pedagogically and shed light on the difficulties faced when trying to teach Bollywood to a non-Indian student cohort. Lucia Kramer (2008) has described how some of the cinema's most fundamental features can create difficulties for her German students (particularly males), who will often reject the films owing to their inferior technical quality and seemingly brainless kitsch melodramatics (Kramer, 2008: 113). There is also a particular cynicism towards the way in which NRI films inaccurately construct and depict the Western world as Indian territory (119). Kramer asserts the need to emphasise Bollywood's heterogeneity, which she sees as 'the basic prerequisite for an adequate engagement' with the cinema (120). She also claims that newer Bollywood films can help overcome some of the above issues, suggesting that the introduction of more contemporary versions of historicals (*Jodha Akbar*), literary adaptations (*Devdas* [2002]) and action films (*Main Hoon Na*) will better engage students and generate discussion: 'Through their negotiation of the Indian and the foreign, and of tradition and modernity on the levels of technology, storytelling, aesthetics and values, recent Bollywood films moreover encapsulate important developments and conflicts in present day India' (120). Similarly, she argues that social criticism need not be purely associated with or reserved for parallel or 1950s cinema, but can be analysed just as effectively in select contemporary mainstream commercial films such as *Swades* (poverty and illiteracy), *Rang de Basanti* (government corruption) and *Lage Raho Munna Bhai* (Gandhism).

Sheila Nayar (2005) has made further recommendations on improving academic approaches to teaching Indian cinema through actively dissolving the Asian cinema–Hollywood binary, which associates the former with psychological interiority (slow pacing and a subdued tone), while the latter is equated with a faster pace 'driv[ing] relentlessly towards a climactic explosion of action' (Nayar: 59–60). One need only look at contemporary Bollywood blockbusters such as the *Dhoom* franchise – comprising three highly successful motor vehicle stunt-based action movies *Dhoom* (2004), *Dhoom 2* (2006) and *Dhoom 3* (2013), which form part of a film trilogy that is something of a first for Bollywood – to see how this is a grossly mistaken assumption. Through having surveyed standard film courses herself, Nayar notes how the specific kind of 'elemental focus on montage and *mise-en-scène*, on lyricism and neo-realism and a gamut of *auteurs*, will have well prepared students for Ray – but not for Bollywood' (63).

Nayar's broader critical work has introduced the notion of how structural similarities between American cinema and Bollywood can be identified by analysing cross-cultural remakes. In drawing cross-cultural parallels, Nayar specifically makes reference to *Speed*, *Lord of the Rings*, *Rambo*, *Titanic* and Walt Disney films (2005: 65). According to her, this comparative approach can help 'expose students to the internal inconsistencies – or . . . the internal variety – that exist within Indian cinema' (63) and can be a useful way of 'dis-Orientalizing' Bollywood by revealing a 'space for ambivalence – about American-ness, about Indian-ness, about the purity of identity' (71). Nayar identifies how this approach allows us to better understand an important paradox within contemporary Bollywood cinema concerning how its film texts appear distinctive and yet simultaneously 'bear the stamp of the experientially familiar' (70). However, whereas Nayar chooses to place emphasis only on the comparative socio-cultural aspects of popular American and Indian films – such as sexuality, marriage and domesticity – my own study of Bollywood remakes (particularly in Chapter 7) explores this paradox by elaborating on the shared *artistic* nuances and formal aesthetic interplay of Bollywood and Hollywood cinematic codes.

Indeed, there are also criticisms regarding the current status of Indian film academia which lament the declining status, appreciation, and academic attention to canonised Indian film artists such as Ray and Ghatak. While some commentators, like Mark Cousins, have suggested that the Oscar success of *Slumdog Millionaire* may instigate a revival of interest in the subtleties of parallel cinema (Cousins, 2009: 81), others like Frances Gateward and David Desser (2006), blame Bollywood for art cinema's continual erosion: '"Bollywood" has frozen out not only India's regional cinemas, its art film *auteurs*, and avant-garde efforts, but also Hindi cinema's own past' (Gateward and Desser: 6). Although I agree that contemporary Bollywood is participating in a kind of 'swallowing up' of previous cinematic forms and thereby stripping them of their superior significance, as I will later demonstrate, the artistic and avant-garde are becoming ever more present within Bollywood films texts themselves[6] via their high-aestheticism and their absorption of avant-garde techniques (particularly concerning anti-realism). Bollywood is also increasingly incorporating cinemas of different states through cross-regional remakes such as *Ghajini*.[7]

Ashis Nandy (2003) has also commented on academia's failure to do much good for popular Indian cinema, which has either been reduced to 'sociological data' (Nandy: 83) or viewed primarily in relation to its middle-class audiences, thus largely ignoring the aesthetic pleasures which appeal to its working-class consumers in India. This Indian film studies bias towards middle-class audiences refers not only to the upwardly mobile audiences within India's multiplex theatre chains, but, I think, also applies to diasporic audiences and the constant academic attention paid to NRI-centred film production. Kaleem Aftab (2002), for example, has cynically concluded that as Bollywood's popularity in the UK is limited to NRI audiences, the cinema chiefly serves to expose and assist the divide between Indian and Western viewing habits and the regressiveness of the British Indian diaspora. Although this may have been the case in the mid-1990s, Bollywood has more recently produced films which no longer simply aim to reflect the feelings of the homesick diaspora. These texts instead engage in a more complex and diverse kind of pleasure, which also addresses the needs, pleasures and experiences of Indian citizens (particularly in the light of India's global shifts and modernisation).

Nandy suggests that the recent academic interest in Bollywood is simply a by-product of the transitory vogue for pop culture, and he accuses film theorists and historians of distancing themselves from the conventional, the gullible and the predictable and for presenting popular cinema as 'inaesthetic, demonic or stupid', fearing it will otherwise impede their desired rigid political-ideological classifications, definitions and conclusions. As Nandy comments: 'recent research deals at greater length with popular cinema in an even more serious and sophisticated manner. Nevertheless the aim is still to produce lengthy, serious and sophisticated reasons for not liking them' (2003: 81). The film historian cannot watch 'without losing ... respectability and without feeling guilty about enjoying something "vulgar" and "cheap"' (ibid.: 83).

Despite the shift in focus towards more global and transnational forms of filmmaking, it therefore seems that Indian cinema's place in Western academia continues to be problematic. As Sumita Chakravarty (2007) remarks following her own experiences of teaching the subject in various American universities,

> a course on Indian cinema . . . must bear the 'burden' of being a course in social history, politics and economics, language and religion. As a stand-alone course on . . . film tradition, it cannot benefit from the 'symphonic effect' that courses more central to the curriculum, such as ones on American or European cinemas, can generate. (Chakravarty: 105)

The above investigations into Indian cinema education give us further insight into how Bollywood has, at times, come to be marginally perceived and (mis)understood, both academically and more broadly, in the West. I would like to make three final conclusive points summarising these insights, which will also help to corroborate my own postmodern study of contemporary Bollywood cinema. Firstly, we must try harder to avoid leaving students of Indian cinema thinking that today's contemporary Bollywood is the same as it was in the 1990s. It is time to start acknowledging and exploring the formal and aesthetic changes that have taken place in films after the industry's economic liberalisation by better incorporating them into our Indian film courses. Secondly, we need to be slightly careful with our demands for authenticity and more sensitive towards moments of cultural appropriation. Simply rejecting newer forms of popular Indian cinema or 'Bollywood' because they are too Westernised and parodic seems unfair, as this too is a reality of (modern) India. As Nandy points out in his aptly-titled essay 'An Intelligent Critic's Guide to Indian Cinema', 'The West today is only partly an external category; it is also an inner vector of the Indian self, an acceptable and legitimate aspect of Indian-ness activised by the society's long exposure to Occidental despotism'(Nandy, 1995: 228). Also, as British Asian Radio presenter Bobby Friction has more recently warned, the modern generation of youth in India may take offence at being rigidly defined *against* Western culture, which they now see as an important part of their identity, and they may protest at having their popular culture confined to (often outmoded) ideas of authentic traditional Indian-ness.[8] There is thus a significant need to investigate cross-cultural appropriation in Indian cinema. Through my own study of Bollywood remakes, I reveal that what may at first seem like inauthentic cultural copycatting can actually be a conscious process of playful mistranslation, leading to much creative innovation, and this method of appropriation could in fact be the key to driving the cinema forward into new territory.

A final important point that this enquiry raises is that, as well as continuing to investigate pleasure and popularity in Indian cinema, we should also pay closer attention to the *displeasure* experienced by viewers of Bollywood films who may ultimately reject the texts. For example, what is it about these films that puts off some Western viewers? Is it really that they have no appetite for song and dance and cannot tolerate anti-realism or excessive displays of open emotion as 'emotionally retarded, if not totally cold-blooded' Westerners (Thomas: 121)? Or is it something deeper-rooted than this: a special kind of film language that Indians are better programmed or conditioned to understand and tolerate? If so, how can one learn and teach this language? Are these Westerners required to adopt a more extreme sense of disavowal in order to enjoy such films? Or are we to assume that this is something too culturally specific, a cinematic mode of spectatorship unique to less discerning Indians? If that is the case, then Bollywood's attempts to become a global or international success seem tragically futile. Whatever the case, I believe that a postmodern reading of contemporary Bollywood cinema can allow us to better appreciate and articulate the aesthetic frameworks of such films.

CONTEMPORARY BOLLYWOOD: NEW DIRECTIONS IN INDIAN FILM RESEARCH

Before I begin my analysis of postmodern practices in contemporary Bollywood cinema, it is important to mention some more recent academic publications that have inspired my own investigation and put forward several refreshing ideas and perspectives, particularly in relation to Bollywood's recent formal-stylistic transformations.

A small number of international scholars have usefully begun to explore Western audiences' consumption and reception of Bollywood films. For example, in challenging the overemphasis on Indian cinema as a conveyor of cultural authenticity (and therefore something only applicable to Indian audiences), Adrian M. Athique (2008) has surveyed the success of newer contemporary Bollywood films among non-Indian Australians, both at film festivals and through self-organised focus group screenings.[9] Athique's outcome reveals a particular responsiveness towards more contemporary, technically advanced films (70 per cent of young Australians exhibited an interest in consuming more of these films), and therefore suggests that 'It might be useful . . . in the imagining of a Western audience, to update the realist imperative of the 1950s and to accommodate the more recent convergence between Indian cinema's song "picturisations" and the post-MTV generation in the West' (307).

There are several key studies that have also provided a particularly valuable insight into India's intersections with Western cinematic culture. For example,

Ananda Mitra's book *India through the Western Lens* (1999) investigated the representation of Indians within Western (chiefly Hollywood) film texts. His study concluded that in the future, Indian diasporic immigrant filmmakers may be inclined to produce 'nomadic identities' which set out to challenge these Western cinematic representations of South Asia, carefully maintaining or negotiating a sense of Indian-ness whilst attempting to situate themselves within the Western market. I would add that this is no longer something exclusive to diasporic filmmaking, but has increasingly become a practice of contemporary Bollywood cinema. Through my own study, I uncover how Bollywood's current representations of Indian identity also attempt to challenge and convert certain Western exoticised images by first appropriating and then subsequently *deconstructing* them from within. I therefore conversely look at how Bollywood represents Western cinema through an *Indian* lens, particularly in terms of its adopting and subverting Hollywood aesthetic codes through its own genre-based films.

Historically tracing early Indian cinema's borrowing of Hollywood codes and conventions, Kaushik Bhaumik (2006) has usefully described this process of Western appropriation as Indian cinema's long-standing and continual method for accessing the modern. However, I believe that this bricolaging and eclecticism has become much more distinguishable and complex in the contemporary climate, and that Bollywood's recent dialogues with Hollywood are no longer necessarily neutral, nor ones of admiration. On the contrary, certain Western cinematic codes are now increasingly being manipulated to serve Indian popular cinema's own postmodern agendas. For example, as Heather Tyrrell has noted in her account of Hollywood's relationship with Bollywood (1999), the latter now presents a firm challenge to Western dominant modes of representation through the way in which it constantly problematises realism – a key postmodern concern. As I later demonstrate in my analysis of contemporary Bollywood films, this anti-realist stance is partly achieved by manipulating Hollywood codes and deconstructing Western notions of realism (reducing the effectiveness of verisimilitude).

Also in relation to Bollywood's cross-cinematic ventures, a handful of scholars have helpfully drawn attention to the unique processes of imitation and adaptation in Bollywood filmmaking. Mira Reym Binford (1988) crucially revealed early on that imitations could facilitate innovation in the Indian cinema. She argued that novelty is almost inevitable, even in texts based on Hollywood models, particularly given Bollywood's disorganised, anarchic and fragmented filmmaking processes. As demonstrated earlier with reference to Sheila Nayar's groundwork on Bollywood remakes, comparative studies can greatly inform our understanding of the differences between, and the bi-directional transferability of, Indian and American filmmaking practices. Work of this kind has slowly begun to emerge and to produce some interesting readings. For example, Tejaswini Ganti (2002) has built on Nayar's work on remakes by investigating how Bollywood filmmakers search out, select and '(H)Indianize' Hollywood films for an Indian audience, although her analysis looks more at transformation during pre-production stages and her textual analysis, like Nayar's, falls short in focusing almost exclusively on narrative content.

In her account of Hindi film remaking, Ganti suggests that in order for a Hollywood film to be deemed suitable for remaking, it must contain plot, character, melodramatic and thematic elements (including sexual themes and moral values) that will be tolerated and 'approved' (287) by an Indian audience. The 'moral boundaries' (288) considered important for a successful adaptation include kinship relationships (which, interestingly, is one of the things the UK non-Indian film students discussed earlier found peculiar and difficult to engage with). Furthermore, difficulties with remaking are seen to occur if the Hollywood text and its protagonist fail to uphold moral values. Ganti notes that Hindi remakes will rectify this problem by including culturally specific social taboos and different 'symbols of deviance' (289). These are seen as missing in Hollywood cinema, which contrarily is seen to have a 'lack of a moral universe' (289). Also, in the process of translation, sexuality in the Hindi film is purely reserved for song sequences and the film will often exclusively centre around a romance where lovers must woo one another. Ultimately, Ganti argues that the successful Hindi adaptation of a Hollywood text involves the addition of three key elements: song sequences, melodramatic emotion (specifically in terms of the narrative) and narrative extension (whereby further sub-stories and diversions are added to the main narrative thread).

However accurate Ganti's analysis of pre-2000 Hindi remakes may have been at the time of writing, many of her assumptions and conclusions now seem outmoded when considered in the current context of Bollywood filmmaking. Sexual imagery can now be found to venture outside and beyond song sequences. Popular films may now address certain social taboos, and stories no longer necessarily need to be family-, kinship- or romance-centred in order to be considered marketable. These changes are largely a result of the liberalising viewpoints and changing tastes of the Indian viewing public – something that Ganti does not seem to consider much in her investigation. Ganti suggests that choices to remake are determined largely by 'worldly' filmmakers (as 'mediators') whose decisions are ultimately tied to the rigid and backward traditionalist tastes of the Indian public (289). Here, the Indian audience is seen as stifling film creativity. They are considered 'monolithic' and 'prudish' (297) by filmmakers – a perception which has since begun to change in view of some of the more experimental, generically diverse and sexually risqué films produced after Bollywood's economic liberalisation.

Ganti also suggests that '(H)Indianization' is necessary as filmmakers believe that Hollywood films are 'not capable of evoking in Indian audiences the psychological or emotional responses necessary for viewing pleasure' (286). But this situation may now have changed in some sections of society given the rise of the multiplex audience and the wider accessibility and distribution of Western popular culture via cable and satellite television. Furthermore, Ganti's argument seems to imply that all remakes that are made (or chosen to be made) are risk-free, accepted and successful, but this is not always the case. For example, Ram Gopal Varma's *Aag* follows virtually the same narrative and character experiences as its 1970s Indian original *Sholay*. This 'self-remake' contains the three elements Ganti suggests are required for a successful remake, and yet the film was rejected by Indian audiences and performed badly. Ganti also asserts that Indian audiences 'derive pleasure only from familiar stars and narratives' (285), whereas I would argue that there are other formal aesthetic aspects of contemporary Bollywood remake texts that attract the audience (for example, the spectacular and figural presentation in recent Bollywood films – see Chapter 7).

The rising trend of self-remaking in Bollywood over the past ten years or so has led to some interesting comparative studies which consider how newer Bollywood film texts *reimagine* older classics. Valentina Vitali's comparative work on *Don* (1978) and *Don: The Chase Begins* (2006) has helped inform us about the way in which the action film genre has evolved from that of the Angry Man era. Similarly, Corey Creekmur's (2007) close aesthetic analysis of multiple cinematic versions of *Devdas* across different eras of Indian cinema history has drawn attention to Indian cinema's inherent patterns of repetition, as well as its relationship to film remaking in general (something I build on through my own investigation of Bollywood film remakes). Creekmur's article offers a more positive perspective on Bollywood's recent remake phenomenon, arguing that contemporary (literature to film) adaptations can also offer us valuable insight into Indian artistic traditions. Furthermore, in her recent account of film sequels, Carolyn Jess-Cooke (2009) also looks at Bollywood sequelisations as a response to Hollywood trends and a means of the industry internationalising itself, whilst also continuing to preserve Indian ideologies. But she asserts that Bollywood's remakes are 'more involved in a process of resistance, subversion and globalisation' (117) and are also 'reconfiguring indianness' through 'a past-bound identity that speaks to the future' (126).

On rare occasions, Indian cinema researchers have attempted to adopt more unusual or unorthodox techniques in order to analyse New Bollywood's unique film language (perhaps aiming to serve as those 'alternative analytical tools' so desperately requested by alienated film academics) and in order to help push the field of Bollywood studies into new directions. For example, Patrick Colm Hogan (2008) uses cognitive neuro-scientific theory to help identify universal principles within contemporary Bollywood films and to dissect the subtle strategies behind their unique filmic coding. In doing so, Hogan explains how certain films, which may on the surface seem trivial, can in fact be highly ironic and playful – particularly texts produced after the 1990s, which he too regards as a renaissance period for popular Indian cinema. Hogan's investigation is most useful in pointing out that Bollywood films may not be palatable to Western audiences because of their employment of different cognitive functions (colour, emotion, music) which require different cognitive responses. Although I do not apply a cognitive scientific approach to my own research, I am also interested in employing new methods to explore the subtleties and strategies behind Bollywood's visual aesthetic structures and modes of signification.[10] My postmodern reading of Bollywood provides a similarly unorthodox approach which may raise eyebrows, but nevertheless helps invigorate our understanding of Bollywood films and the discipline of Indian film studies.

Although the more innovative dimensions of this project come from the application of postmodern theory to Indian cinema, this concept has already been approached (somewhat sparsely) in more recent Indian cinema scholarship. While few scholars have dared to describe Bollywood as explicitly postmodern, much of the research produced on contemporary forms of Indian cinema nevertheless exhibits underlying postmodern sentiments. Indian film scholars have already noted a growing self-consciousness towards song sequences (Garwood, 2006), a rebranding of the cinema as Western 'postmodern pop art' (Athique, 2008), a notable 'post-authenticity' (Rajadhyaksha, 2009) and death or substitution of the real by a kind of Baudrillardian hyperrealism (Srivastava; Gehlawat), a nostalgic evoking of a past through 'retro references', 'ironic affection' and 'slick self-parody' (Athique, 2012) that is not remembered through memory, but rather, artificially overstated through past styles (Creekmur, 2007), a self-reflexive practice employing a new industrial narcissism, polyvocality and 'reflexive capitalism' (Sarkar, 2013), and an increase in the exteriorisation of psychological problems, a dissolving of the modern and pre-modern, and Bollywood's strange apolitical disposition (Nandy, 1998). Even actors and filmmakers within the industry have discussed the cinema's sublime excess, overt sensation, eclecticism and schizophrenic nature (see various interviews with industry professionals in Ganti, 2004). One scholar who has perhaps made the first explicit attempt to classify this latest phase of Bollywood as postmodern is Vijay Mishra. Mishra first indicates how Indian cinema is naturally parodistic of its own 'artificial totality' and inherently self-reflexive in his article 'Towards a Theoretical Critique of Bombay Cinema' (1985) – one of the earliest well-known published theoretical articles on popular Indian cinema. However, in a later publication, Mishra confirms the postmodern aims of contemporary Bollywood as an industry growing 'out of the logic forces of late capital' (Mishra, 2006: 24), and he begins to explore the concept's impact on Indian film production in his critically descriptive entry on Bollywood in the *Encyclopaedia of Communication*:

> The postmodern Bollywood, where the old depth of language and dialogue (hallmarks of classic Bombay cinema as seen, for example, in the 1953 *Parineeta*) is replaced by a 'technorealism' (seen in the remake of *Parineeta* [2005]) at the level of production and the 'mise-en-scene', became the marker of Indian modernity (Rajadhyaksha, 2003). With a difference though – this (post)modernity negotiated a new definition of the spectator and a new definition of the subject of cinema. (Mishra, 2008: 351)

Referring to several key Bollywood films produced after 2000, Mishra explores the cinema's transformation on the level of representation, focusing on the proliferation of different languages and discourses within a single film text and the implementation of computer effects technology that 'seems to overtake the camera' – a feature which he dubs *technorealism*. Mishra also notes how film remakes such as *Devdas* (2002) avoid cinematic fidelity to their originals and instead refer to their own postmodern simulacral textuality (352). Unfortunately, neither of these ideas are explored any further in his concise summary of New Bollywood, but his account crucially instigates a possible space for discussion on the postmodern in popular Indian cinema.

The concept of postmodern Bollywood cinema has since been sporadically (and somewhat perfunctorily) mentioned in relation to contemporary Indian texts. Ranjani Mazumdar (2007) mentions it briefly and specifically in relation to her short reading of *Company* (2002), which she declares postmodern owing to its mimicking of and playfulness with global gangster and action film genre conventions, its use of 'self-conscious lighting' and its actors' 'hyperperformative mode' (192). However, although asserting that the film serves as both 'postmodern representation' and 'the experimental realm of the postmodern condition' (190), she fails to expand and elaborate on either of these points. Similarly, Bhaskar Sarkar (2013) acknowledges an increase in postmodern self-reflexivity in contemporary Bollywood films as a response to the industry's global anxieties (211). However, he regards the 'postmodern' as merely a labelling device (218), and instead uses Brechtian theory to discuss how this self-reflexivity reinscribes collective cultural memory and archives Bollywood and its tropes, ultimately serving as a means of social reproduction.

As discussed briefly in Chapter 1, Ajay Gehlawat's 2010 application of a postmodern praxis currently stands as perhaps the most enthusiastic and direct attempt to analyse New Bollywood cinema's 'essentially hybrid aesthetics' (144). Gehlawat's study references a range of Bollywood films, including (but not as exclusively) a close analysis of post-2000 films such as *Dostana*,

K3G and *Aa Ab Laut Chalein*. Although focusing primarily on song sequences, he provides useful examples of how realistic modes of representation are forsaken for a commercialised 'hyper-saccharine aesthetic' (123) – most effectively in his analysis of *K3G*. Here, geographically specific places (in this case, London) are stripped of their basic reality and instead become an 'impersonated' or simulated 'pastiche of places seamlessly cut and pasted together' (124). He argues that the desired effect of these 'fantascapes' (118) is a destabilising and unfixing of Indian national identity and a reconfiguring of Indian-ness.

Rajinder Dudrah has also recently tried to apply postmodern theory to Bollywood film analysis, this time merging it with sociological approaches in an attempt to expand existing diaspora concepts. His most recent book (2012) includes a short section entitled 'Aesthetics of a postmodern Bollywood film' which briefly explores some postmodern traits through an analysis of *Jhoom Barabar Jhoom* (2007). His reading discusses the film's drawing attention to Bollywood's star system (which I take further in my own analysis in Chapter 6 by exploring instances of genetic textuality), its moments of direct address (speaking to cinema-goers outside real picture halls), its hybridity and eclecticism during song sequences, its drawing attention to story-telling devices, and its blurring of reality and fantasy. Unfortunately, again, the concept of postmodernism is somewhat underexplored or taken for granted here, but Dudrah does acknowledge its value in generating ethnic alternatives to 'white male Eurocentric versions of the modern' (2012: 35). Although he claims that postmodern Bollywood films employ a kind of self-referentiality that is 'of the critical and ironic same' as earlier periods of Indian cinema, he suggests that there is a distinctiveness about post-1990s cinema as it engages in a more multi-layered referencing of popular culture on a specifically *global* scale. Thus he agrees that postmodern theory is 'analogous' with more recent popular cinema – making it 'genuinely refreshing' and 'inventive' (41–2).

Despite being somewhat limited in their scope and few in number, the above discussions of emerging postmodern trends have helped carve a niche for the study of postmodern Bollywood, the significance of which in Indian film studies I now intend to raise through my own rigorous reading of contemporary Bollywood cinema aesthetics.

NOTES

1. Cinema institutions and theatres have used several excuses to explain why they do not regularly screen Bollywood films, such as being charged exorbitant prices from film distributors. There are also ethical issues concerning the rumours surrounding the cinema's alleged funding of underworld and Islamic terrorist activities and its anti-Pakistani sentiments – see Aftab (2002: 95–7). The BFI appears to continue to place more emphasis on promoting independent Indian cinema, as an alternative to Bollywood, as

seen through the programme and industry names featured in its 2013 London Indian Film Festival – see www.londonindianfilmfestival.co.uk
2. This empirical investigation took place from January to June 2009 at the University of Sussex.
3. A 1990s American children's TV series franchise which included costumed superheroes and comic-book-style action stunts.
4. Based on research collated in 2009.
5. As mentioned earlier, these newer commentaries may note the films' MTV aesthetics, bigger budgets and glossy look in the vein of Hollywood blockbusters, but they rarely explore these textual changes in any detail.
6. See my analysis of *Abhay* in Chapter 5.
7. The South Indian film of the same name was remade three years later in Bollywood but retained some of its original key cast and crew, including its director A. R. Murugadoss and leading actress Asin Thottumkal.
8. This argument forms part of a larger discussion I instigated with DJ Bobby Fricton, Indian film journalist Asjad Nazir and Bollywood 'fusion' film directors Jeremy Wooding and Herbert Krill which formed the 'Bollywood Reborn' panel event at the Raindance East Film Festival in London, Tuesday 26 April 2005.
9. Athique uses the example of a film festival tour across Australia in 2004/2005, which 'recorded an attendance of 40,000-odd people of which 80 percent were non-Indians'; and a screening survey with a group of ninety young Australians. All the films he mentions were produced after 2000.
10. It is also important to cite here the work of Lalita Gopalan (2002), who has already drawn our attention to the formal and structural nuances of pre-millennial popular Hindi films via their use of interruptive elements such as intermissions and song sequences.

CHAPTER 4

Postmodernism and India

This chapter considers the much-contested concept of postmodernism within a global context by surveying selected critical writing which has previously attempted to relate the concept to both Western and Eastern cinemas. By providing clear definitions of what I mean by 'postmodern' (since the concept, in particular, is known to manifest itself in many different and often contradictory ways), I am able to locate and investigate Bollywood's postmodern aesthetics.

INDIA: A POSTMODERN PRESENCE

An investigation into postmodern shifts in contemporary Bollywood is best begun by observing the film industry's geographical site of production. A brief descriptive walk through two of India's most prominent celluloid cities perfectly conjures up a sense of what I mean by a *postmodern presence* in contemporary Indian culture (or more precisely, contemporary Indian cinema). In today's Delhi, one can alight from an air-conditioned electric sky-train, walk through an expansive, immaculate, cavernous silvery brushed-steel station (equipped with all the latest computer-generated digital communication technology), only to find oneself suddenly thrown back into the Third World at the station exit. Standing at the entrance to Delhi's state-of-the-art Chawri Bazaar railway station is enough to confound one's sense of place and time. Above ground, within a few metres, hundreds of ragged street-merchants, bullock carts and rickshaw-wallahs stampede under a sky of thick smog, soiled shop signs and tangled electricity cables. All of these tenaciously encircle the shiny new metro station – ironically one of the Government of India's latest development ventures to modernise the city through its transport system.[1] Delhi's cityscape reveals a similar paradox. A vast concrete flyover stretching across the city seems somewhat dwarfed under the towering 175-foot-tall statue of Hanuman, the Hindu monkey god, whose figure looms over the city from every direction.[2] Similarly, in Mumbai, the city's ever-evolving dystopian skyline offers a cacophony of shanty towns and derelict buildings squashed in alongside endless gleaming glass skyscrapers and designer shopping malls – a constant architectural battleground for tradition versus modernisation, the past versus the future. In this city, where Italian sports cars give way to the stray cows that nestle in the central reservations of dual carriageways, the past, present and future seem to coexist with an air of indifference. The poverty-stricken sleep peacefully in television boxes, whilst across the road, the wealthy middle classes purchase their latest collection of one-lakh[3] designer saris.

Andrew Wyatt (2005) has suggested a possible link between this contemporary climate in India and what has been described broadly as the 'postmodern condition' through his study of the country's recent economic shifts. Wyatt argues how late 1990s India has moved away from its 1950s modernist national visions of economic development, and instead towards an 'imagined' economy (where the country now sees itself as already an internationally oriented and important economy) and a 'more fragmented and disjointed approach to economic policy in India' (466). What Wyatt terms 'postmodern India' describes the simultaneous national and international branding of the country (467) (indeed, interesting connections can be made here to Rajadhyaksha's aforementioned discussion around the use of Bollywood as an international brand for India), but his account is not a full acknowledgement of postmodernity on the level of Indian society. Rather, he asserts how certain late capitalist financial structures are creeping into India's metropolitan economy. For example, there is evidence of postmodern patterns of production and consumption in India, particularly with regard to the increased desire for 'intangible and ephemeral goods' (466). There is now more attention given to the building of shopping malls and the retail-leisure industry than to rural agriculture. Wyatt also notes an increase in the variety of cultural products on offer and the 'differentiation in the market for popular culture' in India, briefly mentioning the recent shifts in popular Hindi cinema as a prime example of this (474). He also draws attention to the growing impact of advertising which (by curiously engaging in a kind of patriotic dialogue) has made 'a consumption oriented imaginary part of the common sense' (477) and has also led to a rise in celebrity endorsements of international consumer products.

So what of cinema-going in such an environment? How has this uneven development and economic shift affected Bollywood cinema viewing beyond its days of class-divided picture halls? Rapidly sprouting multiplexes now belittle their since-declining predecessors and house a variety of consumerist treats. From designer clothes stores to DVD vending machines, the Mumbai cinema multiplex has become the epitome of modern luxury in India, be it only for the middle classes. But before one becomes too comfortably settled in the auditorium's premium-class soft leather cinema hall seats, box of masala-flavoured popcorn in hand, a peculiar thing happens: the bellowing sound of the Indian national anthem surrounds us in the darkness, a giant Indian flag envelops the screen, and one is forced to join the rest of the auditorium audience, who are now all standing with hand on heart in a ritualistic salute. This is contemporary India, and it is from this place that a new kind of postmodern Indian cinema also rises.[4] But what do I mean by 'postmodern Indian cinema'? And is it really viable to apply the term outside a Western context?

POSTMODERNISM IN THE NON-WEST

As discussed in Chapter 1, many major theorists of the postmodern have confined themselves to relatively West-centric definitions of the term, most explicitly Fredric Jameson (1991). Despite the counteractive intentions and conflicting interests of various postmodern commentators, there seems to be a commonality between them with regard to *where* this (post)modernity is deemed to be globally situated. Indeed, most have acknowledged universal issues such as globalisation and commercialisation as part and parcel of postmodernity. Most famously, Jean-François Lyotard (1992) has commented upon this 'postmodern eclecticism' where one can 'listen to reggae . . . watch a Western . . . eat McDonald's at midday and local cuisine at night . . . wear Paris perfume in Tokyo and dress Retro in Hong Kong' (8). However, for the most part, celebrated discussions of the development of postmodern art politics have concentrated exclusively on Americanisation, Hollywood and other forms of Western and European cinema and art.

The foundations of postmodernism are very much rooted in the West. Accordingly, there are many thinkers who would hold reservations towards any attempt to theorise the concept's *global* reach, instead asserting its inability to exist in parts of the world untouched by post-industrialism and modernism. How can a society that has never been truly modern be postmodern? How can a concept that revolves around technology, consumerism and mechanical reproduction be appropriated in the context of Third World poverty? There is a danger of taking the term for granted, but I would insist that, in keeping with postmodernism's own principles, stretching the boundaries and maintaining ambiguity in the concept's definitions is essential, rather than simply confining it to a West-centric perspective. Definitions of the postmodern are forever in transition and under negotiation. The popular assumption that the term implies a continuation of or connection to the era of modernism (postmodernism) is merely one of many explanations on offer. Whilst it may have begun as something serving particular and precise objectives, the concept has since grown tortuous and diverse in its application.

Postmodernism has an abundance of defining traits. Some of these are seen to spring from a particular historical context: post-industrialism, Western capitalism, modernism, whilst others – as autonomous stylistic devices – promote the concept's principles, shape its aesthetics and (rather than serving as catalysts) address the *consequences* of a postmodern world. For the purpose of my own investigation into Bollywood cinema, I approach postmodernism as a much more versatile form of cultural practice. I am interested not so much in postmodernity as a historical period of post-industrial Western society, but rather in postmodernism as an aesthetic philosophy or a critical tool, and a non-geographically specific artistic tendency which can be assumed by any culture.

Dominant Western theories have contributed, and continue to contribute, a great deal towards the concept of the postmodern. But although there is still much to be explored in these Western fields, it is vital that we are at the same time able to continually reassess and reach beyond these confines to gain an objectively broad understanding of what the 'postmodern' was, is, and will become. Postmodernism has for too long been considered a fundamentally Western motif. To suggest that this cultural movement operates exclusively within the Western hemisphere is to ignore the fact that its very objective transcends geographical, historical and spatial boundaries. Why should a concept that comprises texts produced for global mass circulation and consumption be so irrelevant beyond the West – particularly as countries such as China (Hong Kong), Japan and India are increasingly powered by international conglomerate corporations and capitalist industries? It is not my intention to suggest that these other unexplored non-Western territories can offer a necessarily better or polarised perspective on the postmodern. Rather, I aim to show that these new areas can in fact help us to reflect upon and adjust current ideas on the concept, allowing the (now somewhat stagnant) postmodern debate to be reawakened and further developed.

POSTMODERNISM IN THE GLOBAL AND EASTERN CONTEXT

A select few have already attempted to apply the term 'postmodern' to non-Western contexts and have contributed to the notion of a *global* or *international* postmodernism. Hans Bertens (1986) particularly notes the early contributions of Ihab Hassan, William V. Spanos and Richard Wasson, who are regarded as the first theoreticians to explore postmodernism as an international movement (38, 44). This global relevance has also been further interrogated by Scott Nygren (1989), Mitsuhiro Yoshimoto (1991), Kwame Anthony Appiah (1991), Hans Bertens and Douwe Fokkema (1997), Ziauddin Sardar (1998), R. Radhakrishnan (2000), and Arif Dirlik and Xudong Zhang (2000). My work does not form part of or spring from any particular school of thought (perhaps unfeasibly, given the subject matter and objectives of this book), but the above-noted critical investigations into global postmodernism have greatly inspired and motivated my research. It is therefore important and worthwhile to explore some of their key ideas and perspectives, with a particular focus on how they define and authenticate the 'postmodern East'.

Within the Eastern terrain, Japan is perhaps viewed as the place where the frameworks of modernity and postmodernity can be situated with the most legitimacy. Japan has been viewed as postmodern in its very essence, particularly through its hyper-consumerist culture, so much so that it has even been imagined as a catalyst for Western postmodernism (Melville, 1994: 280). For example, the technology-saturated city of Tokyo has heavily inspired postmodern cyberpunk fiction. Contemporary Japanese society has been viewed as fundamentally postmodern in various ways, but Masao Miyoshi (1994) offers a précis of the country's key postmodern attributes as the following: (1) a hostility towards logic and rationalism; (2) an engagement with the visual and a world-renowned reputation for packaging and image-making; (3) its 'devotion to simulacra'; (4) its fascination with the sublime (most notably through the popular theme of suicide); and (5) its trademark as an industry of global mass production and reproduction (148). For Miyoshi, postmodernism is a way of gaining insight into contemporary shifts in Japanese society. It also serves as a means of resistance and a way of equalling (if not superseding) the authority of the West.

In his chapter 'Reconsidering Modernism: Japanese Film and the Postmodern Context', Scott Nygren (1989) traces the parallels between postmodernist and modernist movements in Japan and what he refers to simply as 'Western' society. For Nygren, both modern and postmodern cultural movements are unquestionably present in Japanese art, and he contemplates the possibility of an 'alternative access to the postmodern situation' within Japanese society (7). Despite its title, Nygren's essay focuses mainly on modernism, though his argument often appears to relate interchangeably to both Japanese modernism and its 'post-' form (which is somewhat problematic, given the popular polarisation and differentiation of the two concepts). Nygren asserts how Japanese modernism functions inversely to its Western equivalent. He claims that just as Japanese modernist art has been heavily influenced by Western traditionalist metaphysics and humanism, likewise, Western modernism appropriates Japonisme (traditional Japanese aesthetics) as a means of deconstructing its own humanist ideologies. As he demonstrates in the case of cinema, whereas Japanese traditionalist filmmaker Yasujiro Ozu's film style was read as modernist in the West, in Japan, classical Western film conventions were interchangeably adapted to help oppose Japanese cinema's own dominant traditional ideologies. This process of what Nygren terms 'cross-cultural inversion/modernism' raises interesting questions surrounding the dialectics between Western and Eastern modernisms. Particularly in the case of Nygren's noted global interplay of modernist and traditionalist techniques, one becomes aware of the causal effects and destructive consequences of this form of cultural exchange:

> Japanese artists influenced by Western modernism were placed in the odd position of imitating a Western authenticity that in turn imitated Japanese tradition to oppose Western humanism . . . Insofar as Japanese artists sought in Western modernism's borrowing of Japanese tradition a modernism to position against Japanese tradition, they became caught in mirrors within mirrors, an *aporia*, or collapse of meaning. (13)

Viewing Japanese modernism as something created 'on its own terms' (7), Nygren perceives Japanese postmodernism as having an 'analogous but not identical' connection with 'the non-progressivist interplay of traditional and modernist values in Western postmodernism' (14). Unfortunately, Nygren does not extend his discussion here to delineate these connections and differences, nor does he offer explanations of what comparative features Japanese postmodernist texts might possess. But Nygren's account is useful in several ways, namely: in disputing the West-centric origins of Western modernism and relocating them in Japanese traditional art;[5] in promoting the possibility of *alternative modernisms* in the East, operating in a different way from their Western counterparts; in demonstrating an analogous relationship between Eastern and Western modernisms and thus the value of their comparative study; in serving as a reminder that Western definitions of modernism and postmodernism are not quite universal, and that the concepts' characteristics can at times be culturally specific and thus open to interpretation, reconfiguration and inversion; in acknowledging how the tension-ridden adversaries of old and new, past and present, and traditional versus alternative in postmodern art further gain complexity and intertwine when considered in a cross-cultural context; and finally, for proposing the idea that non-Western postmodernism complies not with Western postmodernist but rather with Western *traditionalist* conventions.

Although Nygren tries to account for Japanese modernism, others see modernity as something unfeasible in the East. For example, for Mitsuhiro Yoshimoto (1993), modernity remains ultimately unattainable in Japan, since the concept relies on the division of West and non-West:

The non-West can achieve the goal of modernising itself by the advancement of technology, yet modernity remains always unattainable to the non-West because what constitutes modernity is precisely the exclusion of the non-West from the modern, 'universal' West. The paradox of modernity for the non-West is if the non-West somehow succeeds in obtaining modernity, that would also be the end of modernity, or, in Hegelian words, the 'end of history'. (Yoshimoto: 118)

Again with reference to Ozu, Yoshimoto sees modernism as an inappropriate mechanism for categorising and refocusing the director's films beyond Japanese traditionalist filmmaking.[6] He instead encourages us to view the filmmaker through the postmodern, which does not encourage such a rash break from tradition and avoids 'retrapping him in the discursive field of international modernism' (115). Rather, ' "Postmodern Japan" is constructed in the process of de-historicisation and a parodic mimicry of the critique of modernity in the name of tradition with "progressive potentialities" ' (121).

INTERNATIONAL POSTMODERNISM

Hans Bertens and Douwe Fokkema's book *International Postmodernism* (1997) usefully accounts for the wide variety of approaches to postmodernism in the global and non-Euro-American context, though their study is somewhat literature-specific. This is interesting in itself as literature remains an even more problematic medium in the Third World context than popular cinema, which for the most part is still created for and consumed by the masses. However, as a significant number of the book's chapters explore the concept within a specific national context, it is clear that here the focus is not so much on quantitative investigations of postmodern textual consumption (measuring the proportions of society that access and consume postmodern texts) as on the *methods* and *motives* behind each of these emerging non-Western postmodern literary works. While these postmodern texts may not outwardly instigate postmodern thinking for the whole of a particular society, their postmodern fashioning may nevertheless prove to be *symptomatic* of present shifts in non-Western contemporary culture. Hence, the postmodern strategies and devices I hope to identify through my study of contemporary popular Bollywood cinema should be understood not as socially revolutionary, but as nonetheless representative and reflective of a postmodern conceptual thinking (if not a postmodern practice) already present in India.

Bertens and Fokkema defend their international application of the postmodern firstly by drawing attention to the convergence of postmodern literature and postcolonialism. Comparative studies of these two research areas have proved popular and fruitful (see Tiffin [1988], Appiah [1991], Hooks [1991] and During [1998]), suggesting a complex, problematic yet interdependent relationship between the two. Postmodernism has often been utilised in postcolonial criticism owing to its anti-essentialist nature, its obfuscation of identity, and its tendency to deconstruct socio-cultural monoliths (or 'grand narratives'). However, while the prefix in postcolonialism suggests the superseding or desired overriding of colonialist literature and authority (49), the 'post-' in postmodernism does not necessarily imply the same. It is modernism that seeks to withdraw from the autonomy of traditional practices, while postmodernism, conversely, preoccupies itself with revisiting (be it in order to critique and rework) history, tradition and the past. But along with their differences, the postcolonial and the postmodern do share a likeness in their methods and strategies. Perhaps the most significant connection, as drawn by Bertens and Fokkema, is the way both paradigms achieve development and expansion by surpassing their place of origin. In their study, Bertens and Fokkema examine the global travel of postmodern writing, favouring the 'diffusions and transformations of the concept' over the study of its 'original invention' (298). As in the case of postcolonial literature, sanctioning postmodernism as a globally applicable process helps undermine national and local monoliths and nurtures inclusivity over 'Otherisation'. This approach, even if somewhat romantically idealist itself, at least opens the field by providing alternatives to the concept's previously exclusive and thus limiting definitions. Within a global context, postmodernism essentially becomes a problem if the term is used to refer explicitly to a particular kind of logic within the social system (Sanehide and Ken: 511) and a 'lifestyle based on consumption' (Bertens, 1997: 5). Instead of struggling to locate it within Third World frameworks in that sense, Bertens and Fokkema alternatively present the concept as a universally functioning 'workable poetics' (303), an 'interpretive code' or 'style marker' (298) used as a 'framework to debate the nature of language and the subject . . . [the] provisionality of meaning and truth . . . [the] inevitability of power relations . . . [and] the politics of representation' (Bertens and Fokkema, 1997: 7).

International Postmodernism is also useful for its critical responses to the concept's appropriation within particular national contexts. Although the book's individual chapters cover much of the non-Western terrain, it is interesting to note how India is singled out as a particularly problematic setting for postmodernity from the outset. Unlike countries such as Japan (where the application of modernist principles is better tolerated), India is regarded as a place which socially restricts the postmodern owing to its intransigent and reactionary nature. As Bertens and Fokkema declare in the introduction to their chapter on the international reception and processing of the postmodern, 'local conditions have destroyed the identity of the concept of postmodernism completely in India' (300). Although they do not dwell on this argument long enough to convey what these unique 'conditions' may be, it is clear that they are concerned with the absence of cultural modernism and a problem of assimilation within Indian society. Other local conditions put forward as possible factors affecting postmodernism's execution in certain countries include the lack of tradition or presence of a historical avant-garde, the presence of a neo-Marxist tradition or a communist regime, and a general reluctance regarding or resistance towards any form of American and Western influence.

Notwithstanding these reservations, the materialisation of the postmodern in India is still tackled within this edited collection. In his chapter 'Facets of Postmodernism: A Search for Roots. The Indian Literacy Scene', Indra Nath Choudhuri aims to resolve this problem of incompatibility by proposing a call for new (socio-culturally customised) definitions of the postmodern. Choudhuri opposes the comparative study and application of Western postmodernism in the East through familiar accusations of subordination and West-centrism. However, his attempt to propose instead a 'parallel' postmodernism in India, which he names '*uttara andhikata*', seems somewhat fuzzy in its delineation and intentions. Choudhuri fails to provide tangible examples demonstrating the productivity and value of this new concept, beyond evading Eurocentrism. His suggested effacement of Western postmodernism through the introduction of parallel versions of the concept is seen as a way of 'challenging the very idea of Eurocentrist modernism'. But the critical evasion in this approach is itself similarly problematic, primarily through the fact that any such form of challenge to or critical attack on Western postmodernism would inevitably end up conceding to it to some extent. The subject of critique would unavoidably need to be referred to and thus given a certain level of significance in order to explain the very 'parallels' and differences behind these newer foreign manifestations of the concept. To avoid this kind of exclusivism in my research, I maintain allusions to Western postmodernism and instead view postmodern manifestations in India in the very way in which Choudhuri explains current modernisation practices in India – as an *active response to* (and critical engagement with) *the West*, rather than as simply a passive process of Westernisation (492).

Choudhuri seeks Indian modernity in terms of an introspective turn to tradition and history as opposed to cross-cultural borrowing, but he overlooks India's inherent tendency for cultural appropriation, particularly vis-à-vis its colonial connections with the West. What is more, he acknowledges India's past indigenisation of Western artistic modes as a positive and productive method of achieving cultural innovation and producing alternative experiences and perspectives, listing in particular movements such as imagism, the anti-novel, the anti-play, expressionism, beat poetry, and experimentalism (492). It would be equally unethical (and somewhat condescending) to deny Indians this 'alternative perceptivity', particularly the newer generations, who can find this a liberating escape from oppressive traditionalist cultural regimes. Thus, cultural appropriation could instead be better viewed as a powerful system of rebelling against, critiquing and Otherising the West through mimicry (see Bhabha, 1984).

In overview, Choudhuri's essay proposes that Indian postmodernism should be observed through the Indian subject's 'own realities', independently of the West. But how can one do so when these realities are so inherently tied up with the West, and when the postmodern, by definition, summons the demotion and abstraction of social realities? Despite certain differences in perspective, Choudhuri's account is useful for my own investigation into postmodernism in Indian cinema. Firstly, with regard to his idea of Indian modernity as a reaction or response to the West: Indian modernity is not to be confused with Westernisation or modernisation because it still absorbs and expresses traditional values and shows reluctance towards the technological. For Choudhuri, Indian modernity is not achieved through what is borrowed, but rather through the country's own roots, traditions and realities (494). This idea of accessing and constructing the modern through discourses of the past (tradition, culture, mythology, religion) is particularly compelling, and something I will adapt and explore in my own investigation of Indian cinema. However, Choudhuri is perhaps a little too hasty to draw all our attention to tradition and discount the role cross-cultural exchange plays in helping India conjure up its own experience of modernity. Despite his reservations, Choudhuri usefully acknowledges India's history of imitating Western artistic modes as a way of escaping from the experience of an essentially insular society. I believe it is worthwhile exploring how indigenised foreign elements may exist and work together with the traditional (though by no means harmoniously) to achieve a mutual goal. Choudhuri hints at this coexisting tension when discussing India's conflicting yet simultaneous desire for 'romantic individualism' and a 'reassertion of cultural traditions' (493). Indian modernism is regarded as a way of helping the former manifest itself, and I would add that Indian postmodernism balances and supervises the coexistence of the two. Whereas modernism is usually concerned with Western processes, postmodernism has an affiliation with and dutifulness towards the indigenous. Finally, Choudhuri's account is useful for its claim that the 'Indian mind has always conceived of change within a framework of continuity' (495), thereby suggesting a habitual cognitive tendency towards repetition and a regression into the past, and the constant pursuit of innovation through the ancient – a crucial postmodern paradox and fundamental crisis within contemporary Indian society which, as I shall reveal later, is inherent in much contemporary Bollywood cinema.

Another fruitful investigation into postmodernism in the Asian context comes from Arif Dirlik and Xudong Zhang's edited book exploring

Postmodernism and China. Dirlik and Zhang provide a well-balanced approach to the subject, identifying not only the values but also several key problems and possible objections regarding it. For example, the authors observe a common disdain towards the application of postmodern theory in the East arising from its apparent yielding to Western modes of thinking, or what Xudong Zhang describes brusquely as a 'whoring after Western academic fashions' (Zhang: 404). Consequently, this method of research is seen as often being written off as an unethical 'social fantasy to "catch up" with West' (Dirlik and Zhang: 9). Global postmodernism is reduced to empiricism and nominalism, particularly through its misplacing of First World politics within Third World contexts. Ultimately, the approach is either viewed as simply advocating global capitalism or is dismissed as unsubstantial and vague, drawing connections on the weak premise of 'postmodernism for postmodernism's sake' (ibid.). An even more valid justification for such scepticism is found in the key problems Dirlik and Zhang raise regarding postmodernism's *geographical* and *cultural* displacement in this Asian context. Countries such as China (and similarly, India) could be regarded as too rural and educationally and economically underdeveloped, and thus inadequate spaces in which to foster postmodernity. A certain level of literacy is required for the significance of these cultural concepts to be socially realised, and wealth is required in order to experience the consequences of commodification and consumerist practices, as is a civilised urban lifestyle. In addition, Wang Ning's chapter 'The Mapping of Chinese Postmodernity' also addresses the popular belief that these countries are somewhat socially unreceptive and incapable of absorbing foreign contemporary cultural movements, operating purely on the basis of practicality and relativity. As Ning notes, the West offers 'a multiplicity of choices [whereas] . . . in an economically developing Third World society such as China . . . creation is strongly colored with a sort of utilitarian and cognitive function' (35). But as several of the book's authors unanimously protest, these somewhat arrogant assumptions verge on generalisation and oppression, offering a narrow, naive, colonialist view of the East as a conservative, socio-developmentally-restricted Other. Indeed, Eastern societies do cling to and appear somewhat held back by traditional modes when compared to the West, but this in no way confirms their incompatibility with the postmodern – which itself fundamentally employs past traditions as part of its innovatory strategies.

In response to the aforementioned cultural inadequacies of China, Dirlik and Zhang counterpose and unpick these criticisms, reconceptualising Eastern postmodernism and proposing their own vision of what it might entail. In response to the nativisation and geographical location of postmodernism, they argue that, by definition, the concept cannot be determined by nation, space or temporality. Postmodernism, as a non-nationalist concept, provides us with a way in which to 'grasp and make sense of a complex reality that does not lend itself to comprehension through categories marked by the spatial and temporal teleologies of modernity' (Dirlik and Zhang: 9). The paradoxical co-inhabitancy of industrialised and rural lifestyles in countries such as China and India unusually offers a space in which social progression occurs in a lateral rather than a linear fashion. As another contributor to the book, Sheldon Hsiao-peng Lu, comments with reference to China, the modern, postmodern and 'pre-modern' transpire through 'spatial coextension rather than temporal succession' (Hsiao-peng Lu: 146) – an idea shared with Ning, who declares China a site where the pre-modern, modern, postmodern and primitive are *blended* (Ning: 34). The very term 'uneven development' indicates social progression as well as social dormancy, and thus the possibility of non-Western societies manifesting post-industrial symptoms to some extent. The authors of *Postmodernism and China* draw attention to how the third (and second) world is becoming increasingly pluralistic (once again aided by globalisation) and how, if viewed as such, it opens itself to new cultural movements such as postmodernism, which could eventually be assimilated as a cultural dominant in Asian societies. Although we may be a while away from realising a postmodern Asian society in this final stage, this last point at least removes the fallacy of the East as homogeneous and the tiresome argument that Asian countries are virtually immune to cultural assimilation.

In his counter-criticism, Ning argues against the polarisations of East and West that accompany elitist calls for postmodern exclusivity. As a way of avoiding accusations of mimicry and arbitrary forced connections with Western cultural concepts, Ning suggests that Chinese postmodernism need not be regarded as something brought about by a specific socio-historical condition, but may be seen as a consciously 'borrowed' concept with different means. To paraphrase Ning, non-Western postmodernism is a mutated version of its original, which eventually assumes and produces its own indigenous traits (24). Postmodernism can best be useful as a critical tool, a 'descriptive paradigm', an 'interpretive code' or 'reading strategy' (23). In this case, the concept's relevance in the East can be broken down in terms of its *theoretical* and *practical* tangibility, and these can be dealt with as two separate issues.

Ultimately, Dirlik and Zhang's book is useful for anticipating possible problems with, finding solutions for, and offering suggestions on how to utilise postmodernity in the East. And in fact, despite their varied contexts and locales, all of the above attempts to globally apply the postmodern share several key viewpoints and beliefs. All consider freeing postmodernism from exclusivity and homogenising definitions, and the possibility of removing wholly accomplished post-industrialism from the equation. They suggest that in order to truly observe the postmodern, one must be prepared to take a postmodern approach and be willing to both surpass and rework questions of concept-origin. In aiming to broaden postmodern definitions, all consider the possibility of not one, but multiple alternative postmodern*isms* – each with their own limitations. While the majority of these alternative postmodernisms are situated uniquely in the realm of Eastern cultural production, a magnetic attraction to Western postmodernity is often maintained – at times by conceiving Eastern postmodernism as a possible process of inversion of the concept's original effects and principles. It is through this contrast and inversion that we are able to extend our definition of this cultural phenomenon.

The presence of Western cultural modes in Eastern postmodernism, by way of cross-cultural appropriation, is considered analogous to the fundamental postmodern tension between modernism (the new, innovation) and tradition (past, history). In this context, imitation paradoxically becomes a site for innovation and escape, and postmodern cultural appropriation can become a way of responding to, critiquing and perhaps even internally attacking the Western Other. Arguments made in the interest of protecting the East from converting to Westernised postmodernity are invalidated as such an effort would equally lead once again to trapping Eastern culture within its own national and local monoliths and its subsequent 'Otherisation'.

'UNIVERSALISING' THE EAST

Despite their interesting revelations, the above writers on global postmodernism notably struggle with a need to justify and defend their approach. Criticism aimed at the application of Western-originating cultural theories to non-Western contexts is to be expected, particularly as this can end up reaffirming the notion of Western values as *universal*. Seeking Western aesthetic values in non-Western texts could be seen as unethical, and attempting to do so under the umbrella of postmodernism would go against the concept's own calls for anti-universalism. Universalism is to be avoided, as it supports the West's self-reaffirmation by putting itself at the centre (as a universal point of reference). It consequently Otherises or particularises the non-West while regarding itself as invisible.

As the above discussions have revealed, postmodernism can be made universally applicable, yet can also have culturally unique manifestations. Whilst it may indeed be influenced by Western concepts and techniques, global postmodernism is a place where the West simultaneously self-deconstructs as it informs. The West, once appropriated, is no longer able to be ubiquitous. It is instead opened up to critique and deconstruction. The cross-cultural manifestation and consequent mutation of the original concepts of postmodernism allow previous definitions to be challenged, remystified or superseded. In my chapter on contemporary Bollywood remakes, I reveal how the indigenisation of Western filmmaking modes as a 'universal language' in turn helps to expose this language and prevents it from functioning irrefutably. A global approach to postmodernism may in fact be the answer to seizing the concept from Western elitism and authority once and for all, through a gradual process of reaffirming and reworking existing models.

THE QUESTION OF LEGITIMACY

A final unfavourable critique, briefly addressed in Chapter 1, that could be directed at my attempt to associate Bollywood cinema with postmodern art concerns the issue of legitimacy. Some scholars may argue that there is a danger here of simply identifying coincidental or incidental stylistic correlations between these two art forms and then jumping to the conclusion that these minor correlations mean they both automatically qualify as 'postmodern'. Postmodern techniques refer to ordinary stylistic and textual devices (which can be present in earlier forms of cultural art, such as modernist and tribal art) that have become postmodern only through their being intentionally used in a new way (often politically) and produced within a particular socio-economic context. A text cannot be declared 'postmodern' just because it happens to contain a few of the same isolated stylistic devices found in other texts that have been labelled 'postmodern'. This kind of argument is common and can be responded to in several ways. Firstly, the above statement of the conditions under which a text can become or be labelled postmodern is problematic in that it implies that stylistic devices need to be verified as being *intentionally* motivated by a postmodern political incentive in order to pass as postmodern. This issue of intent is particularly tricky, and is therefore something I will engage with here briefly, and in Chapter 6 in more detail.

In general, my response would be to argue that postmodernism is not always achieved through intention. So many years on, we still contest whether certain films are 'wholly' postmodern. Quite often, the postmodern intentions or effects of a text remain open to debate. The notion of postmodern intentionality leaves no room for interpretation (unless one believes that postmodernism is where interpretation ends). By interpretation, I mean the ability to reread or rewrite the text and take it out of its normal implied context if one wishes. If anything, the postmodern text is ultimately an 'open access' text. What is more, one could ask: what governing role can inferred meaning play in texts which are, for example, fundamentally devoid of depth and averse to meaning-making? Postmodern signification does not stop at production (particularly when we consider its associations with ideas surrounding the death of authorial intent),[7] but also involves the consumer of the text. The consumer's role is particularly distinctive here as postmodern texts tend to be highly self-reflexive, contradictory or chaotic in content, and steeped in intertextuality.

Thus, in this book, I offer my own 'postmodern reading' of contemporary Bollywood cinema.

The contemporary Bollywood cinematic texts I engage with in this book do, in many cases, share objectives with those of established Western postmodern texts. This includes, for example, the rejection and conquering of discourse and meaning by replacing them with pure figuralism and sensation; the desire to simultaneously reinvent, reaffirm and efface the past; the evocation of nostalgia; and the questioning of realism and reality through its magnification. Thus, with regard to legitimacy, although I initially identify a range of Western postmodernism's common stylistic characteristics in contemporary Bollywood cinema, I later narrow my focus on the key traits that have had a more obvious impact and exhibit clearer postmodern principles, perspectives and agendas. This will avoid my taking the term for granted and making any connections that could be seen as merely coincidental.

POSTMODERNISM AS A FORM OF AESTHETIC PRACTICE

Postmodernism can be looked at, often simultaneously, from a variety of positions. It can be examined temporally as a precise period or phase of Western cultural history (post-war, early 1960s to the present day), economically as a major shift in the structure and patterning of consumer trade (multinational capitalism, global exchange, transgression from use value to exchange value), or socially as a cultural epidemic, symptomatic of the degradation or mystification of previously upheld ideological value systems (the waning of post-war bourgeois high modernism).

As was mentioned in Chapter 1, postmodernism has offered us supplementary ways of enunciating and presenting the world. As such, it can be viewed as an abstract cultural theory, offering intellectuals a way of contemplating and contextualising culture in its present state. However, it is also concurrently conceived of as a life philosophy, an adopted lifestyle, a cultural fashioning which can be assumed by anyone. Once adopted, its stylistic modes and principles can help manipulate structures and formations of identity and assist ontological playfulness. For the individual, it offers a means of self-evaluation, self-affirmation or self-abstraction. Productively, it regurgitates, distorts, transforms, innovates, reifies and reinvents. Politically, it can reassert, question, challenge, critique, and deconstruct existing values and ideals. Theoretically, it promises an all-encompassing metaphysics, ruthlessly and ambitiously swallowing up every representation, and every articulated phase of cultural history it comes across. Much like Michael Ende's 'das Nichts' in *Die Unendliche Geschichte* (1979), it aspires to consume *everything* only to leave us with *nothing*. After it has hit, some argue that we are left with a feeling of emptiness. The mind becomes a barren landscape where all creativity and thought has been either stolen or emptied of meaning. However, it is this same void and 'nothingness' that paradoxically draws our attention to the barren landscape before us, encouraging us to replenish and requestion our original pursuit of meaning, innovation and re-presentation.

For the purpose of my investigation into contemporary shifts in Indian cinema, I am interested in these latter approaches to postmodernism as a form of cultural *practice* and a mode of cultural resistance; a stylistic principle assumed in cultural production to help a work withstand existing universalising cultural dominants. In Bollywood's case, postmodern aesthetics are adopted to help it resist the First World economic power that Hollywood/Western cinema holds. However, this resistance is not to be taken as a simple act of evasion by way of 'sidestepping' Western hegemony. Rather, resistance is achieved through appropriating the dominant culture and its internal conversion. Western modernisation is transcended not through distance, but in proximity, through confrontation and *association*. I am also interested in shifting perspectives on the epistemology of postmodernism, and I hope to demonstrate how postmodern Bollywood films can inform us about the nature of the postmodern, allowing us to question its foundations. I believe these films strengthen the concept's legitimacy as a cultural-political enigma, as well as its progressive potential and overall global significance.

NOTES

1. Correct at the time of writing.
2. The brick and cement statue is built as part of a Hindu temple, which sits at its base, on the intersection of Pusa Road and Link Road, Karolbagh, Delhi.
3. A 'lakh' is the Hindi term for a monetary unit equivalent of 100,000 Indian rupees.
4. In January 2003 it became state law to screen the Indian national anthem in multiplex theatres throughout Maharashtra. The video playback of the national flag fluttering to the national anthem has been enforced by the Maharashtra government, which regulates the authority of screening films in movie theatres across the jurisdiction of Mumbai. See Iyer (2002) and Singh (2003).
5. Nygren discusses how key modernist works of artists such as Van Gogh and Monet were heavily inspired by Japanese woodcuts and brocade prints, though the extent of this influence has been contested and is open to debate (Nygren: 8).
6. It is worth noting here that modernism also tends to be a rather difficult and problematic concept in film studies in general.
7. Postmodern theory has built on Roland Barthes' concept of the 'death of the author' (Barthes, 1977).

CHAPTER 5

Postmodern Bollywood

POSTMODERNISM AND FILM THEORY

In the following case studies, I observe a variety of postmodern strategies and conventions operating within contemporary Bollywood cinema. Throughout the remainder of this book, I draw from a selection of seminal postmodern works, including Jean Baudrillard's (1983) formulation of postmodern hyperrealism (the extinction of actual reality and its substitution by the endless saturation of 'simulated' images) and Fredric Jameson's scrutiny of postmodern art as nostalgic, depthless, soulless pastiche, leading to the annihilation of temporality in which past and history collapse into the present. Jean François Lyotard's celebration of the sublime, the presentation of the unpresentable in postmodern art, and the destruction of grand monolithic narratives, will also be drawn upon. Furthermore, in relation to the issue of historical temporality, I have also been informed by Hayden White's (1978, 1996) enlightening work on the blurring of the boundaries of historical truth as fact and as fictional narrative.

My work also draws influences from theorists who have attempted to develop these ideas specifically in relation to the medium of cinema. This primarily includes Scott Lash's (1988) expansion of Baudrillard's concept of the simulacrum through observation of its prioritisation of the figural over discourse and consequent subordination of meaning and signification, specifically with respect to Hollywood's spectacle-based cinema, and Linda Hutcheon's (1988, 1989) retorts against Jameson's ideas of postmodern depthlessness and a-historicism in nostalgia films, arguing instead for a politics of representation and a reworking of the past in postmodern cinema.

In addition to Hutcheon, there are several other scholars who have tried to salvage meaning and value in the cinematic postmodern text. Catherine Constable's (2005) account of postmodernism and film has explored how its inherent intertextuality and visual stylisation can enrich characterisation and assist narrative comprehension. Her brief analysis of *Face/Off* also argues for how character interiority can also be achieved through postmodern techniques. Peter and Will Brooker's reader *Postmodern After-Images* also disputes the blankness and nihilism of postmodern films, this time drawing attention to the deconstructive effects of intertextual devices which challenge distinctions between true original and false copy (Brooker and Brooker, 1997a: 94). Using the postmodern cinematic *bricolage* of Quentin Tarantino as a prime example, Brooker and Brooker (1997b) explain how postmodern films enable 'a more active . . . intertextual exploration than a term such as "pastiche" . . . implies', instead suggesting that these moments of textual appropriation be read as a kind of rewriting or re-viewing (7) and a reinvention, extension and *affirmation* of cinematic conventions (something I will later argue is also true in the case of pastiche and intertextuality in some postmodern Bollywood film texts). Brooker and Brooker also assert the broadness of the concept of postmodernism, explaining that there are many varieties of postmodern films which work in different ways:

> If some examples . . . are at once scandalous and vacant, or 'merely' playful, others are innovative and deeply problematising. If some are symptomatic, others are exploratory. Like postmodern society, cultural postmodernism is various and contradictory: fatalistic, introverted, open, inventive, and enlivening. (1997a: 94)

This wide applicability of postmodernism to cinema is further demonstrated in M. K. Brooker's (2007) study of postmodernism in contemporary Hollywood cinema, which considers a broad variety of Hollywood texts, many produced in the noughties.[1] For the sake of my own investigation, Brooker's work is particularly useful for its consideration of postmodern traits in non-Hollywood cinema. While focusing largely on Hollywood films, the author also explores the possibility of postmodernism's presence in Third World cinema. Via an analysis of Mexico's *Amores Perros*, Brooker questions the validity of Fredric Jameson's claim that Third World culture (which in this sense would include literature and cinema from India) is the only final refuge for unity and authenticity. Rather than seeing Third World cinema as the antithesis of the 'polished' commercial postmodern film, Brooker concludes that, despite its 'lingering humanism and utopianism', Third World film can also be found to 'articulate the global spread of postmodernism' (Brooker: 18). It is also worth noting here that Jameson's contrasting of Third World and postmodern world is problematic, particularly with regard to contemporary Bollywood cinema which, as explained earlier, is now both polished and difficult to categorise as Third World cinema. The notion of 'authenticity' is also difficult here, because contemporary Bollywood cinema is, in many ways, fundamentally inauthentic, as I will explain later in relation to its abundant remaking practices and tendency towards textual appropriation.

POSTMODERN AESTHETICS: KEY CONVENTIONS

For the sake of pragmatism, I have provided a list (Figure 5.1) of all the key postmodern aesthetic features that I engage with throughout my analysis of contemporary Bollywood cinema. These listed postmodern traits, for each of which a brief description is provided, feature most prominently and frequently in the film texts I have selected for analysis. Although I am discussing individual features of postmodernism here, I am aware of the danger of separating off individual characteristics from the overall category of postmodernism as a cultural phenomenon. One can risk losing the dimension of postmodernism by simply citing its individual characteristics. It is therefore important to stress here that these individual characteristics are necessarily part of an overall historical response to the (post-industry status and globalisation) period of Bollywood cinema I am explicitly investigating. Although some of these same fundamental characteristics may be found in earlier examples of Indian cinema, they take on a different value and a different function depending on the historical context in which they emerge. In this case, they specifically respond to the post-industry status of Bollywood in the era of globalisation.

Depthlessness

This fundamental postmodern trait often deliberately draws our attention to the surface of a text. Surface style is emphasised heavily at the expense of signification and hermeneutics (meaning-making). The depthless work moves away from any traditional realistic mode of presentation and is instead inclined towards the *artificial* and the *superficial*. Postmodern pessimists (such as Fredric Jameson) especially criticise this trait for stripping a text of all its meaning and politics. As the text is not 'meaningful' it is considered worthless. It fails or refuses to contribute anything novel or authentic. It has a tendency towards re-production or 'repackaging' rather than actual innovation and imaginative originality. Conversely, other more sympathetic commentators (for example, Linda Hutcheon) have commended the same trait for its radical political strategy in helping enquire into preconceived notions of text and textuality, and enabling the disassembling and disclosure of 'Art' as a concept or institution. In demoting or eliminating meaning in the depthless artwork, we are left to question our own investment in the text, confront its pre-fixed function and institutional labelling, and query our own desires for meaning

1. Depthlessness (elevation of the textual surface, anti-intellectualism)
2. Blank parody (intentional or non-intentional pastiche)
3. The figural (saturation of images, failure of language, politics and deep meaning)
4. Emphasis on sensation (melodramatic, emotional excess over narrative storytelling)
5. Nostalgia (yearning for lost authentic past, return to the past, presence of the past)
6. Schizophrenia and fragmentation (of identity)
7. Self-reflexivity (self-referentiality)
8. Intertextuality (inter-referentiality)
9. Hyperrealism (simulacra, annihilation of the real, questioning or failing realism)
10. Hybridity and *bricolage* (mixing of styles and conventions)
11. *Mise en abyme* (worlds within worlds, stories within stories)
12. Boundary blurring (high/low culture, fact/fiction, reality/fantasy)
13. Deconstruction of grand narratives (master narratives, metanarrative)
14. The sublime (presenting the unpresentable in presentation)
15. Metahistory (history as narrative/fiction/myth)
16. Transcending time and space (non-chronology)

Figure 5.1: Key features of the postmodern in contemporary Bollywood.

and subtext. The depthless work is also positively seen to offer its audience a purer sensory-based experience (see Susan Sontag in Lash, 1988) thanks to its anti-intellectualist approach. This postmodern characteristic is often attributed to mass reproduction and the emphasis on the surface value rather than the 'intrinsic' value of a text, and thus configures with Walter Benjamin's notions of *lost aura* (Benjamin, 1999). In film, this trait is recognisable through a notable heightening of cosmetic stylisation (for example, editing, visual aesthetics and music) over 'substance' (for example, concrete narrative and character psychologies). Despite its shared sensibilities with the avant-garde and some art cinema, the trait is more commonly associated with mainstream popular culture – particularly the genres of melodrama and the action blockbuster in the case of film. Interestingly, many condemnations of the postmodern depthless work echo those of popular Bollywood texts. Both are considered trivial, formulaic, repetitive, predictable, purely commercial, factory-line mass-produced consumer products. They are said to be profit-driven rather than artistically driven (opulence over significance), non-experimentalist, flawed, devoid of artistic merit and sensationalist, and are generally considered unworthy of intellectual engagement.

Blank parody

This term is often used derogatively to refer to postmodern art as an empty copy of an original work; a pointless plagiarism exploiting a dead language (Jameson: 74) which 'mimes the formal resolution of art and life ... while remorselessly emptying it of its political content' (Eagleton, 1986: 132). This particular mode of imitation is devoid of the political or historical content and humour or ridicule that conventionally accompany more credible or productive works of parody. The term therefore has associations with certain notions of *pastiche*. It has been argued that, while lacking an outwardly political or satirical motive, postmodernism's so-called blank parody or empty pastiche can still prove fascinating in its function as tribute or homage. By referring to its original in such a way, it has the potential to ironise, internally critique, and problematise the representation and autonomy of the original work, often *beyond* artistic intention. I explore varied theoretical definitions of postmodern parody and pastiche (most significantly those of Jameson, Hutcheon [1985] and Dyer [2006]) and consider this concept in more detail in the following chapter, which locates parallel methods of postmodern pastiche within contemporary Bollywood remakes.

The figural

This postmodern concept stages the failure of language and instead promotes the authority of the figural (the visual image). In mainstream popular American cinema, the image is normally assumed to serve the needs of the narrative, which drives and directs the text. Discourse is usually centralised (dialogue, narrative, script, storyline), with images functioning secondarily as accessories to the discourse. In the case of postmodern film, however, the triumph of the figural involves the subordination of discourse in favour of the dominance of on-screen images as *pure spectacle*. Consequently, visual moments will often transcend and occur independently of narrative causality, and this can impact upon the text's overall level of signification. Images now operate as empty signs. Ultimately, they do not explicitly tell us anything (signify, denote, story-tell) but instead primarily invite us to see or sense with our bodies without the interference of rationalisation, narrative justification or meaning-seeking.

Despite sharing or accommodating certain aspects of Surrealism, the postmodern figural text differs in its agenda from this previous artistic movement. Whereas Surrealism is often abstract, symbolic, invests in deeper hidden meanings and encourages interpretation, the postmodern figural text has no such intellectual agenda. Images are primarily used to elicit sensory pleasure. And whereas Surrealism clearly operates as a transcendental alternative to the real (constructing a symbolic world), the postmodern figural initially claims to operate within our perceived reality – although this reality is ultimately simulated or amplified, deconstructed, corrupted and eventually invalidated. As a consequence, the recent increased saturation of images in media and films worldwide has been viewed somewhat apocalyptically, particularly by Jean Baudrillard, who sees this postmodern shift towards the figural as indicative of the end of signification and our ability to perceive and represent reality.

The notion of figural postmodern cinema has been chiefly developed by Scott Lash, whose examples extend from popular avant-garde cinema (the films of David Cronenberg and David Lynch) and spaghetti westerns to contemporary Hollywood blockbusters (the *Ghostbusters* and *Indiana Jones* films and the action films of Sylvester Stallone and Arnold Schwarzenegger). I believe that Lash's concept of the figural is the crux of contemporary Bollywood's formal aesthetics, and is what primarily distinguishes this particular breed of cinema. By employing Lash's concept when reading key contemporary Bollywood film texts (see Chapter 7), we gain a greater understanding of the effects and objectives of this newer phase of cinema. Most importantly, analysing Bollywood's figural techniques will help us explore the industry's baptism by fire (or rather, its *agni pariksha*) in the course of its global initiation, and ultimately offer some explanations for the cinema's somewhat problematic transition into the international arena.

Self-reflexivity

This postmodern term refers to texts which address their own textuality. In cinema, self-reflexivity can consist of a film directly or indirectly referring to its own production, or, more broadly, to the world of filmmaking in general. This parodic function facilitates both spectator pleasure (through invested cinephilia) and a more complex mode of self-critique. In the case of the latter, this method of internal commentary aids the postmodern work's ongoing quest to question its own modes of representation. Through self-reflexivity, the text is no longer elusive, but instead becomes the subject of its own political attack. The act of self-referencing is particularly significant in the case of popular cinema, in that it fundamentally disrupts verisimilitude, *revealing* as opposed to *masking* filmic modes of production and textual artifice.

Intertextuality

This broad term refers to the moment upon which a text references or alludes to another pre-existing text. This act of quotation manifests in cinema in a variety of ways, including found-footage filmmaking, where actual original stock footage is re-edited within a new context or appears within the diegesis of a new fictional text, the parodic mimicking or restaging of elements and scenarios from other original texts, or the overlapping and infusion of old footage (from the referred text) with new fictional material. This postmodern function thus incorporates parody, hybridity and *bricolage* – involving the mixing and simultaneous presentation of different genres and styles. Theoretical definitions of intertextuality are as varied and diverse as its applications (see Genette [1982] for an extensive list of the concept's many classifications and guises). It can be found to perform several political functions, but most explicitly, it has the ability to critique and 'recode' its very object of citation.

Intertextuality, and its related trait self-reflexivity, are particularly central to the period of Indian cinema I am investigating. They both encourage new reading strategies, allowing Bollywood audiences to engage differently with the text, and are thus particularly enlightening with regard to how cinephilia can serve as an additional form of spectatorial pleasure for the contemporary Indian film audience. Such perspectives on how Indian audiences receive pleasure from new Bollywood films will hopefully offer a refreshing alternative to the previously cynical notions of the simple and naive Hindi film spectator. Intertextuality is becoming a recurrent aesthetic device in newer forms of popular Indian cinema, which, when employed strategically, helps to break down the boundaries between different genre classifications and aesthetic modes and conventions. This is particularly powerful when Bollywood forces intertextual exchanges with adversary forms of popular cinema, such as Hollywood.

Boundary blurring

This is less a stylistic trait, and more an adopted theme or effect achieved by postmodern aesthetics. The 'boundaries' in question here may refer to those pre-set political, ideological, formal (stylistic), philosophical or contextual aspects of a text, whose fixed positions are gradually weakened by being subjected to various kinds of inversion, manipulation and contradictory juxtapositions. Here, binary opposites (such as past/present and good/evil) are most unusually brought together until they are indistinguishable. One of the classic examples of postmodern boundary blurring is the fusion of high and low art forms, such as opera and pop music. Such a blurring or dissolving of established differences, categories or markers can lead to what Scott Lash has termed as 'de-differentiation' – an inversion of the modernist structural logic of difference which instead favours an aversion to or collapse of difference:

> Postmodernism results from a much more recent process of *de*-differentiation or *Entdifferenzierung* . . . [It is] present in the postmodernist refusal to separate the author from his or her oeuvre or the audience from the performance; in the postmodernist transgression of the boundary (with no doubt greater or lesser success) between literature and theory, between high and popular culture, between what is properly cultural and what is properly social. (Lash: 312)

Although these boundaries are indeed dissolved, this is not intended as an act of universalisation or a way of oppressing difference. Rather, boundary blurring incorporates ambiguity, facilitates diversity, and prevents universality. The inability to distinguish, define and order thereby avoids partiality, inclusion, exclusion and prioritisation, which facilitate grand narratives and dominant modes of discourse. The postmodern aim of working against universal or absolute truths is thus achieved, although somewhat problematically. Particularly with regard to social distinctions (for the most part concerning gender, class and race), boundary blurring can be seen to have dangerous unethical implications, stifling the Other's ability to voice or represent their difference. However, as representations of the oppressed dissolve and are confused with those of the oppressor, the oppressed can just as easily be seen to be empowered (internally manipulating, dismantling and critiquing the language of the oppressor). This postmodern strategy thus proves to be both replenishing and destructive, and partly contributes to the woolly definitions, contradictory behaviours and paradoxical nature of the postmodern. This empowered/disempowered argument is further explored and elaborated on in Chapter 7, particularly in relation to Bollywood's remaking incentives and the act of 'reverse colonialism' in the film *Kaante*.

Fragmentation and schizophrenia

Much like the schizophrenic patient, the postmodern work incorporates a multiplicity of voices and viewpoints. There is no final dominant or fixed identity on offer in the text, but rather, a plethora of multiple clashing styles and subjectivities are presented. The postmodern subject comprises various (often arbitrary) parts: bits and pieces of alternative personae combining to form a fragmented whole. In postmodern film, this schizophrenic tendency penetrates the style (the *bricolage* of different genre conventions), form (multiple diegesis, *mise en abyme* narratives, non-chronology, time and space travel) and content of the text (such as characters with double or split personae and agendas).

The application of this postmodern characteristic in the Indian cultural context is particularly interesting and problematic. When applied to popular Indian film, postmodern schizophrenia threatens contemporary Bollywood's position as a 'national' cinema, as the 'national' often implies and requires the presence of a fixed Indian identity or cultural consciousness. The process of fragmentation within the Bollywood film text involves the breaking down of cultural and national identity, and therefore obstructs rather than advocates any feasible on-screen representations of Indian-ness. The appearance of this postmodern trait in Indian cultural texts is also at times destructive, dissolving distinct difference (and thus, alternative identities) and denying the post-colonial Indian Other an authentic voice or a fixed whole subjectivity. At its best, however, it helps popular Indian cinema to transcend its universal labelling and break away from predictability and closed definitions (its somewhat restrictive classifications, categorisations and generalised conventions) and encourages its reinterpretation by offering up a multiplicity of readings. In view of the fact that Indian cinema has a history of being confined by its cultural and national boundaries, fragmentation liberates Bollywood film texts by making room for experimentation, innovation, inversion and reconfiguration.

It is worth bearing in mind that there have been versions of schizophrenia located in art before the emergence of postmodernism. For example, it is particularly known in the modernist work. However, the postmodern schizophrenic subject remains different from modernism's, which ultimately relies on an individual whole subjectivity. Modernism is in pursuit of interior truth, whereas postmodernism rejects the desire for coherence and uses schizophrenia to create a permanent sense of fragmentation. It assists a meltdown of subjectivity where the self cannot be distinguished from the multiplicity of selves it crosses with.

Hyperrealism

This aesthetic mode is fundamental to the postmodern work's primary agenda, which seeks to question and problematise notions of the real. It employs an alternative method of (anti-)representation, as opposed to established modes of realist representation. Hyperrealist texts employ a visibly artificial poetic realism that claims to be more legitimate and 'more real than the real itself'. The quest for authentic realism is regarded as overrated and reality is suitably replaced by a substitute simulation – the postmodern *simulacrum*. This substitute is constructed through the mutilation and exaggeration of common conceptions and representations of the real. Elements of reality/fact and fantasy/fiction are mixed and fused to the point at which the two are no longer distinguishable, and the ability to represent or conceive any autonomous reality is shattered in the process. Real moments are magnified so much that they appear surreal. By revealing the inadequacy of realist representation, hyperrealism also ultimately undermines modernism's pursuit of a definitive realism and truth.

Hyperrealism corresponds with some popular Indian cinematic notions of realism. Both function as an *extension* to the real and present a flawed or artificially grounded and magnified reality combined with elements of fantasy, which spectators are invited to perceive as conceivable substitutes for the real world – commonly referred to as a willing 'suspension of disbelief'.[2] Hyperrealism appears in different texts with different levels of intensity. More extreme manifestations result in works which completely lack real-world referents, instead creating worlds which are entirely divorced from the real and, in referring only to their own artifice, revel in the marked *absence* of the real world altogether.

Metahistory

Postmodernism's relationship with history is complex. On the one hand it seeks to undermine the foundations upon which history is based. On the other, it draws attention to the historical past and seeks to affirm its significance. 'Metahistory' (see White, 1978) advocates the removal of objectivity from all historical writing (journalism, news reports, historical accounts of past events) and instead exploits and reduces history to a form of narrative storytelling. In postmodern film, this is achieved by scrambling historical facts with fictitious elements (factual narrative is merged with mythology and fantasy) or presenting fiction as if it were historical fact (as with mockumentaries and false documents).

Postmodernism has at times been described as *a-historical* for erasing the distinctions between past and present and diffusing different historical periods. It disorders historical chronology in order to challenge the autonomy of history. Thus, non-chronology and time–space transcendence form part of the postmodern aesthetic. However, this perceived a-historicism is ultimately unconvincing as it deviates from and conflicts with notions of postmodern *nostalgia*, which suggests a desire to 'turn back' or 'return to' the past rather than a wish to escape it totally (as with modernism). Metahistory instead makes room for postmodernism's duplicitous relationship with history, as a mode both of internal attack and of inquiry. In my own investigation of postmodern Bollywood cinema, I will reveal how certain contemporary Bollywood texts contain elements of the metahistorical, particularly moments of temporal playfulness, non-chronology and the blurring of truth/fact/history with fiction and myth. The latter is particularly explored through my analysis of the Bollywood science-fiction film remake *Koi . . . Mil Gaya*, discussed later in this chapter.

Deconstructing grand or metanarratives

This Lyotardian concept points to another political tendency of the postmodern. Grand (also known as 'master' or 'meta-') narratives are defined as the dominant discourses, belief systems, culturally prescribed stories and socio-ideological frameworks that cultural texts tend to operate within. Postmodernism aims to deconstruct and weaken the power of these master narratives, which are seen as too universalising and restrictive, particularly for the marginalised Other. However, this is somewhat contradictorily achieved owing to the double agency and paradoxical nature of the postmodern, which always ends up reinscribing the very things it contests. Postmodern texts initially operate within grand narratives, effacing and perverting them from within. In the context of contemporary postmodern Bollywood cinema, these imprisoning grand narratives could include the indigenous – religious ideologies, Hindutva politics (Hindu fundamentalism), nationalism, patriarchy – and the external, such as Hollywood (as the 'definitive' cinema) and Western rationalism. I will look particularly at how contemporary Bollywood texts disassemble fixed and autonomous representations of Indian-ness, masculinity and modern science, as well as certain universalised (Hollywood) cinematic aesthetic codes.

The sublime

Definitions of the sublime vary in relation to the contexts and theoretical frameworks within which they are used. My use of the term specifically refers to Lyotard's discussions of the postmodern text's aim to 'present the unpresentable' – to present things that cannot be conceived through human reason and cannot be described, conceptualised or represented (given form). Examples of the sublime experience include: the infinity of space, the enormity of an earthquake, turbulent nature, the size of an atom, ugliness, death, love, emotional ecstasy and God. The sublime can only be felt or sensed, and is again one of several nihilistic postmodern concepts that protest against the failure of representation. It marks the inadequacy of the imagination and thus of artistic representation. The attempt to portray the sublime on-screen presents a constant struggle and failure to give form to the formless, and to conceive the inconceivable.

I believe that contemporary Bollywood is a cinema unique for its persistence in trying to present the unpresentable and summon the sublime on-screen – particularly intense emotions such as love. As I will later demonstrate, certain contemporary films have engaged in a kind of aesthetic excess, bombarding the spectator with intricate details and dazzling images in order to simulate and evoke the sublime. It is important to note that although little work has been done on Bollywood's approach to the sublime, the concept has already been regarded as being especially relevant to Eastern art forms. For example, G. W. F. Hegel observed the sublime as a key feature of Chinese, Indian, Persian and Islamic art – all of which adopt stylistic strategies of intricacy, figural abstraction and formlessness in order to overwhelm the observer and inspire them with awe (see Hegel, 1975).

In summary, although they are individually complex, the principal postmodern conventions briefly described above share common goals. They all mark an absence and declare the insignificance of intellectual meaning. They facilitate the fragmentation and abstraction of previously established fixed frameworks and governing belief systems. But despite this, they do not aspire to contribute to any compelling outwardly political agenda, beyond the self-referential. Instead, all comprise an inward textual politics. Any possible interpretations or conclusions drawn will usually concern the text as *text*. By dismantling their own methods of presentation, they render the act of representation either impossible or infinitely problematic. Furthermore, they hail an absence of the 'reality' upon which we normally base our artistic representations. Thus, in the case of postmodern cinema, normative modes of cinematic realism and presentation deliberately malfunction. Finally, they are all inherently hypocritical, paradoxical and contradictory, and as such, they are always subject to contestation.

I shall now try to locate and interrogate many of the above postmodern concepts in contemporary Bollywood film in order to indicate a postmodern shift within the industry, and demonstrate how a postmodern perspective can contribute towards (and rework our existing perceptions of) issues of representation, realism and artistic value within popular Indian cinema.

POSTMODERN TRAITS IN CONTEMPORARY BOLLYWOOD I: *OM SHANTI OM*

Contemporary Bollywood cinema's postmodern inclinations can first be confirmed through an analysis of one of its highest-grossing productions – Farah

Khan's *Om Shanti Om* (2007). Khan's film can be considered a landmark in a potentially growing postmodern Bollywood canon, offering a synthesis of many of the postmodern traits listed above. The film's story revolves around protagonist Om, a junior Hindi film artist (professional extra) in the late 1970s, who secretly witnesses the murder of his beloved movie star idol Shantipriya by her producer-husband Mukesh Mehra on the set of their latest film, *Om Shanti Om*. During his failed attempt to save Shanti's life (by rescuing her from the burning film set), Om is killed in a car accident and later reincarnated as Om Kapoor, the son of a famous film star. Thirty years later, now himself a Bollywood megastar, the reincarnated Om suddenly recalls the tragedy he witnessed in his past life and subsequently devises a plan to trick Mehra to return to Bollywood and finance a remake of his *Om Shanti Om* film, so that Om may expose him as Shanti's murderer in the process.

Khan's film is the first of its kind to construct, document and offer homage to an Indian cinematic canon with such precedence. The film's entire diegesis is immersed in a matrix of references from the past three decades of popular Indian film history. Many of the film's costumes recall film personalities famous from the era, such as Om's outfits, which are modelled on the wardrobe of 1970s acting legend Rajesh Khanna. In the sequence for the song 'Deewangi' (involving thirty 1970s, 1980s and 1990s Hindi film actor cameos) the dance choreography mimics the trademark moves and gestures from each of the actors' previous movies. Similarly, the use of film star lookalikes, bricolaged musical scores (encompassing classical Kathak, rock 'n' roll, gothic opera, and Danny Elfman-esque horror compositions),[3] frequent quotation via 'filmy' dialogue[4] and abundant movie-prop memorabilia all work together to evoke a sense of cinematic nostalgia.

In his discussions, Fredric Jameson argues how postmodernism's lack of new ideas and stifling of creative innovation has resulted in a nostalgic mourning or *yearning* for past aesthetic modes. Any postmodern attempt to resummon past styles and conventions is dismissed as empty pastiche, doing nothing more than damaging the autonomy of historical works. Jameson laments the way in which this form of pastiche causes the past to be swallowed up by the present, destroying our ability to access the past in any objective or pure sense. *Om Shanti Om* (hereafter *OSO*) equally demonstrates the theft of classic Indian cinematic forms and their assimilation into present modes of filmmaking, causing different periods of old/past and new/modern Hindi cinema to dissolve and collapse into one another, although the result of this pastiche is not as fruitless as Jameson presumes.

Initially set in 1977's Film City,[5] *OSO* begins with footage of a song sequence lifted directly from the Indian revenge film *Karz* (1980). This found footage is intercut with shots of Om (played by Shah Rukh Khan), who is seen dancing and mimicking the song sequence's music. The camera frame then widens to reveal Khan/Om among an audience of film extras, supposedly watching a live recording of the sequence from *Karz*. The set pieces and costumes from the original footage of *Karz* are of course replicated for this shot, but so seamlessly is this done that the move from the original *Karz* footage to the replica set with Om is almost indistinguishable, thus allowing the original cinematic sequence to blur with the new one in postmodern synthesis. Furthermore, the casting of Shah Rukh Khan as the 1970s wannabe film star also works to a similar effect. Shah Rukh Khan, whose actual star persona is emblematic of contemporary Bollywood cinema, submerges himself in an older model of the Indian film hero – his character being modelled on 1970s film star Rajesh Khanna. The two actors' different personalities are fused into one character (indeed, it is difficult to tell whether the character of Om is a modern interpretation of Khanna, or a seventies interpretation of Khan), and the film instead invites us to draw connections and continuity between the two personae.

Later on in the film, this collapse of past and present also takes effect in the simultaneous presentation of actors from several decades of Indian cinema. In the 'Deewangi' song sequence, celebrated film stars such as Dharmendra (1960s–70s), Jeetendra (1970s), Rekha (1980s), Kajol (1990s) and Priyanka Chopra (2000s) all come together on-screen. Likewise, the 'Dhoom tana' song sequence brings together deceased actor Sunil Dutt with actress Deepika Padukone (who plays Shanti in the film) through the aid of digital computer effects trickery. The song itself, composed of four verses, fuses four different genres or eras of Indian film music: verse 1 a homage to the Indian classical song and dance number in *Amrapali* (1966), verse 2 from the rock-and-roll cabaret number in *Sachaa Jhuta* (1970), verse 3 alluding to the romantic-comedic duet in *Humjoli* (1970), and verse 4 the archetypal gypsy item number evoking a courtesan dance sequence from *Jai Vejay* (1977).

Jean Baudrillard's concept of hyperrealism can also be found to manifest in Farah Khan's film. Characters such as Om and his mother, Bela, are seen to communicate in their everyday lives through noticeably exaggerated gestures and deliberately hammy overacting. During much of their scenes together, voices are projected to the point of shouting, every emotion from happiness to pain is comically amplified, and facial and bodily movements are eccentric, heavily relying on stereotype – a mocking nod to the performance style of the traditional Indian film melodrama. At one point, Om even refers to Bela as his 'filmy' mother, a familiar Hindi colloquialism meaning *like in the films*, which draws connections between the melodramatic excess of Bela and the on-screen mother figure of 1970–90s Indian cinema. This absurd depiction of the 'reality' of Om's home life strangely works to promote the idea of perceived reality as a fictive construct, particularly when contrasted with the more fictional elements of the diegesis. The 'real life' of the film characters appears more of an artifice than the actual movies being shot in Film City, where the acting and performance gestures often appear to be much more sincere and plausible. Compared with the diegetic world of Om and Film City, it is ironically the cinematic footage shown from Shantipriya's film *Dreamy Girl* and, later, the *Om Shanti Om* remake which engages with genuine emotions and complex character-relationships. Thus, in a classic case of postmodern irony, it takes a fiction-film to reveal the 'truth' about Shanti's death. Cinema, it seems, reveals life better than life itself, which, in the diegesis of *OSO*, is a world of artificial backdrops and fake personalities (Film City). Even when Om's memories of his past life are finally stirred, these memories are presented like old stock film footage: faded images with dust marks and scratches, projected behind him on a film screen. As Hayden White has noted, such efforts to 'blur the distinction between fact and fiction' challenge historical objectivity and restrict our ability to 'discriminate between truth on the one side and myth, ideology, illusion, and lie on the other' (1996: 19).

The idea of the fictional *Om Shanti Om* remake serving up the 'real truth' also correlates with Baudrillard's (1983) theory of the fourth stage of (postmodern) representation or signification, where the signifier (in this case, the film *OSO*) also becomes the signified. It no longer bears any connection to the real world, but instead refers to its own pure simulacrum (see Baudrillard, 1983: 347). *OSO* becomes a film which continuously re-presents other films that quote further films ad infinitum, and where Bollywood cinema represents, signifies, simulates and *real*-ises only its own (false) interior reality. Whilst *OSO* uses several methods to displace reality, it should be noted that in other textual examples, this construction of the artistic simulacrum as a parallel reality pushes Bollywood cinema even further towards experimentalism, offering a heightened and more visceral cinematic sense of the real, as I will explore later on in this chapter in my reading of *Abhay*.

To keep with this notion of cinema-art reflecting cinema-art, Farah Khan's film also includes several instances in which it acknowledges itself as a fictitious text. This self-referencing is evident in the film's opening sequence, where Farah Khan herself appears as a groupie in the audience and begins mocking Om's over-enthusiasm and 'over-acting'. In a quick retort, Om replies: 'What is it to you? Are you the director of the film?' Later on, a similar drawing attention to the story as 'just a movie' is achieved through Om's catchphrase 'There is still some film left in the reel, my friend[s]' (which is finally used to address us, the spectators, before the film's end-credits), and in instances where the audience is literally taken to the movies – such as the cinema auditorium during the *Dreamy Girl* premiere or the mock Indian Film Fare Awards (IFFA) ceremony, India's equivalent of Hollywood's annual Academy Awards.

OSO's self-referentiality is also inclined towards self-parody and self-reflexive critique. In the era of the late 1970s, the Indian film industry is teased on account of its incomplete scripts, its stock characters and dialogue (as seen with the melodramatic mother figure, emblematised by Om's mother) and its exploitation of female actresses (as in the case of Shanti's problematic relationship with Mehra), and for the over-the-top action stunts of the period (as seen in the parodic filming of Om's Madrasi action film, *Mind it*). In the flash-forward to 2007, contemporary Bollywood conventions are likewise mocked through jokes about the industry's current trend for sequels (the *Dhoom 5* nomination at the Film Fare awards) and superhero movies (the comical filming of *Mohabbat Man*). Also, whilst on set for his latest movie, the reincarnated Om ridiculously suggests conveying a mute, deaf and blind cripple's anguish (this is itself critiquing the improbability of many masala film scenarios and characterisations) by having him burst into a sexy disco-dance number. As Om remarks, the relevance of the disco song to the film's narrative and its plausibility with regard to character realism is immaterial. What is important is that it will guarantee its makers a 'hit movie'. Ironically, it is this same disco song that partly guaranteed *OSO*'s success – no doubt a comment on Bollywood films' box-office revenue often largely depending on the popularity of their song sequences and soundtrack-album sales. Furthermore, the 'Pain in Disco' song sequence that follows is saturated with overtly sexual connotations. Shah Rukh Khan's newly toned abdomen and oily, water-drenched body are put on constant display, offering a blatant commentary on the over-emphasised muscled physiques of many male film stars of the post-millennium era.

Additional reflexive commentary on the construction of film star personae is offered in the film through references to actors' film careers. During the Indian Film Fare Awards, Om is offered a best actor nomination for a film called *Phir Bhi Dil Hai NRI* (But My Heart Is Still NRI) – a deliberate play on actor Shah Rukh Khan's having been the male lead in most major films in the Bollywood NRI genre canon, including *Phir Bhi Dil Hai Hindustani* (But My Heart Is Still Hindustani) (2000). Also, the fact that Om is reincarnated as the son of film star Rajesh Kapoor parodies the genealogy of many current Bollywood actors, who have entered the industry by being born into film star families – as with the case of the Kapoor dynasty, whom Om and Rajesh's family name alludes to.[6] Finally, during the film premiere of *Dreamy Girl*, Shantipriya's visual make-up and performance during her 'ek chutki sandoor' scene mimics Aishwarya Rai's performance as Paro in Sanjay Leela Bhansali's *Devdas* (2002) – the role which secured Rai's career as a leading Bollywood actress. This connection signals *OSO*'s unabashed promotional casting of Deepika Padukone as Shanti, also a model turned actress (like Rai) in her acting debut.

In its self-reflexivity, *OSO* also invites an interesting postmodern Marxist reading. The Indian cinema industry is depicted as an exploitative commercial business throughout the film, but this critique is particularly marked through the way in which Farah Khan chooses to demonstrate the industry's transition from the 1970s to the 2000s. At the beginning of the film, Om is seen seeking solace by a walkway under a gallery of late-1970s billboard posters. Surrounding a central film poster for *Dreamy Girl* (comprising mainly a giant image of Shantipriya), we see a collection of hand-painted adverts for consumer goods, which clearly demonstrate the use-value products and market capital culture of the period: Ovaltine, tea, biscuits, Schweppes and Dulux paint. However, when we later see the same billboard thirty years on, these adverts have been replaced by materialist vanity objects – designer watches, mobile mp3 players, jewellery and make-up – signalling the country and industry's shift towards exchange-value consumerism and its growing individualism. Whereas in the 1970s the posters and their featured products target the Indian at home and uphold the idea of 'wholesome family goodness' (classically iconicised by the Indian mother in the Ovaltine advert), the post-millennium adverts literally address the 'global Indian' and their impulse to do nothing but go 'shopping'. This particular example of self-critique reveals how filmmakers can make use of postmodern strategies for dual gain – offering a critique of this materialist culture of product placement, whilst also preserving, practising, promoting and economically benefiting from its glamour and appeal. Again, this political attack from within demonstrates the method through which postmodern works paradoxically reinstate the very things they challenge.

The above postmodern strategy is especially effective in the Indian context, particularly if we take the 1977 poster display to be representative of the traditional values of the period, and the 2007 display as symbolic of the impact of global commerce after the millennium. It is interesting that *OSO* chooses to first view the past (tradition and values) so nostalgically, only to then efface or replace them with an inverted substitute. What happens to the Indian at home and the Ovaltine mother in this new consumer culture set-up? Is this a passing gesture towards India's blind submission to materialism at the risk of tradition and culture? If this is the case, perhaps it is no accident that in the 2007 version, in addition to the painted posters, Farah Khan also removes the view of a Hindu temple in the foreground. Although the film preaches much about traditional values, truth and *sanskar* (the Hindi term for sacrifice, ritual, ceremonial rites and religious service), its protagonists eventually sink back into this very same world of materialist glitz and glamour. While we may follow a narrative about the cheapening and loss of values due to greed and profit, all the while it is made apparent that we are marketing targets for Maybelline make-up and TAG Heuer Swiss watches (most obviously through actors Shah Rukh Khan and Deepika Padukone being the real-life ambassadors for

Figure 5.2: Film City billboards in 1977 and 2007 from *Om Shanti Om* (Red Chillies Entertainment, 2007).

these global consumer brands). Could such moments be considered a means by which Bollywood consciously laughs back at its audience? Whatever the case, *OSO* reveals an Indian society trapped in double standards, torn between the idea of feudal community and the practice of humanist individuality. Bollywood cinema thus doubly serves its purpose as an *advocate* and *adversary* of Indian culture.

TRAPPED IN SAMSARA:
THE THEME OF REINCARNATION

Vasamsi jirnani yatha vihaya navani grhnati naro'parani

tatha sarirani vihaya jirnany anyani samyati navani dehi

['As one gives up old and worn out garments and accepts new apparel, similarly the embodied soul, giving up old and worn out bodies, verily accepts new bodies'][7]
Bhagavadgītā, chapter 2, verse 22

OSO is deeply invested with the Hindu model of *saṃsāra* – the Sanskrit term for reincarnation or regeneration (the continuous cycle of birth and death). The cyclical nature of *saṃsāra* is evoked by the film's palindrome-like title, *Om-Shanti-Om*, alluding to the principal Hindu-Sanskrit circular chanting prayer, and to its song sequences, which include the 'reanimation' of dead film styles and actors through careful digital superimposition and morphing. Similarly, the protagonists Om and Shanti are literally 'reborn' in the narrative, the reincarnated Om 'recycles' Mukesh Mehra's *Om Shanti Om* script and 'rebuilds' or 'clones' its original film set, and in the final sequence, he 're-stages' an uncanny theatrical production of the entire first act, simulating it perfectly from Shanti's costumes to the 1970s set designs. Furthermore, this pattern of reoccurrence is fundamental to the film's narrative structure. Each stage of the story mirrors the next, with the first and third acts more or less paralleling one another:

Act 1 – 1977
Content: Film production of Mukesh Mehra's *Om Shanti Om*.
          The story of junior artist Om and film star Shanti (love story, murder act, death scene on Mehra's *Om Shanti Om* film set).

Act 2 – 2007
Content: Om's reincarnation/reintroduction as film star Om Kapoor.
          Shanti's reincarnation/reintroduction as junior artist Sandi.

Act 3 – 2007
Content: Film production of Mehra's *Om Shanti Om* remake.
          Musical staging and theatrical re-enactment of the story of Om and Shanti (love story, murder act and death scene on *Om Shanti Om* remake film set)

OSO's diegetic framework can be divided into four separate sub-streams: (1) the primary diegesis (the 'real-life' story of Shanti and Om), and three further *extra*-diegetic narratives, all of which overlap with one another and

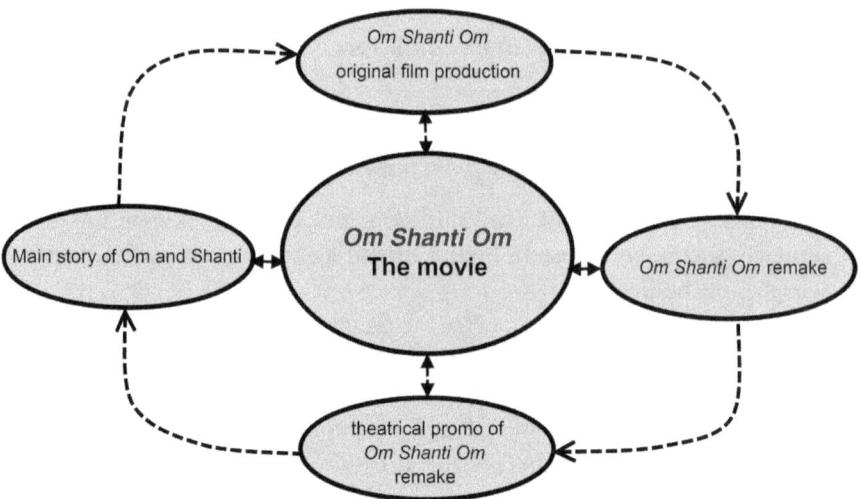

Figure 5.3: The recursive structural framework of *Om Shanti Om*.

mirror the primary diegesis; (2) Mehra's original *Om Shanti Om* film production; (3) Om Kapoor's remake of Mehra's original *Om Shanti Om* movie; and (4) a theatrical restaging of the remake of the original *Om Shanti Om* movie. This type of story frame is familiar within postmodern works and can be seen to follow in the vein of 'Chinese box' or 'Russian doll' narratives (involving worlds within worlds) and the formal technique of *mise en abyme* (recursive imaging). Via such a framework, the film text becomes a gyre of stories within stories, all bound within a main film story (the movie *OSO* by Farah Khan). Furthermore, the movie as a whole is itself ultimately about *all* films and stories within the history or world of Bollywood cinema.

OSO consciously exploits its circular narrative structure, bringing it visibly to the surface of the text. As a result, it exposes a cinema trapped within its own samsara cycle. The film literalises Bollywood cinema's notorious appetite for recycling formulas, plots and conventions, both through its narrative subject matter and its creative execution. It assumes the postmodern impulse for reproduction and imitation, and helps us envisage postmodern art's potential for critical self-reflection through creative reinvention.

Like other Bollywood texts, *OSO* functions through a certain excess of emotion, sensation and spectacle. But it also fulfils spectatorial desire and pleasure by simulating and pastiching images and styles from the past: the classic Bollywood love-story, the religious mythology, or the supernatural gothic. As such, the film is also guilty of *kama* – an unappeasable indulgence in material pleasures or 'carnal' desires (emotion, spectacle) believed to ultimately tie the soul to an endless samsara. In the context of Hindu philosophy, the lack of escape from *kama* prevents the human soul from achieving freedom from samsara and thus liberation (*moksha* – access into Heaven). In Bollywood's case, this can be translated as popular Indian cinema's failure to free itself from formulaic conventions and achieve originality, innovation or autonomy in their purest sense. Farah Khan's filmic depiction of cinematic reincarnation demonstrates and playfully critiques the endless repetition and recycling of popular Indian filmic modes, in each instance assuming a new body, a different guise, but always retaining the same *cinematic soul*.

Regardless of whether or not we wish to perceive this pattern of repetition as Bollywood's eternal curse, despite its stylistic continuities *OSO* remains politically and aesthetically progressive through its employment of postmodern devices, including intertextuality, nostalgia, *mise en abyme*, pastiche, self-reflexivity, hyperrealism and simulation. With reference to this last technique, all modes of reality in the film are constructed through artifice. There is no reality (actual or masked) other than those simulated realities presented through the plastic arts (cinema, music, dance, theatre). All are multiple simulacra within a false universe – the diegesis (Om's world of filmmaking), the *Om Shanti Om* film-shoot, the theatrical stage production, the behind-the-scenes end-credit sequence with director Farah Khan and her film crew, the Film Fare awards mockumentary of actor stars, and so on.

OSO is also progressive in being a Bollywood film which creatively addresses issues of cinephilia and the Indian audience's investment in popular cinema, allowing the spectator's dreams and desires to be realised in the diegesis (the ordinary movie-goer Om eventually becomes a film star). Particularly during the earlier 'Dhoom Tana' and opening title song sequences, we are invited to see through the eyes of Om, who, himself a mere film spectator, is seen to repeatedly imagine and project himself onto the screen in place of the film hero. The film acknowledges and creatively employs this process of cinematic transference. Thus, the spectators may imagine themselves to be Shah Rukh Khan as Om Prakash Makhija imagining himself to be Rishi Kapoor as Monty Verma (in *Karz*).

By drawing its audience towards more extreme melodrama, sensation, and the surface value of the medium, *OSO* concurrently demystifies the glamour value of Bollywood. In true postmodern style, it *subverts* the cinema as it *reaffirms* it. Bollywood is both celebrated and critiqued for its repetition, its hyperbole, its artificiality, its lack of substance, and its failure to present reality. By observing how postmodern functions work within *OSO*, we come to realise that such films may not necessarily be guilty of the postmodern sins outlined by Jameson and Baudrillard (blank pastiche, empty signification, meaninglessness, lack of political agenda), and that these texts instead deserve further examination.

Once we combine *OSO* with Farah Khan's debut film *Main Hoon Na*, which contains similar signature postmodern conventions (see Chapter 6), and her more recent spoof-satire *Tees Maar Khan* (another official remake with a self-reflexive film industry-centred plot, confused narrative, two-dimensional caricatures and a frenetic, exaggerated visual style), we can see that Farah Khan appears to be, perhaps indisputably, India's first official postmodern *auteur*. But the postmodern techniques identified in her films also appear in a number of other contemporary Bollywood films, and it is vital that we map these influences in order to determine the extent of the impact of the postmodern on Bollywood styles and modes of production.

POSTMODERN TRAITS IN CONTEMPORARY BOLLYWOOD 2: *KOI . . . MIL GAYA*

As we have established, postmodern works often blur the temporal boundaries of past and present and dissolve reality into fiction. We can detect a similar blurring of such boundaries in *Koi . . . Mil Gaya* (I Found Someone), a Bollywood film reinterpretation of Steven Spielberg's *E.T.: The Extra Terrestrial*, which attempts to transpose ancient traditions and values onto modern cultural representations. It is worth mentioning here that Spielberg's *E.T.* is itself rumoured to have plagiarised Bengali filmmaker Satyajit Ray's unmade film *The Alien*, whose production was abandoned in the late 1960s by Columbia pictures – the same studio that went on to produce *E.T.* (see Ray, cited in Robinson [2004: 295]). However, since there is very little information on Ray's original script, and for the sake of this investigation, in the following discussion I will refer to Spielberg's film as the original.

The Bollywood film version recalls the original's classical Hollywood narrative, adopting its key themes of friendship, alienation and childhood innocence. Its story centres around Rohit, a developmentally disabled young man with the mind of a child, who befriends a space alien called Jadoo, who has been left behind on earth and needs to get back home. The film embraces many of the familiar conventions of soft science-fiction (science, technology, aliens, spaceships, the paranormal, government and military operations, special effects, unexplained supernatural phenomenon) – a genre previously 'alien' to Bollywood. Before the release of this film, Bombay-based cinema had rarely shown an interest in producing science-fiction films, with Shekar Kapoor's *Mr India* (1987) being the sole science-fiction masala to achieve considerable box-office success prior to *Koi . . . Mil Gaya*.[8] As a result, the *E.T.* remake became famous for using sophisticated modern special-effects technology never before seen in the history of popular Indian cinema.

Despite its noted narrative, stylistic and thematic continuities, *Koi . . . Mil Gaya* (unlike its precursor) does not opt to achieve narrative plausibility through scientific rationale or a Hollywood realist aesthetic. Rather, in this science-fiction-cum-masala musical, diegetic realism is sought through a science-fiction narrative rooted in religious superstition and Hindu mythology. Here, religious mythology becomes the vessel through which one can observe, contemplate and *conceptualise* science. This affinity for a 'vedic science' rather than atheistic science (Alessio and Langer, 2007: 227) is evident in the film in several ways. Firstly, we can consider the importance of magic in both *Koi . . . Mil Gaya* (hereafter *KMG*) and the classical Hindu mythological folk tale. In the case of the latter (the religious text), the magical is associated with godlike powers. Each of the many Hindu deities is known for their individual special powers and ability to perform magic. Both the *Ramayana* and the *Mahabharata* include moments of magic such as levitation, disappearing, shape-shifting, and the ability to fly. *KMG*'s similar emphasis on the spectacular and miraculous is generated through the character of the alien, who is appropriately named after the Hindi word for magic (*jadoo*). In the context of Rohit's mental handicap, Jadoo's powers to heal him are not presented as an extra-terrestrial advanced super-ability, but rather as a 'divine miracle', implying that the sublime wonder in this film is not so much the sci-fi spaceships or the alien, but rather the *mysterious and magical work of God*.

The impinging of the religious upon conventional scientific contexts can also be seen to impact upon certain cause–effect elements of the film's narrative. In *E.T.* the aliens come to planet Earth in order to research and collect plants, but in *KMG*, it is the religious *Om* message in Rohit's father's computer (accidentally reactivated by Rohit) which originally calls the aliens to Earth. The Hindu *Om* chant is described by Rohit's father at the start of the film as a universal code which transcends language (and apparently spatial) boundaries and contains 'the vibrations of the universe'. Jadoo's rescue spaceship is also subsequently summoned by the *Om* computer, whilst E.T.'s spaceship is signalled through his self-assembled satellite transmission device. This conversion of a man-made (or rather alien-made) technical device into a religious symbol serving a religious function (the *Om* computer literally recites a prayer) can be considered in relation to the earlier-raised issues regarding the negotiation between modernism and technical advancement and tradition and primitivism in Indian culture.

It is interesting that the actual moments of extra-terrestrial phenomena in *KMG*, such as the UFO sighting, are so quickly neutralised. The spaceship witnessed by the entire town does not appear to stir much fear or curiosity into its residents, as one would expect. Likewise, Jadoo is almost immediately accepted into Rohit's group of friends. The alien is quickly initiated as one of the gang and the 'Jadoo' song sequence with the children early on in the film confirms this. The sequence is initially set against unusual barren rock formations, colourised with a sepia tint to evoke an alien landscape. However, as Rohit and friends sing of their growing friendship with Jadoo, this environment changes to a natural backdrop of blue skies, mountain valleys, haystacked grass meadows, wheat fields and forests. This natural framing suggests that, unlike *E.T.*, Jadoo is not quite intended to be perceived and presented as an 'Other' to the key characters and audience. In *E.T.* the alien, usually lit in shadows and low-key lighting, is always to some extent depicted as *strange*. E.T. is curious, unpredictable, an oddball, funny looking, or, as Spielberg has described him, deliberately fat and ugly (Gordon [2008: 78]). As Andrew Gordon (2008) has recently stated, E.T.'s story is that of the ugly frog prince – an animal who is later revealed to have the heart of a human. Jadoo, on the other hand, is obedient, rational and even pretty-faced. Before he appears, the mysterious alien fugitive is described by Nisha as a '*jaanwar*' (animal), yet he is quickly 'normalised' through his physical appearance.

The attempt to familiarise and somewhat normalise the alien in *KMG* is also evident through the mirroring of Rohit and Jadoo. In *E.T.*, boy and alien are connected telepathically and physically (when E.T. gets drunk or feels ill, Eliot's body reacts the same way), but in *KMG* these similarities are more explicit. Unlike Eliot, who is the 'ordinary kid', Rohit is by no means considered normal. He is called 'abnormal' by his bullies and is the alien or freak within his social circle. When Rohit eventually acquires Jadoo-like superpowers, he becomes superhuman and thus retains this unique anomalous persona. A biological link between Rohit and the alien is also made explicit when the two characters greet one another for the first time. During the film's intermission, the camera frame freezes on Rohit and Jadoo's shaking hands. In this still image we clearly see that the unusual shape of the alien's hand matches Rohit's, conspicuously replicating the supernumerary thumb of actor Hrithik Roshan.[9] This again reveals a deliberate intention to associate Rohit with Jadoo and neutralise the boundaries of alien and human in the process.

Furthermore, in view of this process of association, mirroring and normalisation, this Indian science-fiction film's object of antagonism appears not to be that which is 'beyond belief', but rather, *non-belief*. In *E.T.*, low, floor-level camera shots are used to film the antagonists (the faceless adults and government authority figures' identities are instead indicated by their suits, walkie-talkies, guns and handcuffs), but in *KMG*, aside from Rohit's school bully, there is no such antagonist. Unlike the menacing American government astronauts who break into Eliot's home, the black-uniformed gas-masked figures that come for Jadoo are left unidentified. Police officials Inspector Khan and Officer Sukhwani are generally sympathetic rather than menacing figures. However, at the start of the film, a group of atheist scientists ridicule Rohit's father for unorthodoxly mixing his religious beliefs with hard science. The audience is encouraged to identify with Rohit's father's frustration and battles against these 'non-believers', and this key moment in the narrative clearly stands as a subtle attack on the monolith of Western atheistic science.

In their postcolonial reading of *KMG*, Dominic Alessio and Jessica Langer (2007) also note the film's abundance of religious motifs, such as its use of the divine phrase 'Om' to communicate with the aliens and its symbolic depiction in the design of the alien spacecraft, its prevalent themes and upheld moral ideals of faith, prayer, worship and self-sacrifice, and the narrative's suggestive moments of divine intervention. The authors offer several reasons for the film's rigid religious backbone. Firstly, the religious motifs are seen to follow the conventional tropes of Western science-fiction, which often embodies the metaphysical and incorporates the 'religious imagination' into its narratives (John Clute and Peter Nicholls, cited in Alessio and Langer: 222). I would add that, although religious connotations are not uncommon in the sci-fi genre, with *E.T.* having drawn its own list of references to Christianity (see Gordon), in *KMG*, religion functions beyond subtext and instead outwardly instigates several of the cause–effect moments in the narrative. For example, it is explicitly 'God' who helps the Pandava team win their basketball game by parting the clouds and helping Jadoo regain his powers. Religion has a particular significance and centrality in *KMG*. It serves a purpose above and beyond genre conformity. It is strategically used to break down the master narrative of science (submerging scientific rationale in mythical superstition) and, most significantly, to help challenge *modernity*.[10]

Alessio and Langer's other explanations for the religious rootedness of *KMG* concern Western modernity. The religious motifs are seen to be, firstly, a conscious *postcolonial* attempt to challenge the homogeneity of Hollywood/Western/colonial cinema, where Western domination is seen to be prevented and replaced by an equally oppressive religious extremism and Hindu nationalist 'forced cultural assimilation' (222); and secondly, a less conscious 'withdrawal symptom' following India's inevitable retreat from tradition and religion towards modernity – a side effect of the 'future shock' (Alvin Toffler, cited in Alessio and Langer [222]) experienced through the country's sudden technological change and modernisation.

The collapse of religion, past and tradition into modernity or the future in *KMG* can best be explored through the text's identification with Hindu deities. Despite the film's innovative style and subject matter, we can tell simply from the way in which Jadoo's character is constructed and presented that Bollywood cinema, despite surrendering to modernity, cannot let go of its past. Jadoo appears not as the infantile, wrinkled, pale, doe-eyed and squeaky-voiced creature of Spielberg's original. Instead, he has blue skin, leaf-like Indian eyes and a deep resonating voice, and is adorned with something resembling a *tilak*, or *urdhva pundra* – the Brahman marking of a half-moon and three horizontal lines which is worn on the forehead in the Hindu religion. Jadoo is in fact the incarnation of the Hindu god Lord Krishna, and comparisons between the two occur throughout the film (for detailed examples

Figure 5.4: Jadoo in *Koi . . . Mil Gaya* (Film Kraft, 2003) as the sci-fi incarnation of Lord Krishna (Exotic India Art Pvt. Ltd).

see Alessio and Langer [222–3]). In Hindu mythological representations, Krishna is often depicted as a young child, innocent and mischievous, much like Jadoo. In the *Mahabharata*, Krishna is portrayed as faithful friend to the Pandava brothers (incidentally a name shared with Rohit's basketball team) sent to earth as God's messenger or helper. Among his many achievements, he is best-known for giving Prince Arjuna personal strength and the power to fight in battle. These character functions plainly and deliberately parallel those of Jadoo, who is seen to befriend Rohit and give him special powers and intelligence to fight his own demons.

The significance of this religious transformation of the alien could be considered in relation to the cultural accessibility of film texts like *KMG*. Is this analogy created to make the extra-terrestrial character more palatable to Indian audiences? Are we to assume that, had Jadoo not had this connection with Krishna, he would be harder to relate to and characterise? In such a case, do these religious connotations therefore prove wasted on Western audiences or elicit confusion within non-Indian viewers? If so, could this assumed nationalist or postcolonial tendency be the very thing that continues to problematise the Bollywood text's international accessibility? Such questions highlight the need for exploring Indian and non-Indian audiences' reception of such films (and their originals), which would perhaps further help unveil the differences between Hollywood and Bollywood filmic coding and viewing processes.

On the one hand, Alessio and Langer argue for *KMG* as an example of a postcolonial cinema which asserts its religious tradition and culture in order to counteract Western modernity and technology,[11] but on the other, they dedicate much of their article to justifying the film's conformity to or adoption of the traits of Western science-fiction, and to explaining the economic motivations behind the film's production as an international commodity. Besides the need to adopt the science-fiction genre to attract global as well as domestic audiences and celebrate India's increased investment in technology and scientific research, the authors direct the question of *why* the film chooses to adopt the sci-fi aesthetic purely towards issues of nationalism. The film is primarily seen to use science-fiction conventions for the purpose of nationalism and assisting its 'Hinduized visual regime' (218). As the authors note, it adopts and 'reshapes' the sci-fi genre to assist its postcolonial agenda — something which I will later explain further from a postmodern perspective. Otherwise, they dismiss the film's science-fiction elements as borrowed 'almost entirely from earlier Hollywood [science-fiction] films, making *Koi* [. . . *Mil Gaya*] a conglomerate of influences rather than a uniquely conceived film in terms of form' (221).

Alessio and Langer are correct in suggesting that the science-fiction genre allows the Bollywood film to evoke the metaphysical and religious imagination, and to juxtapose Indian society and culture against the 'machine' (technology, science). However, their rejection of any originality in the film's form is mistaken. Also, while pursuing their postcolonial reading of the film, they raise (yet fail to explore) the issue of *KMG* as a text which 'challenge[s] the hegemony of Western cinematic production' (227). But why does the film steal references from so many Hollywood films? Surely if the film wishes to challenge Hollywood, this would require a dismantling of Western codes and not a straightforward conformity to and preservation of them. Alessio and Langer consider this supposed attack on Hollywood filmic conventions as simply an example of the film's anti-colonial agenda, but although this may be the case, this unique process of internal critique marks a shift in Bollywood cinema aesthetics which needs be addressed. As will be revealed, films such as *KMG* use foreign generic conventions not only to serve their own alleged socio-political agendas, but also to manipulate and politically reflect on their own genre, aesthetics and textuality.

There are a few issues with regard to *mise-en-scène* and production modes that could be seen to problematise Alessio and Langer's anti-modern and anti-colonial reading of *KMG*. Firstly, regarding its supposed wish to demote modernity and therefore technology, it is inconsistent that the film resorts to innovative special effects and has been publicly revered for having modernised Indian cinema through its technological advances (wire-stunts, CGI, animatronics). Secondly, with regard to the film's alleged semi-extremist nationalist politics, Alessio and Langer discuss the rejection of Western commercialism and consumerism in terms of it being a firm principle of the Indian

Hindu nationalist group the *Shiv Sena* party (224, 226). However, this would fail to explain the fact that *KMG* is unabashedly littered with product placement, including several rather blatant adverts for Coca-Cola.

Instead of simply seeing technology and modernity as perceived 'evils' within the film, I would rather suggest that these are *regulated* through the adoption of cultural or religious motifs. This ambiguous treatment of and attitude towards modernity indicates the film's playful position, instead approaching these issues with a simultaneous desire and dread. Furthermore, rather than seeing *KMG* as offering an outright rejection of the West as coloniser, I would argue that there is a simultaneous attraction to, even adoration of, the 'colonial' in the film which also needs to be acknowledged. It is interesting that many of the songs in *KMG* incorporate Western musical dances (tango, ballroom, tap), and that a traditionally Indian song and dance number is absent from the film. Similarly, the costumes of the lead characters are very much Western or 'modern' (the lead actress is predominantly seen in summer dresses, not a salwar kameez or sari). The sports challenge between Rohit and his school bullies is not a cricket match, but a basketball game (a markedly non-Indian sport), and the entire narrative is set in a hill-station town in Kasauli, northern Punjab, which lacks the iconic Indian architecture (or Hindu temples) which would help give the film a distinctively Indian nationalist backdrop. Finally, it is also noteworthy that Rohit, once in possession of supernatural powers and transformed into a hero, appears to be modelled on a disco-dancing John Travolta or tap-dancing Gene Kelly rather than any known Indian equivalent. All of this Western iconography can be seen to counteract a purely nationalist pro-Hindu and anti-Western reading of the text.

COMPARISONS WITH *KRRISH*

Alessio and Langer choose to avoid recognising *KMG* as a remake of *E.T.*, almost treating the film as an independent work aside from a few incidental, plagiarising intertextual references. While they briefly acknowledge the film's sequel, *Krrish*, the follow-up film to *KMG* is also overlooked in their discussion. However, I believe *Krrish* is worth looking at, particularly for its marked omission of certain science-fiction tropes (spaceships and aliens, the character of Jadoo), its shortage of religious motifs (the religious analogy of Lord Krishna goes only as far as the film's title and the name of the lead character, Rohit's son Krishna), and its move away from science-fiction to its more diluted sub-genre, the superhero action film.[12]

Krrish is predominantly set in Singapore, a place where religion is peripheral and makes way for modernity as the dominant lifestyle. Its cityscape of high-rise corporate buildings and modern architecture signals wealth and progress, but the city is not depicted as suffocating or monstrous. It is beautified. Singapore as the modern city is not the subject of attack, but an object of desire – most likely a result of shooting being permitted there in exchange for Roshan having the film promote the place as an attractive travel destination. *Krrish* was the first film to take advantage of the Singapore tourist board's 'Film In Singapore' scheme. The scheme, launched in 2004, offered a 50 per cent subsidy of on-location filming costs for foreign productions, as well as assistance with restrictions concerning film permits, road closures, and access to key resources (Wong, 2005).

Nevertheless, modernity is still put in its place elsewhere in the film. For example, the dangers of science and technological progress are expressed through superhero Krrish's nemesis (and this time the text's real antagonist) Dr Arya, whose sins are greed, fame, success, power, control and knowledge. Arya's supercomputer which sees the future, allows him to be, in his own words, 'God-like'. His desire to replace God can thus be read as a stand-in warning for technology and modernity's impact on a non-secular society such as India. Whereas *KMG* warns of a coming modernity from the point of an unspoilt rural India, *Krrish* narrates from within the modern – a modernity already in existence. Thus, the objective is no longer to 'protect' the Indian from the modern (as shown through Krishna's grandmother, who learns to let him experience the world and travel abroad), nor to convince Indians about whether or not to embrace it when it arrives. Instead, *Krrish* presents an India which is already internationally situated, globally integrated and culturally hybridised. Krrish is Bollywood's first official Indian cinematic superhero,[13] yet he bears little mark of the traditional Indian. In the film, Krrish is the alter ego of Krishna, who is very much depicted as a nature-child of rural India at the start of the film. However, these two egos remain separate (if not oppositional) throughout the film, and the masking of Krishna when he becomes Krrish ultimately signals the active erasure of his original identity. Krrish's anonymous black-masked and -cloaked appearance suggests a character that exists outside reality and thus any fixed social or national context. Krrish's lack of a real identity, the erasure of his Indian-ness, and his consequent unbound freedom echo the experiences and desires of the modern-day Indian. Contrary to the claims that popular Indian cinema feeds the audience's desire to retain and return to their Indian roots, *Krrish* instead engages in the removal or effacement of one's fixed identity in order for one to attain other identities, or even be freed from identity altogether.

THE POSTMODERN AND THE POSTCOLONIAL APPROACH

Alessio and Langer's reading of *KMG*, if somewhat rigid, is valuable for its recognition of contemporary Bollywood cinema's distinct obsession with and ambivalence towards modernity. Religion may indeed be the 'antidote to modernity' (226), but Hollywood science-fiction codes are simultaneously adopted to contest India's primitivism and backwardness (227). Thus, *KMG* represents the dual desires of a culture wanting to be at once modern and global *and* traditional and autonomous. The film can be considered an ideal metaphor for postmodern Bollywood, a visual culture which now accesses its past through a vernacular of the modern, present or future.

Given the extent to which Alessio and Langer's article informs my analysis of *KMG*, it is worthwhile explaining my reasons for choosing to view the film as a postmodern rather than a postcolonial text. I have already attempted to differentiate the postcolonial from the postmodern. However, my argument for the limitations and incompleteness of applying a postcolonial approach to contemporary Bollywood film is best explained in relation to this key film. As previously noted, there is a reluctance to allow postcolonial texts to enter postmodern discourse under the assumption that this may trivialise the political meaning extracted from a prior postcolonial reading. Both approaches are concerned with the crisis of authority and with challenging monoculturalism, but postmodernism is often accused of reinforcing the very thing it claims to oppose by speaking and operating from within a dominant white Western or European hegemonic discourse. It is thus seen to seize postcolonial texts and stifle their ability to serve any radical political objectives, particularly those concerning issues of race. My postmodern readings could likewise be accused of reinscribing the Indian film texts' marginality while 'robbing them of their raw materials' (Williams and Chrisman, 1993: 13), and forcing them back into colonial territory:

> Assimilation of these [postcolonial] texts into 'postmodernism' ... invokes a neo-universalism which reinforces the very European hegemony which these works have been undermining or circumventing. Thus the so-called 'crisis of (European) authority' continues to reinforce European cultural and political domination ... [making] the rest of the world a peripheral term in Europe's self-questioning. (Ashcroft, Griffiths and Tiffin, 2002: 171)

However, this anxiety and disreputability alone is not enough to disprove the fact that certain Indian cultural works produced post-independence *can* and *do* aspire to appropriate and merge with the West. We may not like it, or want it, but this does not mean to say it is not happening. In the case of *KMG*, it is the colonial subject (or Indian cinema) that willingly chooses to engage with and adopt dominant Western conventions, and therefore becomes an active accomplice to this alleged reinforcing of Western hegemony. Rather than refusing to acknowledge this cultural overlap, it is important to explore the reasons behind and the effects of this active reinstatement of Hollywood aesthetics in popular Bollywood cinema. Thus, my postmodern approach differs in concerning itself with aesthetics and critiquing essentialism, whereas postcolonialism is specifically interested in critiquing, deconstructing and obstructing forms of cultural imperialism – although, as Alessio and Langer reveal in the case of *KMG*, this ambition is not necessarily realised.

Alessio and Langer's fixed focus on the nationalist and postcolonial politics behind *KMG* causes them to almost neglect the aesthetic dimensions of film. It is important to remember the distinction between a 'representation of politics' and a 'politics of representation'. Alessio and Langer read *KMG* as the former, and in doing this, they choose not to dwell on Bollywood's reasons for adopting a Hollywood science-fiction aesthetic (other than tracing back the Indian film industry's sketchy history of occasionally dabbling in the genre). But there is value in exploring this cinematic appropriation since it allows us to observe the way in which various modes of representation are manipulated or inverted, and to what ends. In the case of both approaches, textual analysis reveals how the master narratives behind a text are internally challenged and broken down. However, in Alessio and Langer's article, these challenged master narratives are predominantly engaged with through the film's narrative story and production history. A postmodern film theory approach additionally and more significantly engages with the visual dynamics of film, allowing us to explore this subversion vis-à-vis a more comprehensive study of textual *aesthetics* (stylisation, visual methods of presentation, film form). Alessio and Langer's reading contextualises *KMG* forcefully against a political backbone. As a result, we lose the sense of the text's playfulness and its purpose as a mass entertainment medium and deny the various cultural contradictions inherent in its style and form. Whilst a postcolonial approach leads these authors to locate the cultural specificity of *KMG*, a postmodern approach instead helps us identify moments of textual playfulness, often leading to cultural *ambiguity*. This therefore indicates a final difference in the primary function of the two methods.

DIFFERENCES IN FILM LANGUAGE

E.T. and *KMG* make for an interesting comparison, particularly as the former is very much considered an archetype or landmark of popular American

Koi ... Mil Gaya	*E.T.*
1. Outer space visuals during opening credit sequence	1. Spaceship landing and aliens
2. Car crash and UFO encounter	2. E.T. makes solar system out of levitating objects
3. Rohit smashes Sukhwani's window (comedy)	3. E.T. raids fridge and gets drunk (comedy)
4. Song: 'In Panchhiyon Ko Dekhkar'	4. Drunken Eliot releases frogs in science class
5. Rohit's bullies: motorbike and pushbike chase	5. Eliot and E.T. fly over moon on bicycle
6. Song: 'Idhar Chala Main Udhar Chala'	6. E.T. is dressed up as a woman (comedy)
7. Sukhwani smashes his own windows	7. Halloween costumes
8. Song: 'Koi ... Mil Gaya'	8. Bicycle and car chase 1
9. Storm and UFO encounter in Kasauli	9. Government 'astronauts' enter house
10. Jadoo's magic prank with cricket ball (comedy)	10. Scientists arrive and set up gadgets and equipment
11. Song: 'Jadoo'	11. Bicycle and car chase 2
12. Rohit fights bullies with his super-strength	12. Bikes flying over sun
13. Song: 'It's Magic'	13. Spaceship arrives to take E.T. home
14. Basketball match (including comedy)	
15. Song: 'Haila Haila Hua Hua'	
16. Motorbike chase	
17. Violent fight: Rohit versus Raj's thugs	
18. Rohit beaten up by police officers	
19. Rohit rescues Jadoo from military base	
20. Jeep and car chase	
21. Spaceship arrives to take Jadoo home	

Figure 5.5: Moments of spectacle in *KMG* and *E.T.*

cinema. By seizing the opportunity to rework a classic popular Hollywood text, *KMG* enables us to see how the language and schema of film operate comparatively within popular Indian cinema. This film remake allows us, by observing the breaks and deviations among all its continuities, to consider contemporary Bollywood's inherently varied and culturally different psychologies, perspectives, priorities and agendas, that prove so fundamental to this later form of Indian cinema. The formal differences between *E.T.* and *KMG* extend beyond basic *mise-en-scène* and plotline, and can be further identified in relation to genre conformity, levels of dramatic effect, character functioning, narrative structure and pacing.

One of the most obvious differences between the two films can be seen in the increased number of spectacular moments in *KMG*. Spectacular moments can be broadly defined as whole scenes that function as instances of comic relief or visual spectacle, often operating independently of narrative causality. However, as Geoff King's extensive (2002) work on Hollywood spectacle reveals, these free moments do not always act as a diversion from, or elimination of, narrative. King's study of cinematic spectacle helpfully divides it into four broad subgroups: (1) *action/motion* (stunts and chase sequences); (2) *performance* (song and dance, comedy sketches, celebrity and star appeal); (3) *spectacular vistas* (backdrops, locations, set pieces, production art, special effects, animation); and (4) moments of *emotional intensity* (King: 181). The extent to which each of these elements features in *KMG* mark the film's difference from its comparatively less 'spectacular' original. As the table in Figure 5.5 shows, *KMG* contains significantly more spectacular moments (identified according to King's terms listed above) than its predecessor, even with the exclusion of its six song sequences and moments of emotional intensity.

KMG often pauses its story to engage in emotions and relationships, and entertain its audience via (musical) spectacle. Together, these spectacles and sentimental moments drive the text, whilst *E.T.* bases more of its content on narrative cause–effect relations. Also, given how heavily the themes of sexuality, intelligence or knowledge, physical strength and courage feature in the remake, one could argue that the character development of Rohit and his coming-of-age are more central to *KMG*'s story than its actual supernatural elements, which are merely circumstantial or instrumental.

In the Hollywood original, in-depth relationships really only extend as far as Eliot and E.T., but in *KMG*, the narrative splits into mini-stories, allowing us to view the dynamics between mother and son, Rohit and Jadoo, Rohit, Nisha and Raj (love triangle) and Rohit with his child friends, as well as more peripheral relations between Nisha's and Raj's parents and the comical interaction between police inspectors Khan and Sukhwani. It is interesting to see how the Bollywood adaptation chooses to sidetrack from the main story of the alien (who is not introduced as a character until eighty minutes into the film) in order to explore character dynamics – particularly given the common criticisms about popular Indian cinema's constant neglect of character psychologies (see Thomas).

Furthermore, usually it is the science-fiction narrative that regulates and directs spectacular events in a film text, but in *KMG* almost the reverse is true.

Here, it is spectacle that appears to control and direct the tone and pace of the narrative. Unlike in *E.T.*, where almost every moment is neatly stitched into the storyline, *KMG*'s spectacular moments allow the narrative to ricochet off into different directions and tangents. Lalita Gopalan (2002) has talked of the Hindi song sequence functioning as a disruptive break from the narrative, but in the case of *KMG* the effect is not of abandonment but rather of a *branching out* of narrative. *KMG*'s song sequences can in fact be seen to introduce or trigger sub-plots. For example, it is not until the second song ('Idhar Chala Main Udhar Chala') that we are made aware of the sexual attraction between the film's two protagonists,[14] which then opens up the sub-plot of the love triangle between Rohit, Nisha and Raj. Thus I would be more inclined to agree here with King's view that in spectacle-based cinema, the relationship between spectacle and narrative is one of interdependence (King: 207).

With regard to spectacular vistas, we see that the special effects used to display the powers of the two film aliens also differ greatly. E.T.'s power and intelligence are practically applied: he heals wounds, he makes objects float to demonstrate the solar system, he builds a satellite transmitter, he learns to read and speak English, he makes bicycles fly to help Eliot and his friends escape, and he restores the dying plant which is later used to signal that he is still alive. Aside from similarly helping Rohit escape by making his bicycle fly, Jadoo employs his powers for less practical reasons. They are instead used more for entertainment value and dramatic effect (such as making funny faces out of clouds in the sky during the Jadoo song sequence) or to carry out social functions: he fixes the water-pot to make friends with Rohit, he makes the cricket ball float to amuse the children, he lifts people in the air for mischief, and gifts Rohit with powers out of an act of sympathy, love and friendship. What is more, in the original, E.T. approaches everything with a scientific curiosity, for information and research. Significant time is given in the film to our viewing E.T. getting acquainted with TVs, fridges and comic books. Jadoo does not possess this inquisitiveness, and there is no such period of initiation. Instead he invests his time in playing and socialising with his new-found friends. One could even argue that, more than religion, it is the excessive *humanity* in *KMG* which often compromises the science-fiction elements of the film.

Bollywood's appropriation of science-fiction elements is also compromised or problematised owing to its inherent exhibitionism and magnification. *E.T.*'s film language is all about secrecy and concealment. The film's lighting is largely low-key, with most scenes set at dawn, dusk or at night. In *KMG*, most scenes and subjects are filmed in bright light and full colours (a large proportion of the scenes are set in full daylight), varying from the cool blue-black colour palette in *E.T.* In contrast to *E.T.*, with its low-key lighting, heavy shadows and low angles, there is also a notable level of performativity evident in *KMG* as actors' bodies often fully face the camera. *KMG* intends to offer its audience complete disclosure and an almost omniscient perspective. The remake displays its alien in all his supernatural glory, without shrouding him in shadows or leaving something for the spectator's imagination. In *E.T.*, viewers are often literally and metaphorically left in the dark. It is the difference between this ambiguity which serves the suspense and mysterious elements of *E.T.* and the complete extroverted exposure or 'naked screen' aesthetic of *KMG* that I believe distinguishes the two cinemas. If we take popular definitions of science-fiction, which speak of the genre's compulsion to always hide and conceal things and employ a formal aesthetics (similar to horror) in which figures are often shrouded in shadows, then such attempts by Bollywood to dabble in science-fiction are always to some extent going to be different and difficult.

KMG's loyalty to its adopted genre seems to swing to two extremes, on the one hand deviating from the tendencies of science-fiction, whilst at other times almost caricaturing it. Whereas *E.T.* approaches sci-fi aesthetics with subtlety, *KMG* ventures into a kind of science-fiction-genre *drag*. This can be seen from its opening title sequence, which floods the screen with excessive futuristic clichés: a digital font text in *Star Wars* style rolling credits, superimpositions of shooting stars, galaxies and random flashing lights (consisting of fabrications rather than scientifically referenced images of space), and an accompanying orchestra of electronic synthesisers. This presentation of outer space is too seriously conveyed to be read as parody, yet too excessive and eccentric to be taken as a continuation of the Hollywood science-fiction style. This science-fiction imagery thus hangs off the text like an ill-fitting dazzling costume.

By recycling *E.T.* in such a way, the Bollywood text reworks and transforms the sci-fi genre whilst accommodating its own idiosyncrasies. It obscures and fragments what was originally perceived as a clear cut sci-fi classic, mixing it with elements of romance, melodrama, comedy and musical. Sci-fi imagery and special effects are used for their dramatic effect and to evoke genre, rather than for narrative practicalities. Sensation is important to both postmodern and Bollywood cinema, and the sci-fi genre allows Bollywood cinema to engage in an orgy of spectacle. Also, like the postmodern text, this film embodies multiple story threads; it celebrates excessive and eccentric performance over discretion (realism, verisimilitude) and total disclosure over obscurity, secrecy and mystery – at times flaunting and bombarding the screen with sci-fi markers on such a grand scale that it brings the genre's stylistic tendencies and conventions to our critical attention.

KMG's unsteady management of science-fiction traits reveals how Bollywood refuses to access certain newer genres in a straightforward manner. These genres often need to be translated and adjusted in order to be more palatable to an Indian audience. Although the sci-fi genre has continued to attract more Indian filmmakers (as seen through the production of later films, *Love Story 2050* [2008], *Action Replayy* [2010], *Prince* [2010], *Ra.One*

[2011], *Joker* [2012], *Krrish 3* [2013] and S. Shankar's Tamil film *Enthiran/ Robot* [2010]), it also continues to cause problems for Bollywood cinema as the supernatural will always to some extent be compromised by the ubiquity of religious faith and ritual. While Bollywood endeavours to modernise and liberate itself by adopting Western aesthetics, the Bollywood remake also shows that contemporary Bollywood cinema cannot or will not escape its origins so easily. Whereas many Western sci-fi texts portray the mutation or perversion of nature through science,[15] *KMG* attempts to naturalise science and douse it in religious myth. The connections made between the alien and God in particular signal: (1) an Indian culture only able to access the future through its past; (2) an Indian culture torn between tradition and its aspirations towards modernisation; and (3) the reinsertion of the religious faith ideal via scientific discourse – or rather, the prevalence of religious beliefs over science and technology. Science/technology is usually seen to be the antithesis to religion, but here the two are merged.

Finally, *Koi . . . Mil Gaya* shows how religious myth functions in place of historical or scientific fact in Bollywood cinema, and is used to insert plausibility into the Bollywood film narrative. Religion rationalises the otherwise implausible aspects of the sci-fi genre. Religious mythology is used to locate science-fiction fantasy in 'reality'. In postmodern vein, the film exploits the tensions between tradition (past) and modernity, presenting a world where fiction, myth and factuality overlap and merge with one another.

POSTMODERN TRAITS IN CONTEMPORARY BOLLYWOOD 3: QUESTIONS OF REALISM IN *ABHAY*

Although *OSO* and *KMG* both experiment with popular cinematic traits, some would still argue that they do not quite venture into the kind of experimentalism and political aesthetics akin to an oppositional Indian art cinema. As discussed earlier, scholars and critics of popular Indian cinema have lamented the loss of Indian cinema's artistic and experimental edge, particularly when compared with the national, social, neo-realist and new-wave films of the pre-global era. However, through study of such criticisms, it has become clear that this alleged neglect essentially refers to an absence of (or even ignorance towards) realism in contemporary Bollywood cinema.

Verisimilitude[16] is rarely a concern for popular Indian film. Actors can directly address an audience in order to explain the key themes of the film before it begins, and it has been common practice for crowds of fans to be positioned within the frame and to be seen watching an on-location song or fight sequence as it is being filmed. Having been built on a foundation of musicals and melodrama, the laws and rules of reality are always to some extent compromised in popular Indian film. The fundamental theme of love in almost every film is portrayed as something sublime; it has a power so great that it can transcend the laws of space and time, best demonstrated through the multiple-location song sequence. And as seen above, mainstream Hindi cinema is inherently performative and often self-reflexive of its own artificiality, exhibiting dialogue over conversation and costumes as opposed to clothes (Virdi, 2003: 2). Such unrealistic forms of presentation have aimed to fulfil the audience's desire for films that are larger than life, with 'stories engulfing generations, large periods of time, big influences on a large spectrum' (Akhtar, cited in Virdi: 174) and involving great coincidences, dramatic scenes and religious miracles. These methods of disrupting realism and issues of spectator desire have thus informed our understanding of the Indian film audience's engagement with the popular film text. Manjunath Pendakur (2003) claims to have observed audiences becoming so emotionally drawn into a film that they literally tear up their seats in excitement:

> ... the audience actively transforms watching movies into a performative act ... the cinematic experience and meaning making by the audience is not idle, analytic activity but real engagement with the film. It is often taken to its extreme when the active audience in its excitement of a fight on the screen tears up the seats or gets into a brawl. (Pendakur, 2003: 97)

Pendakur acknowledges the way the Indian audience consciously and actively participates in the cinematic experience, but he is quick to condemn this as an almost hypodermic act, where the emotionally vulnerable spectators are duped into believing in the fictional world of the text. Similarly, Chidananda Das Gupta (1991) has claimed that the Indian spectator is restricted by specific cognitive conditioning, which prevents him or her from differentiating between cinema and real life. Gupta's account of the naivety of Indian spectators has since been rejected by Indian film scholars for oversimplifying Indian spectatorship in this way. I would argue that it is not necessarily that the Bollywood audience does not know that the text is not real, but rather that they are able to understand that *reality does not matter*, and perhaps these 'performative' spectators acknowledge the possibility of investing in art as an alternative to the real. Thus, as realist filmmakers such as Shyam Benegal continue to attack mainstream cinema's inability to connect with and reflect upon real life (Benegal, cited in Binford: 83), others equally criticise the realist cinema as being just as guilty of 'anti-emotion' and 'sterile representations of realism' (Pendakur, 1990: 249). Perhaps it is not questions of value that are most significant in such disputes, but rather the question of the *importance* of cinematic realism.

THE AVANT-GARDE IN BOLLYWOOD

As demonstrated in the case of *OSO*, contemporary Bollywood cinema is wary of its unsteady relationship with the real and takes this as an opportunity to experiment with modes of realist representation. In doing so, it can introduce a kind of avant-garde filmmaking practice that could be taken as a new alternative Indian cinema aesthetic emerging from within mainstream Bollywood.

In his attempt to rethink and challenge previous theorisations of the avant-garde, Peter Burger (1984) has drawn attention to the concept's significant links with mass culture. According to Burger, whereas the historical or modernist avant-garde of the early twentieth century attempted to separate itself from the mainstream, new avant-garde works (such as the 1960s pop art of Andy Warhol) have instead come to embrace popular culture. In response to Burger's attempt to define the avant-garde, Richard Murphy (1999) has therefore insisted that we consider the possibility of an avant-garde that exists within popular cultural forms. Murphy notes how this 'expressionist avant-garde' shares several characteristics of the postmodern, such as self-reflexivity, parody, rewriting, the rejection of claims to truth and origin, and the Lyotardian affirmation of the 'fictionality of all existing cosmologies, metalanguages and master narratives' (Murphy: 263). Furthermore, the expressionist avant-garde realises it cannot resist institutionalisation. Hence, it is able to step across the boundaries of art cinema and that of the commercial industry, and implement the conventions and concerns of both forms of art. This considered, one could argue that although independent art cinema may be diminishing since the glory days of Benegal and Ray, the concerns of such a cinema may in fact continue to develop within an Indian avant-garde that combines the concerns of high-art cinema and mainstream film. By investigating such an artistic drive within popular Indian film, we can identify a cinema that does justice to both issues of realism and the emotional intensity of (more obviously) commercial films.

KAMAL HAASAN'S *ABHAY*

Radical forms of aesthetic experimentation may seem scarce in contemporary Bollywood cinema, but there is evidence of an avant-garde style emerging through some examples of post-millennial Bollywood filmmaking. The South Indian writer, actor, director and producer Kamal Haasan can in many ways be seen to support such a cultural effort. Haasan's films[17] have always maintained cross-regional commercial popularity, but they also demonstrate an attempt to stretch the boundaries of Indian cinema, particularly in terms of formal style. Technically, many of Haasan's films have been known to serve as rare examples of Indian cinema's successful experimentations with visual effects. In his nationalism-themed film *Hindustani* (1996),[18] many of the featured dance sequences involve absurd hallucinatory effects via image manipulation (walking on walls, morphing, and image duplication) never before seen in the cinema. Haasan's films' aesthetic innovations, coupled with often-challenging storylines (*Hindustani* serving as an attack on Indian patriotism and *Hey Ram!* [2000] challenging the integrity and exposing the darker side of Mahatma Gandhi), have not prevented them from achieving reasonable commercial success, suggesting that not all forms of experimental artistic expression in popular Indian cinema are subject to rejection and failure.

Both the avant-garde and issues of realism in Bollywood cinema can be explored through Haasan's 2001 film *Abhay* (aka *Aalavandhan*), which potentially serves as one of the best examples of an alternative and aesthetically political text operating within the boundaries of popular Indian cinema. Despite its commercial packaging, *Abhay* cannot be regarded as a run-of-the-mill popular Indian film,[19] but rather a fusion of several contradictory styles – most significantly reminiscent of Western postmodern surrealist works which aim to distort and diffuse the features of realism and representation.

Abhay's narrative tells the story of twin brothers Abhay and Vijay, whose childhood is destroyed by their mother's sudden suicide and father's consequent remarriage to their adulterous, alcoholic and abusive stepmother, Diane. Abhay, who is particularly affected by these traumatic events, murders his stepmother and as a result suffers a mental breakdown, later causing him to turn into a misogynistic psychopath obsessed with a desire to kill women whom he sees as incarnations of his dead stepmother. Abhay is detained in a prison for the criminally insane while his brother Vijay, who is able to forget his past, enrols in military school and looks towards a happy and successful life as an Army soldier and fiancé of TV reporter Tejaswini. However, still troubled by his conscience (a hallucination in the form of his mother's ghost asking him to avenge her death), Abhay takes Vijay's fiancé as a re-embodiment of Diane. Thus, convinced that his brother is in danger of being subjected to the same female manipulation as his father, Abhay breaks out of the mental institution and attempts to hunt down and murder his stepmother's incarnation, Tejaswini.

Abhay's plot contains several dramatic clichés familiar to popular Indian cinema such as the struggle between an 'evil' villain (Abhay) and an 'honest' hero (Vijay), a beautiful heroine in need of rescuing (Tejaswini), an attention to romance, and the theme of inner-family conflict. However, the way in which the film chooses to present these characters and storylines proves anything but conventional.

ABHAY AS COMIC BOOK VILLAIN

We have already begun to explore the ways in which hyperrealism features in contemporary Indian cinema in analysing *OSO*. However, the impact and effect of this particularly complex postmodern function on the Indian film aesthetic can be further explored through *Abhay* – firstly, through the way in which the film constructs and presents its key anti-hero protagonist. Abhay's physical appearance alone suggests something beyond the ordinary: his bald head and provocative red eyes; his large tattooed muscular body which is continuously highlighted and emphasised through shadowed lighting. In the film's introductory sequence, he is juxtaposed alongside monkeys as he mimics their actions and expresses his animalistic tendencies by repeatedly stating that he is 'half human, half animal'. This, coupled with his constant growling and snarling, his husky deep voice, his distinctively monstrous cackle and his tremendous strength, creates an image of a character verging on the superhuman. Everything about Abhay is exaggerated. His facial features, his dramatic gestures, his animalistic posture and his always dramatic dialogue all help to create a character which to the audience seems larger than life.

Vinay Lal has commented on the 'ludicrously comic' nature of the archetypal Bollywood villain, which in effect produces unrealistic caricatures of real evil: 'some are demons, but for that reason all the more assimilable to rakshashas [demons], the creatures of mythology rather than of history' (Lal: 237). Indian film villains have historically been portrayed through caricature. They are often scarred with facial disfigurements and distinguished by their speech impediments or trademark evil laughter. Amresh Puri, perhaps the most famous actor in Indian cinema to have played a villain (best known in the West for his role as the villain in Steven Spielberg's *Indiana Jones and the Temple of Doom* [1984]), has become famous for having more hairstyles, costume changes and image transformations than most Bollywood actresses. However, *Abhay* is one of the first films to take this form of villainy to such an extreme. Throughout the film, our antagonist is presented as if out of a comic-strip, often resembling Indian comic book heroes like 'Betaal' (the 1960s Indian version is based on Lee Falk's American comic book hero known as *The Phantom*; see Sharma, 1997), towards whom references are made throughout the film. For example, Abhay's personality is marked by a giant picture of his hero Betaal, which is clearly seen painted on the wall in his bedroom as a child. Abhay's character is not presented in this way exclusively for the sake of entertainment value. Rather, it seems that with this film, villainy is being consciously and intentionally exaggerated. The text is engaged in a deliberate attempt to bring the fictionality and unreality of its lead character to the fore, and for this reason it is a film that raises important questions surrounding the notion of reality and representation.

Figure 5.6: Reality is fictionalised and pictures come to life in *Abhay* (V. Creations, 2001).

ABHAY'S WORLD

Although Abhay may be the villain of the movie, the film's focus is nevertheless shared between the points of view of its villain and its hero, Vijay. On several occasions, the audience is given a taste of the world through Abhay's eyes. For example, when Abhay first escapes from prison, we are presented with his point of view of the world around him via a sequence that verges on the surreal. This scene, which follows Abhay through the city's streets at night, is shrouded in an unnatural smoky green light, and presented through a fisheye lens which follows Abhay through various abandoned streets and alleyways.

Unlike the scenes surrounding Vijay's story, which are shot in natural and familiar surroundings, Abhay's street scene conversely resembles a fantasy or dream sequence. As Abhay's hallucinations increase, the audience is brought into a world of giant junk food clowns (Abhay stops to ask a giant Ronald McDonald for directions) and rowing boats and divers which suddenly appear to swim through the town centre. When it seems the sequence cannot get any stranger, cartoon characters appear from television sets and begin morphing into humans (Abhay is prevented from entering a cinema by an usher who morphs from a cartoon character into a human) and we watch as a three-dimensional animated hand of Batman's comic sidekick Robin reaches out of a wall poster and knocks a bemused Abhay on the head in a comedy moment.

This cartoon world is taken to extremes when Abhay visualises Tejaswini crawling out of a poster dressed in a black leather suit and holding a whip – resembling the look of an archetypal comic book vixen. The audience is yet again drawn into a parallel world where ordinary people become fictionalised superheroes. However, although Abhay's world may indeed be full of dream sequences, childish fantasies and cartoon characters, it is even more interesting to note the ways in which this fictional and surreal world is repeatedly confused with reality throughout the film – a crucial feature overlapping with many postmodern texts.

THE EXCHANGEABILITY OF REALITY AND FICTION

Throughout *Abhay*, we see our protagonists and other real-life characters merge into fiction and fantasy. This dissolving of real and unreal elements is also transferred into and prompted by the film's action sequences, which further complicate the possibility of a 'pure' representation of realism in the film. For example, this can be seen through a comparison between two key fight sequences in the film: the first relating to when Abhay slaughters movie actress Sharmilee in her hotel bedroom (after yet again mistaking her for his stepmother), and the second, a climactic breakout between the text's twin protagonists at the end of the film.

The violent scene between Abhay and Sharmilee is presented through an animated sequence where a cartoon version of Abhay continues to attack and torture his female victim. Despite the clear fictionality of this cartoon sequence, the killing scene appears strangely visceral and disturbing. The 'camera' shakes and spins with the action and the sound effects of blood spilling and bodies thumping against a wall sound shockingly realistic. At one point, Abhay's cartoon double is seen to cover the camera lens with his bloody fingerprints, further creating the illusion of reality. Through this sequence we are confronted with an animated world that becomes more 'real' than the real. Thus, through adapting and blending with the cinematic styles of realism (shaking mobile cameras and lifelike sound effects) *Abhay* invests in a kind of hyperrealism.

This hyperrealism is even more significant when we consider the way in which *Abhay* handles its scenes of live action. Almost acting as an inversion of the above stylistic sequence, the final fight between Abhay and Vijay inherits all the conventions of a slapstick cartoon. While the above animated sequence uses accurate, detailed and vivid movement and sound, the latter live-action fight scene is presented through comic parody. The punctuating sound effects

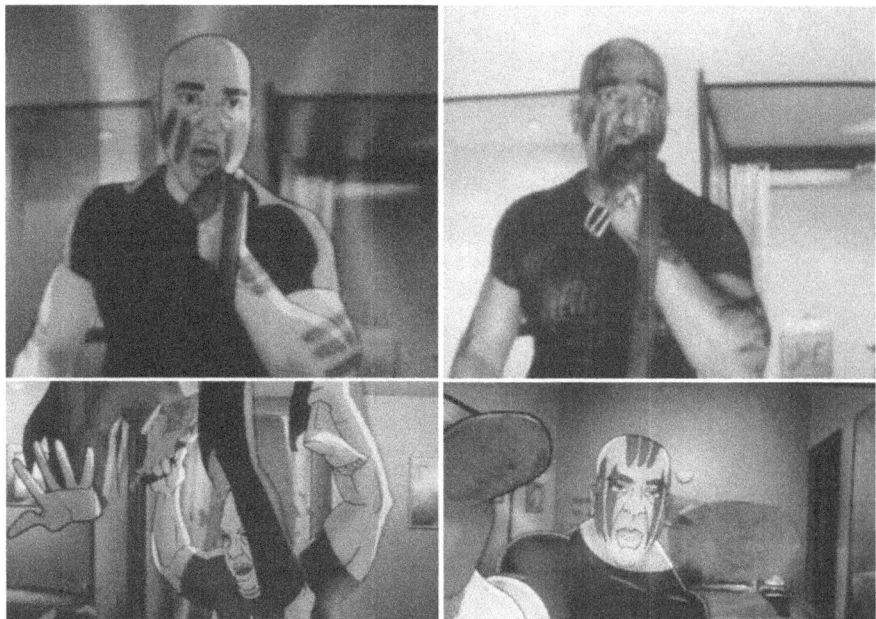

Figure 5.7: Abhay murders Sharmilee in a hyperrealistic animated sequence in *Abhay* (V. Creations, 2001).

used here are cartoon-like. Framing is kept tight and the action is often interrupted with several close-up shots of the characters' eyes – a style very much resembling the images captured in conventional comic-strip art – whilst Abhay is seen to jump into the air in slow motion and swing his brother on his back like a true animated action hero. What is more, when Abhay pursues Vijay and Tejaswini in a dramatic car chase, the fictionality of the scene is further stressed through Abhay, who now actually wears a mask in true superhero style.

It should be noted here that, although integral to the formal style of *Abhay*, cartoon or comic book aesthetics have been increasingly employed in other contemporary Bollywood films, such as certain fight sequences in *Krrish* and throughout Anubhav Sinha's *Cash* (2007), which includes thirty-eight separate instances where the live action switches to animated sequences. In *Krrish*, tight framing, askew camera angles, extreme close-ups and speed trails are used in live action to emphasise the sensorial vivacity of the hero's punches and kicks, whilst in *Cash*, a similar effect of visual intensity is achieved, this time by replacing each protagonist with a cartoon avatar during heightened moments of action and drama.

So absent is *Abhay*'s desire for conventional realism that moments of slapstick comedy are deliberately inserted into its otherwise serious and viscerally violent scenes. Characters walking into poles and lamp-posts and hitting

Figure 5.8: Cartoon comic aesthetics in *Cash* [upper] (Seven Entertainment, 2007) and *Krrish* [lower] (Film Kraft, 2006).

one another on the head spoil the verisimilitude of the violence, preventing spectators from being able to take the live action as real or plausible.

The interchangeability of the stylistic techniques which normally accompany the portrayal of reality and unreality in cinema is also effectively emphasised through the parallels between Vijay and Abhay. At first, Vijay is portrayed as the direct opposite of Abhay, in terms of both his humane characteristics and his visual presentation. He is sane, honest, successful, and lives according to the rationale and ideologies of the 'real world'. However, as the story unfolds, Haasan's text reveals that even these opposites of madness and sanity (or fantasy and truth) are inevitably blurred. *Abhay* is increasingly filled with moments in which the characteristics outlining Abhay and his world of fictional hallucinations can be seen to become diffused into Vijay's. In one scene, Abhay recalls the memory of his meeting Vijay and his fiancé in prison at the start of the film. However, this memory is somewhat altered and they too are suddenly presented to us not as 'real' people, but as comic book characters. Vijay becomes an exaggerated version of himself as a military commando, while Tejaswini is portrayed in the aforementioned form of a comic book vixen. This scene may indeed be a concoction of Abhay's disturbed mind, but the similarities between Abhay's distorted vision and the original 'naturalistic' version are nevertheless significant.

In later scenes, even Vijay's perception of events appears to be influenced by and merged with his brother's. When Vijay arrives at his abandoned childhood family home towards the end of the film, his emotions are no longer portrayed through realistic modes of presentation. Instead, Vijay's reactions are marked by a cut to a close-up of the face of comic hero Betaal. This juxtaposition of real and fictional characters marks yet another attempt by the film to unite the characteristics of the real and unreal. Vijay also eventually begins to hallucinate like Abhay, when he envisages the image of his dead father. Thus, finally (through engagement in the comic book fight sequence mentioned above) Vijay's reality is shattered and he too begins to interact with the unreal world of his brother.

In *Abhay*, the audience is confronted with a world that is explicitly unable to contain the kind of realism that the work of realist cinema wished to expose. Separating the 'real' from artistic representation becomes difficult. Once reality as an ideological concept is broken down, its instability is exposed and we are instead presented with hyperrealism – a confused mix of the unreal, the surreal and the *too real*. As with the case of Abhay and Vijay, reality proves to be a mirrored version or alter ego of the unreal.

Indian popular cinema's relationship with reality is now more complex. As with Western examples of postmodern film, this cinema is bringing more attention to its unreality and its constructedness. The difference is that in India, this self exposition is regarded as having an important if not a *vital* part to play in engaging the audience successfully. Commercial Indian films like *Abhay* show that the audience not only *desires* the unreal, but is able to indulge its playful relationship with and manipulation of the real. There is no need to completely disguise fiction as reality. It can be openly presented as unreal and remain a fabrication, and yet reveal a connection between realism and its aesthetic alternative – the simulacra, the signifier as referent, and the sublime substitute. One should not be so quick to declare an end to realism in Bollywood cinema. Instead we should consider that it is not so much that realism has been lost, but rather that it has been *displaced*. Although realism may not conventionally inhabit the form and style of many Bollywood films, its absence or displacement is jarring and, in effect, it is drawn to our attention constantly throughout such presentations.

THE INDIAN AVANT-GARDE: ART CINEMA ENTERS THE MAINSTREAM

Films such as *Abhay* may hold the key to resolving the conflict between art cinema and mainstream popular cinema in India. Postmodernist or expressionist avant-garde texts such as *Abhay* are able to question, displace and decentre ideologies surrounding the authority of the real as origin (Murphy: 268) and challenge established ideals of artistic freedom and innovation. Such texts are able to occupy both mainstream and aesthetically experimental territories, providing entertainment via spectacle as well as providing a lighthearted critique of cinematic modes of representing realism (verisimilitude) and occupying the interests of both art-house and multiplex or mainstream audiences. The postmodern avant-garde aims to 'deconstruct established patterns of perception without hastily replacing them' (ibid.: 271) or providing a 'necessarily' better utopian alternative – a mistake perhaps made by supporters of modernism and historical avant-garde movements.

Films that continue along the lines of *Abhay* show that commercial cinema can support avant-gardist concerns, and that these aesthetically postmodern and stylistically and commercially driven films still have the potential to be critical, particularly of cinema as an ideological construct. Furthermore, this critique need not even be conscious. Such forms of cinema do not need to produce manifestos or revel in destruction in order to get their point across. In fact, the less conscious a text may be of its critical potential, the less exclusive and corrupted the result is likely to be.[20] Perhaps the reason we puzzle over the lack of artistic cinematic movements in contemporary India is precisely that we have simply looked in all the wrong places. Rather than searching peripheries, margins and niches for innovative and artistic texts, we should consider the sheer volume of films being produced in mainstream Bollywood. There is a great deal of experimentation going on in contemporary Indian cinema today. Boundaries are being pushed, conventions are being subverted and modes reinvented. The personal agendas and aspirations of Bollywood cinema have broadened. The process of creating and offering visual pleasure to audiences now incorporates postmodern irony, invokes cinematic canons, addresses the artifice of filmmaking and fiction, rouses and articulates cinephilia, celebrates the hostile interplay of different cinematic modes, inverts and attacks traditional conventions, and nurtures aesthetic experimentation.

The above case studies show that it is possible for mainstream Indian cinema to entertain and critique, to conform and subvert, to affirm and problematise, to produce art yet make money. However, this presents no utopia, silver lining or happy ending for the medium, for the interdependency and constantly apparent tensions visible between each of these binary objectives remind us of Bollywood's inexorable predicament: popular Indian cinema is caught in a trap, a cycle that ties it to convention, consistency, custom, repetition and reproductions. Its aspirations for change (vis-à-vis modernity, evolution, progress, sophistication, global appeal) result in a paradoxical turning back to the past. Whether or not we consider Bollywood to be truly postmodern, the concept (at the very least as a stylistic mode) has helped us to articulate this predicament and understand its benefits and hindrances. A postmodern perspective unveils Bollywood's current attempts at innovation and evolution. By adopting postmodern traits, the industry can attempt to serve its divided objectives of outward global expansion on the one hand, and internal self-preservation on the other. What was previously a West-centric theoretical framework now actively helps raise our appreciation and understanding of contemporary Bollywood films and uncovers an entirely new phase of Indian cinema. Likewise, in turn, by placing it in the context of Indian cinema, we are able to see how postmodernism's global application broadens its impact and brings to our attention its many new potential materialisations and aesthetic applications.

Now that we are able to see how the postmodern can be applied to the analysis of New Bollywood cinema, we can study it in more detail (via a more intensive textual analysis) as a body of texts, or perhaps even a movement or genre, in order to consider further instances of aesthetic innovation and political issues at stake. It is important to note that the majority of the films mentioned in this chapter are, in some form, cultural appropriations of other texts. Although I do not wish to suggest that postmodern occurrences in contemporary Bollywood films stop at remakes, there are certainly a strikingly significant number of post-millennial Bollywood texts that lend themselves to the postmodern, yet also engage in remaking practices. Remaking appears to be one of the most characteristic features of New Bollywood cinema, and I believe its connections with the postmodern issues discussed above are more than merely coincidental.

NOTES

1. The author's long list of postmodern populist films includes *Austin Powers: International Man of Mystery*, *Charlie's Angels*, *A Knight's Tale*, *Ocean's Eleven*, *O Brother, Where Art Thou?*, *Wayne's World* and *Who Framed Roger Rabbit*.
2. The term, originally coined by Samuel Taylor Coleridge in his *Biographia Literaria* (1817), refers to the audience's investment in (and acceptance of) the fantastic, even impossible, elements of an artistic work for the sake of entertainment. It refers to the act of literally suspending one's judgement of a text's plausibility in order to immerse oneself in its fictional world.
3. The 'Dastaan-e-Om Shanti Om' song sequence is a visual amalgamation of Emily Brontë's *Wuthering Heights*, Andrew Lloyd Webber's/Gaston Leroux's *Phantom of the Opera*, the music videos of rock star Meat Loaf, and Baz Luhrmann's *Moulin Rouge*.
4. 'You're not getting bored are you?' and 'In friendship there are no sorrys or thankyous' from *Maine Pyar Kiya* (1989), and 'Frankly my dear, I don't give a damn' from *Gone with the Wind* (1939).
5. Film City is the real name of the Indian film industry's officially-based studio complex in Mumbai.
6. The Kapoor family comprises five generations of actors, producers and directors. The lineage includes legendary actor Raj Kapoor, and the legacy has more recently (2007) been continued by newcomer Ranbir Kapoor.
7. Translated via www.bhagavad-gita.org.
8. Earlier examples include *Chand Par Chadayee* (1967) and *Elaan* (1971).
9. The actor is famous for his deformed hand, which has become something of a signature trademark in his films.
10. Indeed, scientific rationale is fought somewhat hypocritically with another grand narrative – Hindu religion – but I wish to suggest that such a polarisation ultimately leads to a mutual cancelling-out effect, thus weakening the solidity of both ideologies.
11. The authors give the example of Rohit reminding his IT teacher that 'man made the computer, the computer did not make man', which reveals the film's binary opposition of humanity and morality over technology and machine (223).
12. It is worthwhile noting that *Krrish* is still directed and produced by the same supposedly pro-Hindu BJP backing director, Rakesh Roshan.
13. The superhero concept had, however, been experimented with earlier in Hindi films like *Shiva Ka Insaaf* (1985), which also associates the figure of its superhero with a Hindu god (Shiva).
14. The adolescent sexuality between Raj and Nisha is classically and symbolically represented in the sequence through their playful dancing and getting soaking wet in the rain.
15. Interestingly, this familiar sci-fi topic later becomes the central moral subject of the follow-up film *Krrish 3*, and the religious context so crucial in *KMG* seems largely diluted if not extraneous.
16. The verisimilitude I refer to here is the social or cultural variety (public perception of reality or truth) as opposed to the generic kind (conformity to the rules of a particular genre). See Steve Neale's discussion of Tzvetan Todorov's two definitions of the term (Neale, 1990: 47–8).
17. Haasan is credited as an actor for *Abhay* and *Hindustani*, and as writer and director for *Hey Ram*. However, he is still widely considered and described as the *auteur* of his films owing to his collaborative involvement in all creative stages of filmmaking. For example, *Abhay* is based on the 1984 novel *Dayam* written by Haasan.

18. This film is also known under the title *Indian*.
19. I shall avoid explicitly referring to *Abhay* as a Bollywood film, since it and many other Kamal Haasan films have been produced by the Tamil film industry in Chennai (known as Kollywood) and not in Bombay. However, I would argue that the film's Bollywood co-stars, its Hindi dubbing and repackaging for the north Indian market, and its promotion in Bombay film press circles allow the film to fall into a grey area regarding whether or not it can be considered part of the medium of Bollywood cinema.
20. This is perhaps a return to Jean-Luc Camolli and Jean Narboni's category (e), where ideologies and systems are corroded and dismantled by being restated and integrated in a film (Comolli and Narboni, 1969: 817).

CHAPTER 6

Indian Cinema: A History of Repetition

We have already begun to identify that Bollywood cinema's postmodern tendencies partly stem from its investment in remaking and recycling past film texts, styles and conventions as a means of internal commentary, creative innovation and subverting conventional modes of representation (such as cinematic realism). In the following, I provide further examples of such instances of postmodern appropriation in contemporary Indian cinema, demonstrating how widespread such processes are among the diversity of films produced in Bollywood in the 2000s decade. To inform my research, I have viewed and compared over one hundred modern Bollywood remakes alongside their alleged film originals (observing patterns of similarity not simply in narrative content but in style and form, which help to determine appropriation rather than coincidence in formally unacknowledged remakes). Although this study has covered several of the film texts that appear in Nayar's aforementioned discussions of popular 1990s Indian film remakes (1997, 2005), the majority of the films I have chosen to discuss here emerge specifically from within the post-millennium decade. I intend to draw attention to the sheer output of remakes in this period in order to signal a new phenomenon of remaking that is symptomatic of the recent impact of postmodernism, globalisation, modernisation and internationalisation in India and its film industry. In the following discussions I shall employ the term 'remake *genre*' as I believe that the contemporary Bollywood remake has inherited a particular set of (postmodern) agendas and stylistic conventions. It can be recognised as an artistic work with unique form and content, which offers its audiences a particular kind of gratification in viewing and engaging with it.

My Appendix offers a long list of Bollywood films which have either been confirmed as remakes (by their filmmakers) or which the media, academia, or fans and viewers in online forums have simply speculated might be remakes. It therefore broadly includes disputable or unsubstantiated remakes which have emerged from public hearsay, as well as conspicuous plagiarisms, certified homages, and explicit literary adaptations. The list is by no means exhaustive (it excludes numerous remakes of South Indian films), but it does present a substantial body of films demonstrating the strong remaking trend in Bollywood, particularly in the noughties. The purpose of my study is not to indisputably confirm each and every film listed as a clear-cut remake (indeed, several of the remakes analysed in this book refrain from outwardly disclosing or acknowledging their sources), but to enable and encourage others to explore and determine the level and effect of appropriation in such films.

By exploring a wide range of film remaking modes, which function and perform on various levels from scene-specific citations and allusions to the more blatant 'rip-offs' and movie tributes, I aim to expand our current understanding of the various categories and functionalities of cinematic remaking. I will also provide further illustration of how remaking can powerfully assist a dismantling of familiar filmic conventions. In the latter part of my investigation, I look at a series of remake films specifically focused around masculine themes and a male ensemble cast, demonstrating how these male-oriented films have spawned a new breed of Bollywood remakes which subvert cinematic representations of the 'coolness' and 'masculinity' of the Bollywood anti-hero.

My investigation into Indian film remakes will be less about documenting the historical emergence of these films (a mammoth project in itself) or the conditions in which they were made, thus following a different line of investigation from Ganti's anthropological work on remakes, which looks at pre-production decision making and scripting processes (as discussed in Chapter 3). Instead, my study will be more analytically focused on the remake text's formal techniques and devices. I will study the semantics and iconography as well as narrative structuring of the film texts. Key areas of analysis will consider technical or stylistic exchanges between original and copy, shifts in character and audience perspectives, thematic focus and prioritised content, the balance of style versus story (substance), audience reading and decoding processes, and the inversion of thematic, stylistic and cultural codes.

THE FILM REMAKE

Film remakes and adaptations still occupy a relatively narrow space within Western film studies. The remake text often has the misfortune of having a stigma attached to it. It is inherently a source of comparison against its esteemed original, through which we enjoy critiquing, condemning and demoting the copy. The remake text seems incessantly to fall victim to the laws of fidelity and the defenders of elite film or literary canons it often alludes to. The question of whether Hollywood's remakes – in the form of sequels, homages, literary adaptations, updates, parodies, makeovers, and series – engage in this textual 'cannibalisation' (Stam, 2000: 61) for the sake of quick profit, nostalgia, or simply because they have run out of new ideas, is a fashionable point of debate in remake and adaptation studies.[1] Meanwhile, literary adaptation theory largely preoccupies itself with four key concerns: autonomy, fidelity, the supremacy of the literary original, and the problems of translating *word-story* into *image-story*.

The issue of textual fidelity (a remake's loyalty to its original) has fuelled criticism and dominated remake discourse. In his survey of pre-1980s Hollywood movie remakes, Michael B. Druxman (1975) comments on the danger fidelity holds for the remake:

> ... people cling to their precious memories of a grander cinema in days gone by and ... almost no remake – despite its quality – can shatter the fondness a spectator might hold for the original version he saw in his youth. It's called nostalgia. (24)

However, such discussions distract us from other more positive traits of remake cinema. As Brian McFarlane (1996) notes, the fidelity argument prevents the drawing of attention to adaptation as 'inevitable artistic (and culturally rich) progress; the more interesting process of transference ... [and] the powerfully influential production determinants in the film remake which may be irrelevant to the original' (McFarlane: 10). Thus, theorists have attempted to shift the focus away from comparative quality analysis, and towards interpretation. For example, Robert Stam (2000) has proposed that we look at adaptations as 'translations' (62), encouraging a study of the way in which original texts are manipulated and altered to produce new meanings, perspectives and experiences.

Scholarly work on film remaking is limited yet dense and diverse in its ideas and perspectives. For example, some theorists argue that remaking is a fundamental part of all cinemas, and that the term is applicable to all texts since every film is guilty of re-presentation or prior conception (Andrew, 2000: 29). As Stam comments, 'All texts are tissues of anonymous formulae ... conscious and unconscious quotations, and, conflations and inversions of other texts' (64). Others, however, have tried to classify and order the term (see Druxman, Greenberg [cited in Verevis, 2006: 8–9], Leitch [2002: 45–9] and Eberwein [1998]). Gerard Genette first used the term 'transtextuality' to refer to special and unique instances of repetition, and attempted to divide, organise and group these instances of cinematic intertextuality into various sub-genres: paratextuality, metatextuality, hypertextuality, architextuality, celebrity intertextuality, intratextuality, genetic textuality and auto-citation (for detailed definitions of each see Genette, 1982). Likewise, more recently, Robert Stam has confirmed the complexity of the remake-adaptation as a subject of study by noting its many tropes, including reading (shedding new light on the original text through critique or creative misreading), dialogisation (engaging the original text in a dialogue or conversation with other texts), cannibalisation (the remake text's openness to a polyphonic and infinite number of textual influences) and transmutation (specifically here, changes to an original text's plot events and characters) (Stam: 62), as well as its transformation processes: selection, amplification, concretisation, actualisation, critique, extrapolation, analogisation, popularisation and reculturalisation (68).[2] Theoretical studies of visual adaptations have also pointed to their broader importance in media and film studies – for example in relation to general issues surrounding postmodern reproduction, and with regard to the act of *storytelling* itself. As James Naremore (2000) envisions: 'The study of adaptation needs to be joined with the study of recycling, remaking, and every other form of retelling in the age of mechanical reproduction and electronic communication. By this means, adaptation will become part of a general theory of repetition' (15).

Another underexplored aspect of the textual adaptation is the cross-cultural remake. A few scholars have produced interesting accounts of cross-fertilisation and boundary crossing between various foreign national cinemas and Hollywood, most notably remakes from Hong Kong (Aufderheide, 1998; Bordwell, 2000), Eastern Europe (Horton, 1998) and France (Wills, 1998; Mazdon, 2000). In her book *Encore Hollywood: Remaking French Cinema*, Lucy Mazdon (2000) focuses on the ways in which remaking, or more precisely the 'aesthetic cross-fertilisation' of French and American cinema, facilitates *and* interrupts the formation of French or American cultural and national identity (26). Mazdon highlights the importance of determining 'how ... the signifying structures of the original text [are] replaced by target culture signifying structures in the remake' (ibid.), arguing that remakes do not simply copy, but that they *produce new identities*. Mazdon first explains how cultures use the process of cross-fertilisation to differentiate themselves (through their own nationalist cinematic traditions) and mobilise their sense of national identity. However, she later reveals how remaking can also end up interrogating and calling those very same identities into question (125) – particularly when the values and beliefs of the original text's culture are reinscribed into the target culture of the remake (26). The act of remaking can therefore draw our attention to 'the instabilities and hybridity which constitute the filmic text' (125). To paraphrase an important question posed by Genette, there is an urgent need to investigate cross-cultural adaptations and ask what dynamics and dimensions are involved in such films, where language, cultural traditions, psychology, and even narrative sense may differ greatly between original and remake (Genette, cited in Horton and McDougal: 4). Such discussions have almost denounced discourse on textual fidelity in favour of studying the way in which remakes resist and perform in opposition to their originals (Dika, 2003: 20).

The majority of theoretical work on film remaking has focused on Western and specifically American cinema. Particularly in the case of Hollywood, the remake text is associated with the following distinctive characteristics: the presold text, the reiterated formula, a bigger budget, updated technical effects, extensive marketing and publicity campaigns, blatant commercial filmmaking methods, as well as often explicit incentives – 'guaranteed' financial gain, cultural imperialism and 'defensive production' (where a popular foreign text may threaten to compete with or steal its inland box-office spots [Verevis, 3]). Remakes have offered Hollywood studios economic efficiency via their recyclable plots and recycled studio-owned material (Druxman: 14) and quick profit through non-remakes (films simply bearing the same title and author name of previous films, as defined by Druxman [15]), plus the chance to repackage old texts successfully with the help of nothing more than updated dialogue, star casts and technical advancements in sound, colour and ratio-format (ibid.). But although the aforementioned appraisals are certainly relevant to scholars investigating, say, the commercial filmic adaptations of Shakespeare, Jane Austen, or the original Batman franchise, they do not suffice to explain the phenomenon of all other forms of remake cinema – such as the Bollywood remake.

American cinema has several decades of solid movie remaking behind it, but the same cannot be said of Bollywood, for which a concentrated output of film remakes is more of an abrupt millennium phenomenon. As previously discussed, mainstream Indian cinema has seen many formal changes in recent years, including a booming series of well over a hundred self-remakes, sequels and foreign film adaptations. The latter category's best-known examples include *Kaante* (2002) [*Reservoir Dogs* (1992)], *Koi . . . Mil Gaya* (2003) [*E.T.: The Extra Terrestrial* (1982)], *Krishna Cottage* (2004) [*Ringu* (1998)], *Sarkar* (2005) [*The Godfather* (1972)], *Fight Club: Members Only* (2006) [*Fight Club* (1999)], *Partner* (2007) [*Hitch* (2005)], *Ghajini* (2008) [*Memento* (2000)] and *Daddy Cool* (2009) [*Death at a Funeral* (2007)]. Of course, we can still find some earlier evidence of such appropriation in films such as *Mr India*, which works almost as a cultural inversion of Steven Spielberg's 1980s film *Indiana Jones and the Temple of Doom*, and further back in the 1950s with screen legend Raj Kapoor's involvement in reworkings of Charlie Chaplin films, Frank Capra's *It Happened One Night* (1934), and Vittorio De Sica's *Shoeshine* (1946). In addition, as mentioned in Chapter 3, Hollywood narrative adaptation in 1990s Bollywood cinema has already been explored by Nayar (1997, 2005) and Ganti (2002). But despite these earlier examples, what I wish to emphasise here is the shift in remaking from something previously occasional and cursory, to a now much larger-scale investment and cultural trend that is being recognised by the Indian film media and embraced by the industry and its audiences as never before. But what has sparked Indian cinema's sudden wholehearted and extensive investment in this special form of repetition now, having previously comfortably conformed to more familiar (now outmoded) stereotypes, stock conventions, and traditional methods of movie making? Before addressing the ways in which Bollywood remakes can operate as a form of resistance and innovation, it is best to begin with a brief account explaining Indian cinema's inherent hunger for textual appropriation in more detail.

Repetition and adaptation have been considered *fundamental* to Indian cinematic tradition. Film historians have revealed how today's Bollywood industry evolved from the dramatics of Sanskrit Drama, Parsi theatre, folk myths and ancient religious texts.[3] One particular religious mythology, the *Ramayana*, has been repeatedly looked upon as a framework for almost every commercial masala movie ever produced vis-à-vis its Proppian stock characters of the gallant hero who must rescue an endangered damsel from an evil or demonic villain (Propp, 1968).

As we have already established through Rosie Thomas's account of Indian cinema, Western criticisms of Hindi films have thrived on this compulsive custom to repeat the same clichéd and repetitive stories, characters and outcomes: '. . . the story-line will be almost totally predictable to the Indian audience, being a repetition, or rather, an unmistakable transformation of many other Hindi films, and . . . it will be recognized by them as a "ridiculous" pretext for spectacle and emotion' (Thomas, 122). Even despite Robert Stam (2000) and Dudley Andrew's (2000) declaration that *all* cinema is inherently re-presentational, or Steve Neale's (1990) discussion of repetition (alongside novelty) as intrinsic to all film genres, repetition still seems to have a deeper-rooted significance in popular Indian cinema. According to Vinay Lal (1998), the Indian film medium, like its nation's culture, is trapped in past traditions, each time inevitably reproducing the same past ideas and results. Thus, as Lal comments:

> Whereas the Western concept of continuity construes it as 'only a special case of change', in Indic traditions the language of continuity, which assumes that all changes can be seen, discussed or analysed as aspects of deeper continuities, occupies a predominant place. Change, in other words, is only a special case of continuity – and this is best exemplified in the Hindi film. (232)

Although the Hindi film industry has long been in the business of recycling formulas, it has rarely resorted to such blatant repetitions as Druxman's 'direct' or Thomas Leitch's 'true' remakes (see Verevis: 7–12) which carry the same title and character names – with the exception of movie versions of religious classics (the *Mahabharata* and the *Ramayana*) and filmic adaptations of literary classics such as Saratchandra Chattopadhyaya's *Parineeta* and *Devdas*. In the case of *Devdas*, the story of the lovesick, doomed alcoholic has been remade at least nine times. It was remade in 1928 by Naresh Mitra as a silent movie, in 1935 by P. C. Barua in Bengali (redone in Hindi a year after), in 1953 in Tamil and Telugu by Vedantam Raghavaiah, in 1955 by Bimal Roy, in 1974 in Telugu by Vijaya Nirmala, and in 1979 in Bengali by Dilip Roy. More recently, 2002 saw the release of two more versions – one by Bengal's Shakti Samanta, and the high-profile Bollywood blockbuster by Sanjay Leela Bhansali – while in 2009 Anurag Kashyap attempted to update the story with his modern-day Hatke rendition *Dev.D*.[4] However, it is important to remember that these remakes are *literary* adaptations and not copies or sequels of original film screenplays, which had previously only emerged rarely in mainstream Hindi cinema. Earlier examples such as *Nigahen* (the 1989 follow-up to *Nagina* [1986]) and *Return of the Jewel Thief* (the 1996 sequel to *Jewel Thief* [1967]) are both regarded as critical and financial flops.[5]

Perhaps the most popular and long-standing reason given for Indian cinematic remaking is the industry-spread belief that this act of borrowing or copying foreign cinema is symptomatic of the sheer lack of good writers in Bollywood, as has been stressed by film directors such as Nagesh Kukunoor and remake connoisseur Vikram Bhatt:

> If you hide the source you're a genius . . . There is no such thing as originality in the creative sphere . . . When you begin creating a work, you look around for inspiration – a real life character, a sound, a tune or something that stirs you, something that you wish to replicate . . . If the Indian market begins to invest in writers, more people will see it as a career option and you'll have fresh ideas rolling in . . . Till that happens, I would rather trust the process of reverse engineering [remaking a film] rather than doing something indigenous. (Bhatt, cited in Banerjee, 2003)

Fortunately, despite the above claims of starved creativity, others have suggested alternative reasons which point towards remaking as a form of creative transformation. As Ganti (2002) has revealed, foreign film scripts often first require a certain amount of cultural filtering by filmmakers, but contrary to her attention to film storyline, moral values and emotional narrative themes, these adjustments also take place on the level of visual representation and aesthetics, as I will later demonstrate. Indeed, the remake offers Indian audiences a way of better understanding or accessing foreign film texts (through greater cultural proximity), while conforming to a Bollywood-specific *film language.* Hollywood texts, for example, will have been (often unofficially) culturally franchised in order to successfully appeal to the Indian audience, who may not fully comprehend or identify with the foreign original.⁶ However, I would add that contemporary Bollywood's remaking incentives have also been stirred as Bollywood has shifted away from the confines of the native Indian viewing public and towards a worldwide *global* audience. This pursuit of global recognition and Bollywood's acknowledged popularity with the NRI diaspora are both primary catalysts for the cinema's increased modernisation and experimentation. The recent boom in self-remakes through revisions of several 1970s and 1980s Bollywood classics could also be seen as the (somewhat belated) active formation of an Indian film canon and the signalling of a nostalgic Indian cinema endeavouring to eternalise itself. Perhaps this inclination to remake marks a phase of Indian popular cinema that is finally nurturing a conscious desire to improve and update itself, now mindful of the aforementioned criticisms of its primitivism and 'backwardness' in comparison to its Western (and Eastern) cinematic rivals. The remake therefore serves the frustrations of a cinema wanting to escape from itself, led by a new generation of filmmakers who seek to replace movie moguls (such as Yash Chopra and Mahesh Bhatt) who had preserved the industry for two decades, and it is the perfect platform for a newer 'cooler' global Bollywood where previously non-Indian filmic forms, styles and characters can flourish. Once it has borrowed from and indigenised external foreign cinematic modes, the remake potentially promises Bollywood a status akin to Hollywood. At times, it offers empowerment through a seeming act of *reverse colonialism* (a concept which I will return to in the following chapter) – a device that dislocates its employed hegemonic Hollywood codes. At others, it stands as a symptom of the collapse of Indian identity in the wake of globalisation, making cross-cultural mixing a possibility, if not a necessity.

Technical progression is another factor that may play a part in Indian cinema's move towards remake films. Before the release of post-millennium films such as *Koi . . . Mil Gaya*, Bollywood had invested little time or money in technologically advancing its movies. Filmmakers account for this by arguing that there has never really been a *need* for a technical investment in their films, particularly given the Indian audience's alleged lack of a discerning viewpoint, their tendency to overlook technical flaws, and their ability to extend their suspension of disbelief *just that extra bit further*.⁷

Given the Indian audience's cultural orientations, it seems that religious devices and narratives centred on the theme of human compassion have effortlessly fed their appetite for fantasy and escapism – leaving little need for or interest in indigenising Western fiction-fantasy genres which would more often require the assistance of special effects technology. However, despite previous reservations, it now appears that the Indian film industry and its audience are finally ready to embrace a cinema of *technical* attractions.[8] With the recent discovery of new special effects aesthetics in the form of CGI, time-slicing or 'bullet-timing' and green-screening (most notably established in the Hollywood sci-fi film *The Matrix* [1999]), Bollywood has been inspired to produce a range of action movies, often alluding to action sequences from Hollywood blockbusters – signalling the beginnings of the Bollywood-Hollywood remake. Recent films such as *Mujhse Shaadi Karogi*, *Awara Paagal Deewana*, *Jaani Dushman* and *Krrish* all contain sequences openly mimicking the virtual cinematography of *The Matrix*. Farah Khan's 2004 action blockbuster *Main Hoon Na* also contains similar allusions. In this film, Shah Rukh Khan plays Major Ram Prasad Sharma, an Indian commando who has gone undercover as a college student in order to foil a terrorist plot to sabotage a peace pact between India and Pakistan. During his mission, Ram finds himself chasing a gang of terrorist henchman with only the aid of a rickshaw. We watch him exit a road tunnel in slow motion, narrowly escaping the explosions from a CGI petrol tank that bursts out from behind him. The chase sequence is accompanied by a musical score of frantic beating drums and classical raag (Indian vocal percussion). However, as we watch the rickshaw hurtle down a hill, rebound off a rock and launch into the sky, we hear this music suddenly merge into a parodic rendition of the theme tune to *Mission: Impossible* (1996). The camera encircles this hyperreal moment of action, prolonging and intensifying it as the henchmen (and cinema audience) gasp in amazement at Ram's stretched-out body, now frozen in mid air, shooting a gun in *Matrix*-esque bullet-time – handgun in one hand, rickshaw in the other. This postmodern technorealism not only increases the wow-factor of Bollywood action sequences, but has also impacted upon the generic framework of Indian action films as a whole – something I explore later in Chapter 7 in relation to action film remakes.

Despite the different reasons outlined above, I would emphasise that Bollywood's most recent boom in remaking is ultimately a product and vehicle of modernisation, globalisation and global postmodernism. It corresponds to India's unsteady obsession with modern advancement (as seen through *Koi . . . Mil Gaya*) and is a 'historically specific response to the postmodern circulation and recirculation of images and texts' (Verevis: 23), as self-reflexively illustrated by film remakes like *Om Shanti Om*. As such, the consequences of this current phase of Bollywood cinema could not only prove to problematise Hollywood codes and conventions once they have become wholly indigenised, but could perhaps even prove ominous for Bollywood's own film language.

Figure 6.1: Farah Khan's postmodern parody of *The Matrix* and *Mission: Impossible* in *Main Hoon Na* (Red Chillies Entertainment, 2004).

RESEARCHING THE BOLLYWOOD REMAKE GENRE

There are several key questions that need to be asked of Bollywood remakes which I believe may help enrich our understanding of contemporary Indian cinema, inspiring new definitions as well as increasing the scope of remake theory and research. Firstly, with regard to textuality and referencing, we need to establish which elements of the original text these Indian remakes tend to borrow from, how frequently and systematically they do so, and how an original citation is used and manipulated to serve the remake-film's own ideology (McFarlane: 10). Is there a particular aspect of a foreign film text that draws Bollywood towards adapting it? Does Bollywood (like Hollywood) actively search for foreign stories to steal, or is the attraction more organic and incidental? Do these Indian remakes invest purely in the narrative content of the Western original, or does this borrowing stretch to other aspects of the text's form and coding? And do these Bollywood remakes fit within the categories defined by theorists such as Genette, Leitch and Druxman, or do they occupy a category all to themselves, with entirely different characteristics and incentives?

Questions concerning viewing and reception processes are also important. One needs to consider how these remakes can operate as both readerly and writerly texts – that is, how they enable the audience to participate both as consumers of the text's pre-determined meanings *and* engage in their own meaning-making via the films' self-reflexive layers of textual referencing (Barthes, 1975). Are some Bollywood audiences even aware of the intertextuality within the Indian film text which alludes to Western films? If not, how do they comprehend and receive these alien aspects of the remake text? And is the aforementioned hostility of Western critics and audiences towards Bollywood films intensified by their recently increased appropriation? Is there something deeper-rooted in the style and semiotics of newer film texts and the *way* in which they remake and appropriate their texts that may make them even harder to digest?

Regarding the impact and consequences of Bollywood producing foreign remake films, I would also ask whether the original film source is able to maintain its autonomy, authenticity or affect once translated by Bollywood, or if its exploited signifiers are somehow altered or given new meaning. Could the Bollywood remake, as a 'hypertext',[9] be destructive towards its Hollywood original, whereby exposed Hollywood devices are made vulnerable and less able to hide behind the illusion of verisimilitude which fundamentally regulates the Hollywood mode in certain genres?[10] Lastly, in relation to artistic merit and labelling: How does the fact that Bollywood is not effectively confined by laws of plagiarism and copyright affect the way in which it copies and borrows from other texts? Can we learn anything from remakes which have not been institutionally defined or labelled as such? Is a Bollywood remake of a Western film really a remake if there is no discourse surrounding the text to support this link? Given its distinctively unique film lingo, stylistic preferences and thematic barriers, can Indian cinema ever remake a Hollywood film in the direct sense? These are all questions I hope to answer through my investigation and analysis of Indian film remaking.

PARODY OR PASTICHE?: A NOTE ON INTENTIONALITY

Intentionality plays an important part in discussions surrounding cinematic remaking. Parody is in particular a remake category viewed as an explicit and deliberate act of political humour, as opposed to an instance of incidental quotation. According to Linda Hutcheon (1985), parody is distinguishable as an act of constructive critique, which actively seeks to distance and differentiate itself from its subject. Here, the process of copying an original text offers a means of *commenting* upon it – thus audience pleasure is received not so much via the act of repetition as from the counter-readings on offer: the change of meaning or the semantic shifts that have been imposed upon the original source through a process of abstracted reflection, involving exaggeration, misdirection, deformation, defamiliarisation and inversion.[11] Hutcheon's definition of the parodic moment involves a sophisticated subject who recognises and reads an author-implied evaluation or critique of a primary text within the metatext, and she argues that this intentionality is 'essential' to the functioning of parody. It is important to stress that many Indian remake films do not explicitly employ a parody of this kind (with the exception of films like

Om Shanti Om), since this particular definition implies a verified conscious attempt to portray a remake as a copy in order to offer some form of sophisticated political critique. Alternatively, however, others, such as Dan Harries, have argued that the power to read parody lies with the reader and that the parodic function of a film text is completed and thus determined by its spectator (Harries: 107). Harries somewhat devalues authorial intent by stressing a film text's potential plurality of meaning and by pushing the idea of an active spectatorial pleasure derived from inventing meaning:

> As ironic discourse, parody would possibly need to be decoded as having some authorial intention . . . but this does not necessarily rule out the potential for reading no intention into a text . . . With such refashioning, the parodic text is viewed as being intended as a 'reformulated', multivoiced text . . . a spectator can generate meaning out of the text's significance without any consideration of how the parody was intended by its producer. (ibid.: 106–7)

Indeed, when there is neither audience awareness of, nor acknowledgement made to a film's intertextuality, Indian film remake texts may be in danger of coming across as 'mindless' copies devoid of play and critique. But Harries' argument reminds us of the value of cinematic interpretation, and reminds us that authorial intent is not essential to it. One may even be so bold as to say that intentionality is in itself somewhat overrated, particularly in the case of the remake. For as Robert Eberwein rightly argues:

> Are we limited in our interpretation to those relationships that the director consciously wove into the fabric of the film? It seems a rather simple-minded stance, and one that most artists would reject . . . the diversity of cinematic modes of alluding and the sheer number of allusions themselves in films ought not to be ignored merely because intentionality cannot be proved. (Eberwein: 142)

By demoting intentionality, Harries' redefinition begins to offer us a way of considering parody's potential in Indian remake cinema, though certain remaining elements of the category still seem somewhat unsuitable. For example, humour-focused parody ultimately aims to deconstruct, mock and hold a certain disdain for its target text. Bollywood texts often lack such an obvious political reflexivity or critical evaluation of their target texts. Unlike Hollywood films, Bollywood films do not almost exclusively borrow from films that have been widely promoted, discussed in national media circles, or canonised by art institutions and film critics in India (aside from the occasional self-remake). There is often no guarantee that the majority of the pan-Indian audience is even aware of the original, as in the case of the films of producer/director Vikram Bhatt, whose impressive profile of Bollywood-Hollywood remakes (including versions of *What Lies Beneath*, *Jagged Edge*, *On the Waterfront*, *There's Something About Mary*, *The Whole Nine Yards*, *Fear*, *Unlawful Entry*, *State of Grace* and *Cellular*) have almost passed as disguised originals. The Bollywood remake film functions more on the level of *secret* or *concealed imitation*, or what Bhatt himself terms 'reverse engineering', and thus *pastiche* may be a more useful term for it.

Richard Dyer (2006), in his book *Pastiche*, defines pastiche as an alternative to parody in that it does not deconstruct but rather reconstructs its target text. It imitates for the sake of imitation, favours similarity over difference, and has a more neutral attitude towards its original. Dyer, similarly, states that in order for pastiche to exist irony and intention are required, and that non-intentional pastiche indicates a failed attempt (Dyer, 2006: 3). He even draws connections between *pasticcio* (pastiche as combination, *bricolage* and hybridity) and the Indian masala genre, though he quickly abandons this association by condemning the opportunistic and nonsensical manner in which different ingredients are 'crammed' into the popular Indian film text:

> [Popular Hindi cinema's] opportunism in cramming in feelings is still subject to rough notions of not having too much of any one thing or not putting all the searing or all the hilarious bits together, and with no sense that it is inappropriate to combine so many different things. In other words, masala is not pasticcio. (Dyer, 2006: 11)

Harries' and Dyer's definitions of parody and pastiche may not wholly suffice to explain the kind of intertextuality that functions in the contemporary Bollywood remake, but they can at least help identify and indicate certain problems and irregularities that this method of copying creates for the Bollywood text – particularly in terms of its unsteady reception by (particularly non-Indian and Western) audiences. As Harries mentions, *excess* is one of parody's key strategies of spectatorship. Moments of excess in cinema are often signalled and read as parody by audiences, most explicitly in the case of the camp genre. In the Western text, excess as a parodic strategy automatically invites counter-readings and thus can be seen as problematic with regard to the international appeal of the contemporary Bollywood film. As discussed earlier in reference to my observation of Western film students, when a Western audience attempts to 'read' a Bollywood film, heightened actions and emotions can be mistaken for excess and therefore as parody, inciting laughter and a mockery of the text. Thus, for example, when referencing *Reservoir Dogs*, Indian remake *Kaante*'s excessive style and action could automatically invite a double parodic reading of both the primary and the secondary text. Neither

Hollywood nor Bollywood conventions can be naturalised. As irony is absent from the allusions and exaggeration appears without humour, this, coupled with Harries' notion of active meaning-making, can lead to interesting and unusual viewer positions and responses.

Parodic referencing is often employed in Hollywood films to turn serious matters into comedy. However, Bollywood remakes will also frequently do the opposite when parodying Western texts. For example, the internationally released cross-cultural remake *Ek Ajnabee* introduces one of its leading characters (played by Arjun Rampal) through a kung fu fight sequence, which uses the stigma-ridden comical 1974 music track 'Kung Fu Fighting' by Carl Douglas as a non-diegetic accompaniment. Ironically in *mock-heroic* style – Dyer's term for pastiche that aims to reproduce a low or trivial subject in an artistic, sophisticated or high style – the parody here is used not to ridicule but to add sophistication, class or 'coolness' to the character or scene (Dyer, 2006: 39). This strategy is persistent throughout many contemporary Bollywood-Hollywood remakes, and is therefore something I explore in more detail later in relation to male-oriented film remakes. Through its textual parody, *Ek Ajnabee* unfixes or deliberately misplaces the comical connotations associated with the song, inverting its stigma to suit the film's own aesthetic agenda. This form of borrowing, again, may have unusual implications for the experiencing of such texts by Western viewers, who may instead recognise and associate the song with tongue-in-cheek chopsocky films and therefore identify with Rampal's character as comical or ridiculous rather than serious and 'cool'.

In considering the many Indian remakes which deny or withhold their textual sources, one can also see the problem of what Harries terms the 'sophisticated naïve viewer' (Harries: 110). When allusions are not acknowledged, audiences may take references or borrowed styles literally. In the case of the Bollywood remake, some Indian audiences may come to take Western/Hollywood iconography and visual techniques as authentic to the style of contemporary Bollywood, which in turn impacts upon and complicates notions of convention, tradition and genre. Imitation can thus be a valuable and progressive strategy rather than empty, and should not be so readily associated with simple repetition. The imitative remake is an especially interesting (and problematic) object of analysis, as it is neither pure copy nor original. Rather, it is a *supplement* that acts as a pre-text to its original (Worton and Still: 7). As Worton and Still point out, remakes are revealing in that they can be 'usefully seen as textual modalities of recognition and transgression of the law' (9). Though Indian cinema has been born and bred under the style and influence of pre-existing texts (such as those of Hollywood), this should not stand in its way of it being also viewed as an innovative and educative cinema. Contemporary Bollywood cinema is a special case of imitation that simultaneously imitates itself, its Other, the familiar, and the arbitrary, as the following case studies reveal.

CELEBRITY AND GENETIC INTERTEXTUALITY

The films I have selected for my study reveal Indian film remaking in its most diverse modes, from the mirroring homage-remake to more subtle and temporary forms of remaking such as quotation, citation and intertextual referencing. Bollywood remakes encompass various forms of intertextuality, but one of the most remarkable kinds, to which I wish first to draw attention, is 'celebrity textuality' – the functioning of the star (and singer-stars) as an intertextual device. With regard to the film star personality:

> The very concept of a film star is an intertextual one, relying as it does on correspondences of similarity and differences from one film to the next, and sometimes too on supposed resemblances between on-and-off-screen personae. (Worton and Still: 176)

Several key theorists (most significantly Dyer, 2004 and Dyer and McDonald, 1997) have written on the function of the star persona within Hollywood filmmaking. Likewise, celebrity textuality, having a similar if not more central significance in Bollywood, has also attracted some limited theoretical criticism (see Mishra, 2002). The Indian film star persona is, even in the more experimental climate of the contemporary Bollywood industry, frequently subject to stock characterisation, stereotype and genre attachment. Certain lead actors will often better succeed in specific character roles which allude to their previously similar and acclaimed performances. For example, actor Sanjay Dutt's gangster role in the comedy *Munna Bhai M.B.B.S* will comically allude to his more serious profile of gangster films such as *Khal Nayak* (1993) and *Vaastav: The Reality* (1999), as well as to his real-life involvement in drug crime, black money laundering and the Bombay underworld.[12] What is more, Bollywood movies are famously driven by the audience's identification with the vocal talent of backing singer superstars such as Asha Bosle and Lata Mangeshkar, whose voices are often similarly used to connect certain actors or movies to previous characters and films. Perhaps one of the best examples of this is in the 1994 film *Hum Aapke Hai Kaun* [Who Am I to You?], where the audience is invited to make connections with this film and 1989 'super-hit' *Maine Pyar Kiya* [I Fell in Love] (made by the same film production company) through the use of the same star singer Lata Mangeshkar's voice for the female lead, and the reappearance of several songs from the soundtrack of its 1980s predecessor.

In his account of the different categories of the remake, Constantine Verevis (2005) also examines the significance of this particular form of filmic referencing within Hollywood cinema, which he terms *celebrity* or *genetic textuality* (20). However, I believe this particular mode of remake referencing is even more prominent in Bollywood, most tellingly in the case of the famous Bachchan family. The connection between the Bollywood superstar Amitabh Bachchan and his rising star son, Abhishek Bachchan, has been played with in several contemporary Bollywood film scripts, such as the *Bonnie and Clyde* pseudo-remake, *Bunty aur Babli*:

DCP Singh [Amitabh Bachchan]. Why did you get into all this?
Bunty [Abhishek Bachchan]. I wanted to be someone important.
DCP Singh. And you became . . .?
Bunty. Forget it. You wouldn't understand.
DCP Singh. Why? Why wouldn't I understand?
Bunty. Because he never did.
DCP Singh. Who?
Bunty. My father [turns to look at DCP Singh]. He's just like you. [pause]
DCP Singh. Are you trying to con me again?

In his chapter tracing the construction of Amitabh Bachchan's star profile, Vijay Mishra (2002) describes his celebrity as a special case of stardom, in that it moves beyond Dyer's morphology on the basis of 'political economy, marketing and distribution' (147). For Mishra, Bachchan senior 'transcend[s] the status of stardom to become a text in his own right' (156). His 'ubiquitous' star persona[13] is constructed through alternative methods, most significantly a 'carefully modulated and subtly self-conscious' manipulation of the film's 'song and dialogic situations' (155), and thus he becomes a 'parallel text' in himself. If Amitabh Bachchan is indeed a text as Mishra suggests, this implies that he is also open to quotation and rewriting. Thus, for example, in *Bunty aur Babli*, this is achieved through the deconstruction of Bachchan's star 'costume', consisting of his 'stereotyped voice, constructed physiognomy and gestural repertoire' (127), which are parodied by playfully transferring the characteristics onto his actor-son Abhishek, who evokes his father's early-career persona via his costumes, dialogue delivery and acting style.

An even more revealing example of this genetic or celebrity referencing can be seen in the Bachchans' 2005 collaborative production, Ram Gopal Varma's *Sarkar*. Varma's acknowledged tribute to Francis Ford Coppola's legendary *Godfather* trilogy is perhaps one of the rarer examples of Bollywood-Hollywood remake, in that it is presented as a direct homage to Coppola's original. *Sarkar* opens with a signed note from director Varma, who declares:

'Like countless directors all over the world, I have been deeply influenced by "THE GODFATHER". "SARKAR" is my tribute to it.' This blatant acknowledgement of the film as homage-remake does not only openly invite a comparison to the original, but also emphasises the film's interpretative and intertextual relationship to an established worldwide film canon on top of which Coppola's classic sits comfortably. Varma's reworking follows Subhash Nagre, a wealthy resident and unofficial Mafia Don in Mumbai. In facilitating an almost parallel government, Nagre takes justice into his own hands and in effect earns the respect of the people – thus earning the title 'Sarkar' (translating as 'Sir', 'Boss', or 'Government'). Following a murder of a local politician, Nagre is framed and imprisoned by his enemies through the assistance of his weak and bitter eldest son. Nagre's younger son Shankar thus sacrifices his life plans to take on responsibility for maintaining the Sarkar supremacy, seeking vengeance, and freeing his father. Though the film's narrative bears a strong resemblance to that of *The Godfather*, the story is relevantly historically situated within the existing political climate in Mumbai and current anxieties over the prominence of the Mumbai underworld. While *Sarkar* serves as an interesting source of comparison with its celebrated original, beyond its many references to its Hollywood counterpart lies an even more interesting and unique form of intertextual referencing relating exclusively to the film's two lead protagonists: Amitabh Bachchan/Subhash Nagre (as Marlon Brando's Don Vito Corleone equivalent) and his on-screen/off-screen son Abhishek Bachchan/Shankar Nagre (as Al Pacino's Michael Corleone).

Miriam Hansen (1991) has explored the way in which the presence of film stars (in her case, those specifically of the Hollywood silent era, such as Rudolph Valentino) 'undercut the narrative and scopic regimes' of a film, stimulate a discourse external to the film's diegesis, and enhance 'a centrifugal tendency in the viewer's relation to the filmic text . . . thus [running] . . . counter to the general objective of concentrating meaning in the film as product and commodity' (Hansen: 246). This centrifugal tendency is increasingly present in contemporary Bollywood films like *Sarkar*. Varma's choice to cast father and son is interesting particularly in relation to how the Indian audience is left to interpret and experience the film. Amitabh Bachchan's godfather role in *Sarkar* uncannily mirrors his famous persona as the godfather of Hindi cinema. On writing on the phenomenal persona of Bachchan, Mishra explains how the film star has come to resemble a godlike or religious figure in India, whom devoted fans have worshipped for over three decades – particularly evident during the actor's involvement in a near-fatal accident on the set of his 1983 film *Coolie*, which threw the nation into a virtual state of mourning (see Mishra, 2002: 144). This image of Amitabh Bachchan as a national power figure is even more significant when we consider the actor's real-life involvement in state politics. The actor was once an MP and a close friend of the Gandhi family, before getting caught up in a financial scandal and later being rumoured to have connections with the Mumbai gangster underworld (ibid.: 140). This background profile immediately dissolves the barriers separating real-life fact and the fictitious filmic world of *Sarkar*. The use of Bachchan's biographical profile becomes yet another textual source for the film, and in effect is used to manipulate the audience's identification towards and judgement of the lead character. Subhash Nagre (aka 'Sarkar') is all at once a law-breaking gangster (within the film diegesis) *and* heroic idol (as a much-loved and respected film star). Thus the connection between the film and Bachchan's off-screen persona uncannily allows the audience to experience a deeper reading of or insight into *Sarkar*'s characters and thematics.

In addition to this celebrity textuality in *Sarkar* there is a genetic textual dynamic, which arises from the audience's awareness that Amitabh Bachchan is the father of Abhishek Bachchan, who analogously plays his son in the movie. To illustrate the value of this particular intertextual device, I want to draw attention to one of the film's climactic scenes, where Shankar/Abhishek Bachchan visits his father Sarkar/Amitabh Bachchan in prison, and the inevitable transference onto him of his father's roles and responsibilities takes place. As father and son share an emotional moment of bonding on-screen, the audience members find themselves passing through several worlds, realities and narratives simultaneously as the film text allows them to decode and interpret the scene in a multiplicity of ways: (1) as an allusion to the actors' real-life father and son relationship, subject to much discussion in popular widely read Indian media gossip columns; (2) a symbolic depiction of Amitabh Bachchan passing his fame and status as Indian cinema's leading actor on to his son, who has with each film increasingly grown to adopt his father's acting style, image and on-screen persona; (3) an underlying commentary hinting at Bachchan Senior's real-life political agenda and underworld connections; (4) an analogy of the real-life tensions created by the gangster underworld and its power over the Bollywood film industry and its stars;[14] and (5) the equivalence of Bachchan senior and Bachchan junior, as great Bollywood actors of their generation, to Hollywood legends Brando and Pacino.

Coupled with the nostalgic star cameos and self-parodic performances of actors in *Om Shanti Om*, this kind of tensioned, overlapping multiplicity of reading in *Sarkar* and playfulness in *Bunty aur Babli* demonstrates the value, insight and innovation that remaking and intertextual referencing can bring to the Bollywood film viewing experience – contrary to the arguments of those who wish to simply dismiss the technique as a crass and empty method of duplication. Later films such as *Drona* (where genetic textuality is this time achieved through the relationship of on- and off-screen mother and son Jaya Bachchan and Abhishek Bachchan), *Billu Barber* and *Rab Ne Bana Di Jodi* (see Chapter 8 on Shah Rukh Khan's self-referencing in these films), or Zoya

Akhtar's *Luck by Chance*, could be similarly explored to reinforce the fact that, far from being a rare novelty, these intertextual methods are becoming more and more a staple device of Indian filmmaking.

NOTES

1. As James Naremore (2000: 7) highlights, adaptation theory has particularly gained sophistication since the 1960s via the structuralist and poststructuralist poetics of Barthes, Genette and Bordwell and Thompson.
2. Unfortunately, despite this long list of processes, Stam does not provide concrete definitions and explanations for all of them. Nevertheless, I have noted them here to indicate the diverse ways in which adaptation has been found to operate within or affect a text.
3. For more on the repetitive structuring principles of Hindu mythology and oral traditions in India, see Corey Creekmur's Freudian analysis of repetition in *Devdas* films (2007).
4. Since this time two further Pakistani and Bangladeshi versions have followed.
5. It should be noted that South Indian director Satyajit Ray produced two follow-ups to *Pather Panchali* (1955) prior to this. However, Ray's films do not form part of the mass-consumed popular cinema that Indian audiences identify with; therefore I have excluded his work from my account of popular Hindi film remake series.
6. The notion that non-Indian audiences need to have a Bollywood film culturally franchised before they can accept or tolerate it does not fully account for the Western censure of this cinema.
7. This is not to suggest in any way that the Indian spectator's gaze is less civilised or less informed. A significant portion of the Indian film viewing public avidly consumes Western or alternative modes of filmmaking, yet equally takes pleasure through this subject position when viewing Indian films.
8. I make a connection here to Tom Gunning's essay on early cinema, which describes it as a spectacle- or visual-trickery-driven 'cinema of attractions' (Gunning, 1990). References to Gunning's concept have been made before in popular Indian film criticism, but I would argue that the term is more aptly applied in relation to the cinema's latest turn to special effects.
9. Gerard Genette's umbrella term for any text that transforms or relates to another (Genette, cited in Verevis: 20).
10. I acknowledge that the level of verisimilitude varies in Hollywood depending on genre; for example, it is less concentrated in comedy films. However, the majority of the remakes I look at in this study occupy more 'serious' genres, which normally rely on a certain level of generic and cultural verisimilitude (gangster, action, thriller, heist).
11. For a more comprehensive list and explanation of these methods see Harries.
12. Dutt is known as 'Bollywood's Bad Boy' for his connections with infamous Mumbai mobster Dawood Ibrahim and for being suspected of having planted bombs prior to the 1993 Bombay riots. He was previously arrested under the Terrorist and Disruptive Activities court and imprisoned for illegal possession of arms. The actor also has a known history of drug addiction.
13. Bachchan has been referred to by the Indian media as the 'one-man industry' or 'King of Bollywood' on account of his influence over the public as a national treasure and the mass popularity of his films due to his star presence.

14. Bollywood stars and directors are known to be repeatedly exposed to blackmail and death threats from the Mumbai underworld, which has often tried to launder black money by financing films.

CHAPTER 7

Contemporary Bollywood Remakes

SHIFTING TOWARDS THE FIGURAL:
SANJAY LEELA BHANSALI'S *DEVDAS*

Further insight into postmodern aesthetics in the contemporary Bollywood remake can be offered through an in-depth analysis of one of the genre's earliest, most prominent examples: the *Devdas* lineage. As mentioned earlier, filmic re-presentations of Chattopadhyaya's novel are profuse. However, for my analysis, I want to draw attention to two of the most popular and widely regarded versions: Bimal Roy's 1955 classic, and Sanjay Leela Bhansali's 2002 version – a divergent alternative to Roy's pseudo-original.[1] The somewhat ritualistic inclination to juxtapose the superiority of an original text against its 'inferior' remake applies greatly in the case of these two films. Roy's film marked the start of a classic era of socio-realist[2] films in India, held in high regard for their refreshingly underplayed performances, their compassion for humanity (as social commentary and morality tales), and their attention to 'real' characters. Contrarily, Bhansali's remake is a flagship for the contemporary Bollywood blockbuster, famous for its operatic style and record-breaking budget (costing Rs 500 million, it was the most expensive Indian film in history at the time of its release). However, simply debating which film is better and why will neither satisfy nor advance our understanding and appreciation of the Bollywood remake genre. What is more, as my investigation will reveal, it seems inappropriate to judge Bhansali's remake against Roy's original when the two films have been produced not only in separate decades, but also through a completely different *genus* of cinema.

There is an almost unanimous sense of disregard present in much of the discourse surrounding Bhansali's *Devdas*[3] and his work as a director, which parallels Western criticisms of postmodern and low popular art forms. The circulation of Bhansali's *Devdas* within high and low art circles reveals a familiar paradox: the film (a national and international box-office hit) was loved by mass audiences, yet was panned in critical film reviews worldwide. It was a characteristically populist mainstream Bollywood production in India, yet was promoted in high-art film festivals (Cannes) and exhibited in art-house cinemas in the West. Bhansali's film therefore exists simultaneously as art cinema (through its exhibition) and 'depthless melodrama' (through its critical reception) – a label that the director has become much accustomed to in his career. In her book *100 Bollywood Films*, Rachel Dwyer (2005) comments on Bhansali's trademark cinema of 'excess'. With reference to his international debut *Hum Dil De Chukeh Sanam*, she comments that 'although the film boasts beautiful clothes, sets and locations, Bhansali is showing the beginnings of the excess that was to mar *Devd*as . . . the main Haveli [mansion] seems to open out into different landscapes and climates in strange continuity breaks' (Dwyer: 116).[4] Dwyer and critics alike have struggled with the implausibility, unreality and overt stylisation of Bhansali's works – all of which apply chiefly to the recent *Devdas* remake and underline its extreme digressions from Roy's socio-realist original:

> The 2002 adaptation, although it had some wonderful musical and visual scenes, is a series of moments, where the storyline is spoilt . . . by the all too often kitsch quality of its visuals. The emphasis on the *mise-en-scène* overwhelmed the love story to the point at which it seemed to become almost irrelevant. The zamindars [land owners of colonial India] are presented as glamorous and supremely wealthy in the manner of bazaar art, whereas at this time (this version is set in the 1930's) they were in decline. (Dwyer: 68)

This frustration with the historical inaccuracy of *Devdas* is a familiar reaction to the 'heretical' film remake. As Stam comments, the adaptation which threatens the authenticity of the original will often be viewed as a deformity, as religious sacrilege, and invite charges of 'outraged negativity' (Stam: 54). But I would add that the very fact that many of Bhansali's films transgress the laws of history and plausibility (perhaps occasionally even in a conscious act of rebellion) also indicates the postmodern sensibility of these contemporary texts. Bhansali's confusion of historical facts corresponds to the a-historicism or temporal and spatial discontinuity that enhances fragmentation in many postmodern works.

BOLLYWOOD AND THE POSTMODERN REGIME OF SIGNIFICATION

Audience and critical reviews of *Devdas* describe it as 'spectacular', 'extravagant', 'operatic', 'lavish', 'picturesque', 'beautiful', and 'opulent' – terms that continue to dominate from its international reviews to its DVD packaging.[5] Bhansali's film therefore also supports Scott Lash's concept of postmodern cinema's move towards a discourse of the figural.[6] Lash's theoretical contributions to postmodern film theory are useful here on several levels. In his essay 'Discourse or Figure? Postmodernism as a "Regime of Signification"', Lash deals with a polarisation of the literal and the visual in cinema. He draws his ideas from Lyotard's earlier writings, which establish and differentiate the terms 'discourse' and 'figure', Susan Sontag's esteem for an 'erotics of art' and a 'sensual', 'energetic' cinema, and the Artaudian theatre of cruelty. Particularly in the case of the latter two, the sensory and the visual are privileged over didacticism and discursive meaning. This surrender to a principally figural mode of theatrical presentation is what Lash identifies as a key characteristic of all postmodern cinema.[7]

While some of the perspectives in Lash's essay may be too specific to be widely applicable to mainstream texts (his use of Sontag's argument, for instance, focuses too much on anti-meaning and the avoidance of interpretation), his attempts to apply his 'regime of signification' to popular modes of postmodern filmmaking can also inform our understanding of contemporary Bollywood cinema aesthetics. For example, connections can be made through the notion of bringing *sensation* to the surface of the text and the depriviledging of dialogue and intellectualised hermeneutics, for which, interestingly, Bollywood cinema is often critically condemned. Whereas formalist, modernist and realist aesthetics would assume a 'worthy' work of art to be one which *discursively* attempts to represent or critique the world, Lash's postmodern aesthetics celebrate those texts that bring sensation and overt figuralism (beyond intellectualised meaning) to the fore:

> ... even in mainstream cinema, narrative content is increasingly losing centrality and giving way to a more image-centred 'spectacular' cinema ... [and] in non-mainstream, critical cinema, a new image-centred mode of signification, based on an alternative 'regime of pleasure', may come increasingly to displace the most pervasive type of critical cinema which is modernist, discursive, and intellectualist. (Lash: 314)

Lash embraces popular Hollywood texts (such as the early action blockbusters of Spielberg, Sylvester Stallone and Arnold Schwarzenegger) under this new concept, though he quickly separates this 'postmodern mainstream cinema' from texts such as the films of David Lynch – which he contrarily terms '[t]ransgressive postmodernist cinema'. Unlike the postmodern mainstream variety, transgressive postmodern texts allow the spectator a critically accessible and unfixed viewing position. They more consciously and deliberately problematise reality through a film's subtext or context. These films have more associations with avant-garde techniques such as surrealism (indeed, from the outcomes of my analysis in Chapter 5, we may be able to describe *Abhay* as a film that falls into this transgressive category). Ultimately, as Lash notes, his postmodern aesthetics are more concerned with those 'unpleasant' texts which 'have a notable absence of a vision of a better world' (Lash: 331). Populist Bollywood films clearly do not fit this mould, as they are largely anchored in pleasure and utopian fantasies. But despite this (particularly since his theorisations remain relatively incomplete and under-explored by others), there is the potential here to try to expand on some of Lash's ideas regarding popular postmodern cinema, and utilise them to demonstrate the productivity of contemporary Bollywood's cinematic modes.

There are several postmodern sensibilities listed in Lash's work which tie in well with the characteristics and criticisms of contemporary Bollywood cinema and (more specifically) Bhansali's *Devdas* – particularly the film's aforementioned foregrounding of desire, its presumed 'draining of aura' from its original and its lack of critical distantiation. The film also exhibits Lash's de-differentiation process – denying the difference or separation of aesthetics, theory and cultural art from the real world, reality and the social. Similarly to *Om Shanti Om* or *Abhay*, Bhansali's *Devdas* facilitates this blurring of art and life, although this time the film text does not see itself as an artificial work severed from reality. Rather, it asserts itself as a *sublime version of reality*. In many contemporary Bollywood films, the intensity of human emotions is transfigured onto the cinema screen in deliberately extreme (often absurd and excessive) ways in order to project feelings as *close to life* as possible. Thus, for example, moments of characters bursting into song and dance and other forms of exaggeration in the films are very much treated (and read) by their regular audiences as 'natural'. Defenders of Bollywood cinema argue that it is this increased visceralism of Indian films which separates them from other modes of filmmaking (particularly Western realism) and provides audiences with a unique empathetic pleasure and experience of the world. Also, with regard to the figural, both Lash's postmodernist cinema and Bollywood texts like Bhansali's *Devdas* advocate a distinctly visual sensibility, a devaluation of formalism, and 'operate[s] through the spectator's immersion, the relatively immediate investment of his/her desire in the cultural object' (Lash: 314).

In his essay, Lash references the Nietzschean notion of art as not representative, but rather as an 'extension' or 'supplement' to life – a philosophy that aptly explains the aspirations and logic behind Bollywood cinema. As was discussed earlier in relation to the cinema's history of censure, popular Indian films have (even if not through conscious critique) always been known to deform and exaggerate reality. Regarded as unnecessary and incidental, realism is often omitted by design. Plot becomes 'an excuse for a succession of spectacular events', or in Bollywood's case, an excuse for immersion in song and dance (Lash: 326). In Bollywood cinema, the image is not always constrained or subordinated by meaning. It will often free itself from the 'dictates of narrative' (317) for the sake of immersing itself in the sensory, as seen in its sometimes disruptive song sequences. However, as with Lash's postmodern 'pornographic' cinema of spectacle, contemporary popular Indian films frequently depart from realistic representation (and realist aesthetics) to a greater extent than their predecessors, for example by allowing fragmented images of the body and sexuality to dominate over dialogue and narrative – as epitomised by the cinema's trademark MTV-style song sequences. Lash's concept can thus help us begin to answer the scepticism-ridden question of the *value* of contemporary popular Hindi cinema. For it is now neither narrative nor sociopolitical enlightenment, but rather the pleasure in the image, the spectacle, and the sensory expression of emotion, that drives the cinema. The influence of the figural within contemporary Bollywood cinema infiltrates the film text, affecting a wide spectrum of cinematic devices, and this is notably evident in Bhansali's *Devdas*.

A SYNAESTHETIC CINEMA

Perhaps the thing that is most striking about Bhansali's adaptation is the film's opening sequence, which has been described by some as a scene so hysterically melodramatic it is almost unendurable. Critics describe the scene as a moment of 'dramatic claustrophobia' (Elley, 2002: 25), a 'grotesquery of emotion' (Singh, 2002: 90), where spectators are 'suffocated' by its elaborate *mise-en-scène* (Johnston, 2002: 20). However, these excessive melodramatics should not be dismissed as an accident or product of the director's carelessness. Rather, it is intentionally and strategically created through the collaboration of the film's director, costume artists, musical composer, cinematographer, production designer and actors.[8] The scene is perhaps particularly problematic for crossover audiences as it is too lavish and hyper-emotional – exhibiting a cinematic language too alien or inaccessible to modern Western audiences. The first scene opens with jauntily-angled crane shots of a mansion resembling a giant Roman temple. Cameras track behind Devdas's mother running frantically through the halls of her palace-like home, arms open wide as the near-screaming voices of Devdas's family members overlap to rejoice about

Devdas's return home after ten years. No character establishment is offered at this point through the narrative or dialogue. Instead, the wealth, status and background of this family is indicated though the grand architecture of their 250-foot-long home[9] which, barely fitting into the camera frame, is overwhelmingly and blatantly put on display. This display of wealth is key to the film's overall visual rhetoric. As Mandakranta Bose notes, the film is so focused on wealth that 'money does not just make the film, it is the film' (Bose, 2007: 192). Sound and noise also function pivotally in the sequence and significantly add to this experience of excess. During its opening segment, the noise in *Devdas* is as striking and obtrusive as the visuals. The amplitude appears maximised (perhaps to the point of distortion) and there is a distinct lack of pauses and silences. The orchestration of music, dialogue, sound effect and silence lacks 'focus' (the careful selection and exclusion of sounds – see Sergi, 2004) and such a density and layering of sounds compromises the clarity of the sequence, inevitably resulting in 'cacophony' (ibid.: 150–1). Furthermore, during conversational exchanges between two or more characters, the dialogue appears compressed, as if silences have been removed to quicken the pace of the scene. Devdas and Paro's mothers, Kaushalya and Sumitra, even when standing only a foot away from each other, project their voices and shout their dialogue as if acting on a theatrical stage. There is also an unusual over-sensitivity to surrounding sounds: Foley effects of even the softest of sounds – the raindrops from a leaking roof, the crystals of a hanging chandelier, a distant outdoor water fountain, the bangles on Paro's arms or the bells on her dress – are all amplified in volume to assist this multi-sensory, exaggerated introduction.[10] This deployment of noise as an *effect* could alone be enough to instil a feeling of suffocation in a viewer previously unaccustomed or unconditioned to such highly charged opening film sequences. Dudley Andrew has spoken of cinema's extra-literalness in comparison to the novel, particularly regarding its ability to be 'synaesthetic' (engaging multiple senses simultaneously). In many ways, a film like *Devdas* epitomises this notion of synaesthetic cinema by intensifying its *mise-en-scène* (Andrew: 61).

In her unique account of the synesthetic experience in cinema, *The Skin of the Film: Intercultural Cinema, Embodiment, and the Senses* (2000), Laura Marks describes film as a membrane that allows the audience to access sensuous memories. For her, particular forms of sensory cinema (which she labels 'intercultural') draw upon the senses to evoke cultural memories and a diasporic yearning for the homeland. However, these sensory experiences are not available to all. Accessing cultural memories requires prior experience and is thus always culturally exclusive:

> If one's sensory organization privileges other senses as well as vision, it will be easier to experience an audiovisual object, like a film, in a

multisensory way. If it does not, the object may appear inert because the viewer cannot perceive its multisensory quality. (231)

If this is the case, it is possible to assume that the sensory organisations offered in a film such as Bhansali's *Devdas* may clash with or even offend the sensorium of Western audiences. The rejection or displeasure expressed towards such a cinema could in some cases be understood as what Marks describes as 'sense envy'. She argues that rather than simply rejecting a film because of its unfamiliar representation of sense experiences, we need to be more aware of our 'fear of others' sensuous geographies' (247) and be prepared to hold our own sensory limitations responsible for our inability to experience these films fully:

In mainstream cinema, references to the nonaudiovisual senses tend to appear as cinematic excess, as extra treat on top of the richness of audio-visual representation. But for intercultural artists, memories of touch, smell, taste, rhythm are not 'extra': they are the very foundation of acts of cultural reclamation and redefinition. (231)

This distinction made between mainstream and intercultural cinema proves problematic for Bollywood, which could be seen to position itself under both categories. Bhansali's *Devdas*, for example, is an unmistakably commercial film, but its sensory elements are also tied to its cultural and artistic traditions. Produced for a global audience, its sensory self-exoticism does appeal to the diasporic non-resident Indian's nostalgia for homeland, although the emphasis on diasporic longing which Marks places on intercultural cinema is less relevant here. The film does indeed enhance its images in the manner attributed to mainstream cinema, but it does not use its sensory excess solely in order to provide a 'wealth of information', where the sense represented 'merely complements the films' verbal and visual images' (231). Rather, Bhansali's film evokes the senses in a way that is excessive and commoditised in order to convey a particular kind of political aesthetic.

DRAWING PARALLELS: *DEVDAS* AND THE INDIAN MINIATURE PAINTING

In order to further explore Bhansali's visual style in some depth, I would like to turn to another Indian art form, somewhat smaller in scale, which is also marred by similar criticisms: the Indian miniature painting. The foundation principles of the now-sparse Indian miniature (developed and circulated in India most notably between the sixteenth and eighteenth centuries) lay in illustrating a reality beyond a certain vantage-point, a world expressed through the language of symbolism. The paintings adopted an aesthetic mode incorporating 'gesticulating' figures, visible brushwork, multiple viewpoints, and a playfulness with perspective, as well as an active attempt to merge and 'unfold' multiple dimensions in a single image. For example:

> The [Mogul Indian miniature] painters found a solution to the problem of spatial projection through European examples and repeatedly painted the distant views of towns set on craggy hills, winding roads . . . [but] such passages seemed hard to rationalize with the rest of the composition, which was conceived in bird's-eye view . . . [also] they never conjured up a planned chiaroscuro. (Chakraverty, 1996: 33)

The credibility of Indian miniature art was hindered by its contradictions in perspective and stylistic incoherences or 'imperfections', such as night scenes lit as if in full sunlight and distant objects occupying disproportionately larger space than those in the foreground. Trees and foliage painted with shaded layers creating the illusion of depth were disruptively positioned onto floors with a two-dimensional effect 'enhanced by a flat application of the pigment' (Chakraverty: 53). The images were attacked for their hurried brushwork, often a result of the 'freak idiosyncrasies' (71) of their character figures: women with elongated fingers and eyes 'almost touching the ears' (Jodhpur-style, ibid.: 71), who were drawn in unusually exaggerated poses, often presented simultaneously in frontal (flattened) or three-quarterly (three-dimensional) views. Also, with regard to overt visual detail, the paintings were seen to be hindered by their excessive and 'forceful' application of bold colours, which particularly in cases such as the Pahari style, never lowered their strength of tone regardless of the size, type, distance or positioning of an object-feature in the picture frame (Chanderohri, 2001). Such criticisms thus inevitably led to Western intervention, significant stylistic alterations and, arguably, the subsequent demise of the Indian miniature painting. As Anjan Chakraverty explains, the blame for the dying art form lay partly with the East India Company's derisive critical assessments of miniature craft work, ironically set up to help promote the trade. The following citation, which Chakraverty takes from a late nineteenth-century British civil servant's account of a local miniature artist at work, demonstrates the simultaneous admiration and disdain incited by the excessive style of the Indian miniature:

> His colour is often exaggerated but it is always warm and rich and fearless. The native artist is also patient . . . painfully elaborating the most minute details; no time is considered too long, no labour too intense to secure perfection in imitation or delicacy in execution. The greatest

failing in native artists is their ignorance of perspective and drawing . . . and it is fortunate that this want is most easy to supply . . . (B. H. Baden-Powell, *Handbook of the Manufacturers and Arts of the Punjab*, cited in Chakraverty: 355)

This demand for the de-abstraction and installation of realist aesthetics in the miniature painting parallels the aforementioned comments made by Dwyer regarding Bhansali's naive craftsmanship and the general condemnation of Bollywood cinema's inferior, almost primitive modes of filmmaking. The critic Sheila Johnston (2002) almost mirrors the above patronising comments on Indian miniature artwork when she similarly comments that '*Devdas* is a bloated banquet with minimal nutrition for the grey cells, but a few spicy morsels to tease the taste buds along the way' (Johnston: 17). Johnston goes on to positively critique the film only via its comparisons to Alfred Hitchock's *Rebecca* and a feminist reading of the narrative – reducing its visual abstractions to something gluttonous (ibid.), tiring, inflated and unnecessary.

In the case of the Indian miniature, defenders of the paintings have argued that these visual abstractions were deliberate and intentional and that they should not be condemned, but celebrated for their unique qualities – their abstract, sensuous, sublime images conveying a world beyond the eye of conventional realism. The paintings were meant, like true art, to *stimulate*. The intensity of their colour, detail and hyperrealist aesthetics all contributed towards an attempt to depict and grasp a truer sense of emotions such as passion, elation, romance, love and seduction. With this in mind, I likewise invite a similar argument to be made in the case of Bhansali's *Devdas*.

One of the most striking similarities between the Indian miniature and Bhansali's film is in the construction and presentation of the female subject. As with the miniature, the representation of the female figure in *Devdas* (2002) pushes towards hyper-femininity. Not only are the female leads adorned head to toe in elaborate jewellery, draped in daring bold colours and heavily embroidered designer fabrics (actress Madhuri Dixit's costumes for the film reportedly weighed as much as 30 kilos each, and one famously fetched Rs 2.5 lakh in a film auction), but each and every detail of their visual make-up accentuates their femininity. Fingertips and feet are decorated with intricate henna patterns, even for shots lasting only a few seconds. Carefully applied eye make-up abnormally extends, enlarges and throws open the eyelids. Lead protagonist Paro's excessively lengthy Rapunzel-style hair extensions give her a larger-than-life quality and, as discussed in Chapter 1, the casting of hyper-feminine actress Aishwarya Rai in this role only further accentuates this excessive femininity. Several of Rai's choreographed dance sequences give at least the illusion of her fingers, arms and torso stretching with abnormal flexibility – much like the gesticulating figures of the Indian miniature. In fact,

CONTEMPORARY BOLLYWOOD REMAKES 157

Figure 7.1: Ornately decorated and framed, Paro in *Devdas* (Mega Bollywood, 2002) resembles a figure in a fine Indian miniature painting (Exotic India Art Pvt. Ltd).

Paro analogously personifies the miniature, right down to her kiss-curls, which almost pay homage to the trademark fine-brushstroke hair strands commonly found framing the faces of the paintings' female subjects, particularly those in the Kangra and Guler styles (Chanderohri, 2001: 62).

Another stylistic aspect of the miniature that is shared with Bhansali's film is the extension of optical views. Set design, art direction, lighting and cinematography are combined to present a perspective beyond realism's often single-angle, mono-dimensional viewpoint. This can be exemplified by the opening shot of Devdas' family home. As was mentioned earlier, the purpose-built Roman temple-like mansion is overblown in size and distorted through the use of a wide-angle lens and tilted cameras. The visual presentation of this family home continues to resist subtle realism by displaying interiors through multiple viewpoints: omniscient bird's-eye and mid-air shots suddenly switch to eye-level tracking shots following characters running through corridors. Throughout the film, static shots are often disrupted by subsequent point-of-view shots of spinning dancers, a scene through a pair of binoculars, or the blurred vision of a tearful-eyed Devdas. Also, just as the miniature obscures depth of field by blending three-dimensional architecture with flat-profiled figures, Bhansali utilises a generous lighting set-up and frame composition to achieve a similar effect. Depth is not created through the usual contrast of light and shadows, but rather, is abstracted through the manipulation of light and the layering of visual stimuli within the frame. For example, in scenes set in Devdas' and Paro's family homes, distant windows and door frames are subjected to a vivid lighting set-up, bold colour scheme and sharp focus of equal strength to the foreground. Every section of the film set (and camera frame) is decorated, and rarely is there a back wall or corner of the frame left empty and unlit. Images in the foreground appear to merge in with the background, such as the dancers in Chadramukhi's Kotha palace, whose costumes resemble the colour and fabric of the hanging drapes behind them. The details of the Rangoli-pattern painted floors appear raised and merged with the outlines of the figures that dance upon them.

The clarity of detail of distant objects encourages multiple points of distraction within the frame. The spectator's eye scans the screen frantically, unable to focus on a single object in the frame, lacking the aid of a conventional set-up of blurred backgrounds, shadows and perspective. This abstraction of the film's visuals is further emphasised through frame composition layering techniques. For example, in her first song sequence in the Kotha, Chandramukhi is seen walking down the Kotha palace staircase. The composition is a complicated one, made of many layers which simultaneously exhibit and focus upon far-off views as well as props and set pieces directly in front of the camera. Hence, in this particular image set-up, the composition is (from foreground to background) thus:

Fountain spray (close-up, right corner of frame) curtained pillar →
ornate Chandramukhi on staircase → decorative wall, window opening
and pillar → exterior fountains lit in brilliant-white light → a moodily lit
marble building → another background building with decorative turrets,
lit yellow → spinning nauch-girl in turret window → deep blue night sky

What is interesting about this busy visual set-up is how its contained objects
and scenery, whether placed in front and nearer the lens or behind and far
away, all appear at focal point. In effect, the scenery fights for the viewer's
attention, creating multiple distractions and encouraging a fetishist gaze. It
is this constant, meticulous process of ornamenting the frame and this unabashed exploitation of façade that move Bhansali's film beyond realism and
towards a multi-dimensional figural overindulgence. From this example alone
we can see that what we may at first regard as photographic inaccuracy, error,
or amateurism can in fact offer us something that the mirror-to-life image of
realist cinema's camera cannot.

Bhansali's *Devdas*' visual complexity stretches even further beyond its
gargantuan mansions, stained glass hallways, chandelier-scattered palace halls
and jewel-encrusted costumes as the story's characters also disclose and communicate to one another via the figural. This can first be observed with regard
to the film's opening eighteen-minute delay before the face of its protagonist,
Devdas, is revealed. The film's lead character is at first unusually hidden from
us, not only playing upon the audience's desire to see superstar Shah Rukh
Khan in the classic role, but more importantly, pushing them to a point at
which they care not so much about *who* he is or what his intentions are as about
what he looks like. When Devdas finally appears, his image is styled upon the
vintage fashion of 1930s England, complete with an Englishman's hat, cravat,
coat and smoking cigarette, which become a dominant visual character trait
throughout the film. Similarly, when Paro (Devdas's lower-caste childhood
sweetheart and neighbour) first hears that her long-lost love has returned
home, very little dialogue is used to convey her thoughts. Instead, her emotions are made evident visually or sensorially: from the use of highly saturated
colours and images of fluttering doves to rapidly tracking cameras following her
running down a seemingly endless corridor, the fabric of her silken sari trailing
behind her. (This visual depiction of Paro differs greatly from Roy's version,
which subtly hints at her emotions through static shots, strategic silences and
a predominant reliance on dialogue.) Of course, a more visualised style is not
uncommon to Indian cinema, but it is the sheer *excess* and prioritisation of this
style in Bhansali's *Devdas* that I wish to stress and draw attention to.

FIGURAL EXCESS VERSUS LOW-KEY REALISM: BHANSALI AND ROY'S ADAPTATIONS

It is not sufficient to say that Bhansali's visually excessive reworking of Roy's film is a naturally progressive result of modern updates in film technology, as would be commonplace when comparing a modern remake to its classic original. Bhansali has found it necessary to create an entirely new cinematic language for *Devdas* in order to allow us to perceive its characters in a new light, to get closer to a more literal (or rather, hyper-literal) experience of the story's sublime themes: passion, devotion, sacrifice, eternal love. The 2002 adaptation of *Devdas* makes an interesting shift towards multiple viewpoints compared to its statically shot predecessor, as can be seen in the key moment when Devdas first lays eyes on his beloved Paro. In Roy's original, we see Devdas walk into a bare room, catching Paro lighting a diva. Paro, stunned by the sight of Devdas, burns her hand on the match she is holding. The two are locked in a gaze while the hidden, still eye of the camera and sudden silence support the privacy of the moment. In the contemporary version, however, the scene is presented more dynamically as the audience is invited to experience the moment through a multiplicity of gazes. As Devdas moves towards a sleeping Paro, the camera moves right up close to almost touch her softly lit face as she lies shrouded in moonlight, stained glass shadows and flickering candles. The scene subsequently shifts between such extreme close-ups to long-shots, tracking shots, and point-of-view perspectives of Devdas observing Paro. Furthermore, in following scenes, we find ourselves voyeurs peeping through binoculars, omnisciently floating through corridors and down the stairs of grand mansions via crane shots and unedited long-takes. Thrown into the chaos of the moment, we spin and get dizzy with the dancers (as in the film's sequence for the song 'Dhola Re'). We fall with the characters as they drop to the ground, with even our vision blurring as Devdas takes his last breath in the final scene of the film.

Unlike in the contemporary adaptation, cinematography in Bimal Roy's *Devdas* is utilitarian and does not draw attention to itself. In the blockbuster remake, however, cameras move all over and around the characters – fragmenting and shifting the position of the audience by switching between shot-reverse-shot gazes, third-person spectator views, voyeuristic gazes, and character point-of-view shots. This issue of positioning the audience is also interesting when we consider *where* incidents are placed within a key scene. For example, we notice the difference in suturing strategies in the scene where Paro receives a letter from Devdas, denying the love between them. Whereas Roy's version distances us from the moment at which Paro screws up the letter in despair (verisimilitude and an impersonal static observatory shot of her prevents any chance of an overtly intimate and subjective viewpoint), the

2002 remake instead throws us and our viewpoint into the fire with the letter. The cinema screen burns with the letter in an extreme close-up before us and our personal engagement with this moment is thus encouraged. Through an enhanced visualisation of this incident we feel more involved and entangled as our viewpoint (literally thrown into the fire) mirrors the emotional state of Paro.

One can also look at environments and settings in order to determine the polarisation of visual set-ups in the two films. Roy's production is set in a naturalistic environment. Most of what we see contributes to the rural realism of the story: forests, village roads, crop fields, muddy farm roads and river banks. In fact, the only obvious symbolic use of the story's setting is a lotus-flower bud, which blooms to bridge the passing of time from childhood to adulthood of the lead characters. In Bhansali's film however, this symbolism is so frequent we can scarcely keep up with it. We barely have a chance to interpret a symbol's meaning before we are confronted with another. Every environment or setting the character or audience is brought into is used for aesthetic gain: the pond in the courtesan's palace which Chandramukhi dips her hair into seductively to entice Devdas; the mirror in Chandramukhi's bedroom which shatters dramatically when she turns to see Devdas, indicating the chemistry between them; the river Devdas sinks into as he drowns in alcoholism; the tree whose red petals shower over Devdas as he lies on his death bed. For some audiences and critics this excessive need to over-saturate the screen with symbolic images can become too much, as demonstrated through my earlier examples of the film's negative Western critical reviews and my analysis of student responses to Bollywood films in Chapter 3. So why does this cinematic technique appeal and work in Bollywood cinema? Why are audiences of such films drawn to this aesthetic style? And what do films like this reveal about the Bollywood audience's tolerance, understanding and perception of the relationship between image and word on-screen? Is it perhaps possible that the Bollywood audience has come to be more tuned into and dependent on the poetry of the cinematic image? From analysing films like Bhansali's *Devdas*, it certainly appears that Bollywood cinema, with its uniquely figural cinematic language, can at times come to depend on the image as much as the Western film depends on its narrative discourse.

DEMOTING THE DISCURSIVE

Bhansali's remake almost evades cinematic discursive frameworks, particularly with regard to narrative storytelling and dialogue. In Roy's film the emotions and sentiments of characters are 'told' rather than shown. Relationships are developed through narrative. The first hour of the film focuses on the lovers' childhood friendship, while the contemporary version disposes of this background story, aside from a few seconds of flashback footage. Rather than documenting or staging events and conversations to explain the bond between Paro and Devdas, *Devdas* (2002) expresses this more explicitly through its sensuality and imagery – at times almost akin to a picture book storytelling sensibility. In Roy's film, locations (such as Chandramukhi's dancing room) are often lit in a rather low-key way and camera shots are almost always tightly framed around the characters' bodies. Our knowledge of Chandramukhi's wealth or Devdas's love for Paro is therefore often dependent on narrative and discursive clues. This form of narrative presentation is not merely a consequence of technical inefficiency and low production costs at the time Roy's film was made, but is an intentional hesitation and restraint that form part of Roy's classic socio-realist style. Thus Bhansali, in breaking with this realist aesthetic, tries instead to represent the film's issues, themes and emotions through his saturated visuals.

The demoting of discourse in Bhansali's remake is also evident with regard to its dialogue, as seen in the reuniting of Paro and Devdas at the start of the film:

Paro. The desire to meet the sea turns the stream into a river.
Devdas. Then why take time to show me your face?
Paro. Like sighting the moon after ages, I fear I shall leave you breathless.
Devdas. [laughing] Not even the moon is as vain.
Paro. Why should it be? The moon is scarred.
Devdas. Fair enough Paro, then we shall wait 'til moonrise to see which leaves me breathless, the moon's radiance? Or your vanity?

The dominance of imagery in this passage of film dialogue is partly symptomatic of the language used at the time the story is set (early twentieth-century Bengal), which is fundamentally poetic and descriptive. Nevertheless, the way in which the image invades conversation throughout Bhansali's film is distinctive when the film is compared to its realist predecessor. Dialogue, discourse and narration function at different levels in the two films. Most noticeably, in contrast to the above visually driven dialogue, Roy's *Devdas* uses two vagabond minstrels as a narrative device to verbally explain the situation and feelings of young Paro, after she has been abandoned by Devdas:

Come and meet me dear Krishna . . . come and meet
Come dear Krishna, your Radha's roaming all alone looking lost
We all miss you so terribly in Vrindavan dear Lord
The day your topic comes up, our haunted eyes overflow
Even now we worry in mind, what will happen in future

For your Radha's roaming, lost lost
You still haven't sent us news about yourself
We still have no news from you
Every girl in Vrindavan has gone mad crying over you
Come and console them, show your face o lord

Throughout the above song sequence, the movement of the camera is discreet. It is restricted to two camera set-ups (a long shot and a medium close-up) and a few cuts catching the facial expressions of the three on-screen characters. In this scene (and the film as a whole) the image functions as a frame for words, dialogue and narrative. The minstrels' song is situated very much in reality (a diegetic musical moment as opposed to a dream sequence). Here, the minstrels remain fairly static and their religious songs are coincidental, detached representations of Paro's situation. In the 2002 remake, however, songs are less devices of omniscient narration and become actual projections or re-enactments of the characters' fantasies, thoughts, desires and emotions. They shift between real events (Chandramukhi's dance-hall numbers) and symbolic events (the Krishna and Radha song) and thus often move beyond storytelling into figural emotion and sensation.

Just as with cinema's attempt to remake or retell the novel, Bhansali's remake can transfer Roy's film's narrative, but not its original *system of enunciation*. In speaking for Western remakes, Brian McFarlane notes that whereas the novel's enunciation operates wholly through verbal signs, film varies between the visual, the aural and the verbal (McFarlane: 26). Bhansali's *Devdas*' ratio of these three forms of enunciation is somewhat different, as the film operates predominantly through the first two *sensual* sign systems. Roy's version also features songs which connote the feelings of characters, particularly in the case of the dancing courtesan Chandramukhi. However, her feelings are still often under-represented and subtly hinted at in her dance sequences when compared with Bhansali's Chandramukhi, whose framing, choreography and 'operatic' emotive vocals all contribute to revealing her inner emotional state. Thus again Roy's adaptation, as a classic of Indian social realism, maintains a distance in its song pieces, while Bhansali's film exploits the virtues of song and dance for heightened sensation and affect.

As well as highlighting the prioritisation of visuals in the postmodern film text, Lash has stressed how these images come to act independently of narrative, signification and meaning to a point at which symbolism and connotation become irrelevant or obsolete. Bhansali's *Devdas* may not do this to the extreme of, say, a David Lynch movie, but the film certainly shows moments of this pure, exclusively figural presentation. As mentioned earlier, critics have attacked the film's failure to narrate, represent or signify. Bhansali reduces the story of Devdas to 'a series of moments', the storyline is 'spoilt' and cannot function normatively owing to the 'overwhelming' emphasis on 'kitsch' visuals. *Mise-en-scène* becomes so dominant that the love story of Devdas and Paro 'becomes almost irrelevant'. In this particular remake the hierarchy of word and image are reversed. Narrative and discourse now inversely function to frame the image. Bhansali's *Devdas* becomes so absorbed in its visual dimension, it consequently dispenses with narrative, historical accuracy, plausibility, realism, and signification (at least in its conventional and palatable sense). One could also argue that in doing so, the film challenges these grand frameworks, inviting us instead to view a more liberated, less repressed, and purer sense of the film as a 'cinematic' art form.

Dilip Kumar, lead actor of the 1955 classic, once commented on Roy's intention to make films that were 'close to the soil' and his inclinations towards a minimalist style that involved 'trying *not to do* rather than doing'.[11] This tendency led to underplayed roles (particularly with regard to Kumar's acclaimed performance), producing a completely different Devdas to Shah Rukh Khan's later interpretation – who cries with bloodshot eyes, shouts and yells drunkenly, staggers around stubble-faced, unwrapped dhoti[12] in hand, and has been attacked repeatedly by critics for 'over-emoting'. Khan's Devdas almost works against everything that Kumar's characterisation stood for. With Roy's and Bhansali's adaptations therefore, we have two films offering two entirely different cinematic interpretations of human passion. However, it is the later version that exudes passion, obsession, tragedy, romance and devotion in its most visceral form. One can understand and appreciate Bhansali's method of remaking as akin to (to borrow from André Bazin's description of film adaptation) an 'electric transformer transforming the 'voltage' of the original', where 'aesthetic energy is dissipated . . . differently according to the demands of the camera lens' (Bazin, 1948: 25). By increasing the visual and dramatic energy of the film (to the point of absurdity, abstraction or risking authenticity) Bhansali aims, in postmodern fashion, for the *sublime* – to present those intangible emotions (passion, devotion, sacrifice, eternal love) that cannot be described, conceptualised through narrative, or represented through conventional modes of representation; those *unpresentable* emotions which Roy chose to suppress. In such a pursuit for the sublime, Bhansali willingly risks allowing his film to fail to represent in a manner that is deemed acceptable, plausible and conceivable to Western audiences. Regrettably, for all its visual barrage, noise, and high-voltage unabashed indulgence, it may not be so easy to overcome our impulsive discomfort towards this form of cinema. However, through considering the above, Western critics, theorists and audiences may begin to appreciate the complexity, craftsmanship and unique affect of such a cinema, rather than dogmatically and futilely condemning it for being figurally excessive.

Following the success of *Devdas*, Bhansali released *Saawariya* five years later in 2007. Based on the short story *White Nights* by Fyodor Dostoevsky ([1848]

2012), the film appeared yet another platform for the director's figurally excessive style, perhaps even more indulgently than *Devdas*. Cinematographer Ravi K. Chandran has described how every frame of the film was constructed like a painting, with its use of saturated colours and space lights which created a ' "painterly" mood lighting'. Chandran describes Bhansali's desire to paint the screen: 'His aim was to make the images for *Saawariya* more like paintings rather than just photographic images. So we started by looking at the paintings of artists like Frederick Arthur Bridgman, Fred R Wagner and William Louis Sonntag as references' (Saawariya Presskit, Saawariyafilm.com). It is perhaps no accident then that, in 2008, multinational conglomerate the Sony Corporation announced it would be releasing *Saawariya* as its first Bollywood Blu-ray. As a relatively new technology in India, Blu-ray promised to offer Bollywood audiences a more sensory cinematic experience: an enhanced depth of field, sharpened visual detail, vivid colour saturation and TrueHD sound. *Saawariya*'s rich painterly palate of jet blacks, deep blues and scarlet and its bold contrast lighting perfectly demonstrated the new technology's increased bit-depth. Bhansali's penchant for sharply detailed set-pieces and enhanced depth of field aptly boasted Blu-ray's high resolution. Furthermore, its ambient sensual soundtrack maximised the format's uncompressed and multi-channelled audio enhancements. Contemporary Bollywood's ongoing investment in high definition cinema has led to a greater emphasis on visual effects, colourisation, and most recently, experimentations with 3D technology,[13] which has included Bhansali himself announcing a rerelease of *Devdas* in 3D (IANS, 2012).

Saawariya was followed by two more films exhibiting Bhansali's unique aesthetics: *Guzaarish* in 2010 and *Goliyon Ki Raasleela Ram-Leela* in 2013. Although arguably driven by more serious themes (disability and euthanasia) and lacking the colour saturation of *Devdas*, *Guzaarish* still conformed to the director's signature style, this time achieving visual excess through a complex play with lighting. Similar to his 2005 disability-drama *Black*, the film dramatically accentuates shadows and silhouettes with a cooler palette, while still utilising grand scale set pieces, a vast depth of field, image layering techniques, and ornamenting the screen as in *Devdas*. For example, protagonist Ethan's mansion bedroom ceiling is covered in an abundance of picture frames, which act as visual distractions, so much that they appear to skew the perspective. With *Ram-Leela*, a Bollywood adaptation of William Shakespeare's *Romeo and Juliet*, Bhansali engages in a strange postmodern feedback loop with director Baz Luhrmann, having already referenced Bollywood-inspired *Moulin Rouge*'s set design in *Saawariya*. In keeping with his penchant for overlapping different time periods, *Ram-Leela* is explicitly a-historical: traditional Gujarati costumes are made using a combination of century-old antique and contemporary fabrics, elaborate rustic mansions and giant wall murals of Hindu gods are combined with 1950s cars, denim jeans and neon-lit porn-DVD shops decorated with Betty Page-printed drapes. In the film's song 'Ram chahe Leela' classical Kathak dance and yogic postures are performed to a fusion of rock and devotional rhythms. The figural is on display through locations, such as the Saneras' garden (an overgrown chaos of vegetation and statues), and sequences often slowing down purely to focus on the flowing fabrics of the characters' ornate costumes. Even the film's dialogue switches from sophisticated and poetic rhyming couplets to coarser metaphors and colloquialisms.

In light of the above, one could argue that Bhansali's cinema is cinematic in the purest sense of the word vis-à-vis its foregrounded and dynamic visual aesthetics. As Robert Stam reminds us, cinema is

> a composite language by virtue of its diverse matters of expression – sequential photography, music, phonetic sound, and noise . . . [it] 'inherits' all the art forms associated with these matters of expression. Cinema has available to it the visuals of photography and painting, the movement of dance, the décor of architecture, and the performance of theatre. (Stam: 61)

SELF-REFLEXIVITY AND SELF-REFERENTIALITY IN BOLLYWOOD: *DIL CHAHTA HAI*

We have already begun to look at self-reflexivity as a central postmodern device in the contemporary Bollywood text, particularly in the case of *Om Shanti Om*. I will now provide further examples of its functioning in order to illustrate how it is part of a wider phenomenon in contemporary Bollywood. Self-reflexivity has rarely been a focal point of Indian cinema criticism, yet it frequently figures in the contemporary Bollywood film text, particularly if we permit it to function independently of authorial intent. As discussed previously, whilst it may be treated as a novel feature in the modern Hollywood text – operating outside or against the principles of verisimilitude (for example, as in the comedy spoofs of director Mel Brooks) – Bollywood, which is often contrarily devoid of verisimilitude, may allow its self-reflexive moments to manifest repeatedly in film after film, with little critical or innovatory recognition ever being drawn to them. In Hollywood, a text may receive critical attention and acclaim for its ingenuity or daringness to step outside and look back at itself (*Being John Malkovich, Pleasantville, The Truman Show*). In Bollywood however, it has come to form part of the often taken-for-granted nature of popular Indian cinema – repeatedly used and perceived as an integrated, *non-disruptive* device inciting routine humour, momentary cinephilia, and audience pleasure. Common self-reflexive moments in contemporary Bollywood films include the drawing of attention to film as text though the popular use of the phrase 'this is not a movie, this is real life' in film dialogue. Most explicitly, Sanjay Gupta's *Musafir* (a 2004 remake of Oliver Stone's *U-Turn*) uses similar dialogue to reflect on the narrative and stock character conventions of the film and play with the audience's expectations of the unfolding narrative action. The film's antagonist (archetypically played by Sanjay Dutt) spends much on-screen time referring directly to the film's current plot and action, literally addressing himself as 'the villain' and the lead character as 'film hero'. He also openly cites or alludes to other popular Indian films – particularly those that have starred actor Anil Kapoor, who plays opposite Dutt as *Musafir*'s protagonist. For example, various references are made to one of the most famous films of Kapoor's early career, *Ram Lakhan* (1989).

Another popular self-reflexive function in Bollywood is the film-within-a-film scenario, in which lead characters are portrayed as struggling actors attempting to break into the Bollywood industry (*36 China Town*, *Mast*, *Luck By Chance*). The films of Ram Gopal Varma are perhaps best-known for their narratives set in the filmmaking world: *Mast* (focusing on a young boy's obsession over a film actress), *Rangeela* (a love triangle set in the backdrop of the Hindi film industry), *Company* (involving underworld money laundering through film production), *Satya* (the female lead plays an aspiring actress), *Naach* (portraying a wannabe Bollywood dance choreographer), *Sarkar* (one of the key villains is a corrupt film producer) and *Darna Zaroori Hai* (two of its short stories centre around a member of the film audience, an aspiring actress and a film director).[14]

Self-commentary is also made effective in contemporary Bollywood through different modes of narration. Song sequences also now increasingly act as extra-diegetic commentary, reflecting on the film story or foretelling events to come. For example, during a climactic cliff-hanger moment in *Don: The Chase Begins*, the song 'Aaj ki raat' [Tonight] is shot with the film's key characters facing the camera/audience and asking them 'Aaj ki raat hona hai kya? [What is going to happen tonight?]'. What is more, one verse in the song (sung by the anti-hero Don) discloses the plot-twist at the end of the film by singing about Don's getaway plan to 'quietly sneak away' with his girlfriend under everyone's noses. Several contemporary films have also featured narrator-figures, who will interrupt the narrative in order to interact with the audience and comment on the characters and action. Two examples include India's Oscar entry for 2006 *Paheli* (in which two Rajasthani puppets comment on the story-action throughout the film) and the *When Harry Met Sally* inspired *Hum Tum* (where the diegesis and themes are discussed by two cartoon characters from a comic book).

Furthermore, it is becoming more common for actors to step outside their roles and look at, talk to, and interact with the audience. In Karan Johar's

KHNH, film extras stop and face the camera to indicate what day it is in the countdown to the lead characters Rohit and Naina falling in love. For example, in one scene, a man calling for a taxi faces the camera and shouts 'Day 1'. This technique of creating a calendar through visual cues continues throughout the scene; a business man, a student, a waiter, and a passer-by all stop to reflect on and punctuate the storyline. Movie star personae are also similarly played on within the film. At the start of the film, Shah Rukh Khan's character is given a somewhat exaggerated tongue-in-cheek introduction – a dramatic fanfare accompanying a *Titanic*-style 'king of the world' pose as his ferry approaches New York city, and the juxtaposed shots of other characters' desperate prayers for a saviour-like hero to come along. This moment signals to the audience, whose attention is drawn to the casting of Bollywood's most famous lead actor in an archetypal heroic role. They are reminded of their own investment and submissive pleasures rooted in the Bollywood star system.[15] The film's closing song sequence also explicitly situates the text as part of the Yash Johar production company lineage (Dharma productions) as we see its female lead occasionally replaced by momentary cameos of actresses Kajol and Rani Mukherjee, who both appear in the company's previous hit films (Rani Mukherjee in *K3G* and *K2H2*, and Kajol in *K2H2* and *DDLJ*).

Among the various self-reflexive techniques employed in Bollywood film, self-parody is perhaps the most dominant. As Harries comments, parody itself operates with the postmodern potential to *reinforce* and *counteract* the film canons and genres it works within: 'As parodies arrive to scavenge worn-out conventions and their accompanying over predictability, some critics argue that this signals the end of the tradition and its approaching moment of extinction' (Harries: 123). Thus, when looking at Bollywood self-parody (and indeed, when considering the contemporary Indian remake in general) it is important to bear this destructive potential in mind. Admittedly, the above examples of continuous self-reflexivity may be disputed as offering nothing beyond visual gags, directorial in-jokes, or brief moments indulging and evoking audience cinephilia. However, I would argue that a closer look at such cinematic moments can reveal more complex ways in which self-reflexivity functions in these films. In order to explore this complexity and investigate the importance of self-parody as a valuable feature of Bollywood texts, I will conduct an in-depth analysis of a key song sequence from one of contemporary Bollywood cinema's most acclaimed films.

Farhan Akhtar's new generation film *Dil Chahta Hai* (hereafter *DCH*) has been regarded as a milestone in popular Indian cinema and in many ways marks the beginning of what I have proposed to be a significant shift in contemporary Bollywood film aesthetics. As Rachel Dwyer notes in *100 Bollywood films*, *DCH* touches new ground in a multiplicity of ways – its slick look, its updated representations of modern day youth with stylish haircuts and designer clothes, its global international settings (Australia, Goa), and its deeper exploration of character relationships (Dwyer, 2005: 71–2). But despite deserving much credit for its fresh take on love in the modern age (the film as a whole is not a remake), *DCH* cannot be associated with a return to sophisticated realism and originality in mainstream Indian cinema either. Although its script and story are largely original, *DCH* still exhibits key elements of postmodern imitation in cinema, this time through one of its most popular song sequences entitled 'Woh ladhki hai kahan?' [Where is that girl?].

In this sequence, protagonists Sameer (Saif Ali Khan) and Pooja (Sonali Kulkarni) walk into a Hindi cinema theatre and pass a poster, reading the title of a pseudo-movie called *Woh Ladkhi hai kahan*. We are allowed a quick glance at the poster's lead hero and heroine, who look uncannily familiar (1). Following a cut to the auditorium interior, we are presented with a point of view shot of a blank cinema screen from the upper balcony (2). As the 'movie on the screen' begins, the camera cuts between what is on the 'screen' and reflects back to catch the expressions of Sameer, Pooja, and the auditorium 'audience' as they watch (3). The song sequence on the 'screen' first appears as a black-and-white homage to 1950s Hindi cinema (4), perhaps most directly quoting Guru Dutt and Mala Sinha's roles in *Pyaasa* [1957]). What is more, the lead performers in this parodic scene are played by none other than Khan and Kulkarni (5). The camera cuts to Sameer and Pooja in the auditorium, who look at each other in shock, recognising none but themselves in the film (6). After a moment of bewilderment, the two decide to submit to this fantasy and begin to laugh at the screen (7). The second verse of the song switches to a parody of 1960s to early 1970s Bollywood cinema, accompanied by appropriately amateurish special effects of the period: a studio-set car supported by a moving-scenery backdrop, with several film extras on bicycles implausibly riding along beside it. The scene's lead singers (the 'on-screen' Sameer and Pooja) comically stand up and dance inside the car, rarely looking ahead in a driving pose, and even sit on the bonnet while the car is supposedly moving (8). The final section of the song ends with a parody of 1990s Bollywood conventions. The 'screen' Pooja appears as an exaggerated version of popular actress Madhuri Dixit, supporting a badly wrapped chiffon sari and a false-looking wig. Her performance is deliberately unconvincing, melodramatic to the point of absurdity, and her dance movements are staged as extremely tongue-in-cheek clownish convulsions (9). In the last few lines of the song, the camera cuts back to the auditorium 'audience', where the real Sameer and Pooja are now standing up singing to each other (10). Suddenly the 'audience' in the auditorium around them also bursts into dance, mimicking the hand-gestures of the goofy 'on-screen' choreography (11). The scene ends with a return to the point of view shot of the auditorium cinema 'screen', which now reads: '*The Beginning*' (12).

Figure 7.2: 'Wo Ladhki Hai Kahan?' A parodic journey through popular Hindi cinema in the 1950s, 1960s and 1980s in *Dil Chahta Hai* (Excel Entertainment, 2001).

On one level, this sequence can be conceived of as a moment of lighthearted relief and amusement, a comic interval serving as a break from the more serious and dramatically charged scenes which directly precede it in the film narrative. On another level however, the kind of pleasure being offered to the audience in this scene is far more complex. What can we make of this scene, seeing that this film largely chooses to veer away from stereotypical old-fashioned Bollywood conventions? Is this Akhtar paying homage, or trying to indicate the staleness and artificiality of the kind of Bollywood films that the audience would usually find pleasure in (in which case, this sequence is potentially quite damaging to traditional Bollywood cinema)? The scene stands apart from the film's other song sequences, which depart from familiar conventions, though *not* always through the eye of realism (for example, one of the film's equally fantastical song sequences is situated inside a painting – including smudged images, over-enhanced colours, high exposures, and CGI graphics of jumping dolphins). Thus, although it may be more 'realistic' than the traditional Bollywood masala film in one sense, *DCH* often explodes into multiple modes of existence – the real, the cinematic, the symbolic, and the hyperreal.

The 'Woh Ladkhi Hai Kahan' sequence consists of a multiplicity of self-reflexive moments. The film text sets its own characters up and instigates audience pleasure through the following self-reflexive techniques: dramatic irony [a film poster hints at what is to come (1)] whereby the viewer's voyeuristic gaze and position as spectator is reaffirmed if not *doubled* as the act of cinema-going becomes part of the story-subject. The real world and film world overlap or align [point of view shot inside auditorium (2)]. Much like Pooja and Sameer, we the spectators see ourselves mirrored in this scene and we read our own pleasures in the faces of the diegetic 'audience' [shot of 'audience' in auditorium (3)]. The film text acknowledges and evokes its own historical roots [1950s black and white film parody (4)]. Casting, role play and performativity are exposed and lines are drawn between the lovers on the 'screen' and the characters in the diegesis. Desires are paralleled and transferred from spectator to the on-screen characters, and from the on-screen characters to the fantasy personae on the diegetic 'screen' [film watchers Sameer/Khan and Pooja/Kulkarni take on fantasy personae (5)]. Pooja and Sameer register and respond to their own artificiality whist we, the spectators, indulge in seeing their functionality as the source of light comedy and 'innocent love' openly addressed in the film and mockingly projected back at them in exaggerated form [Pooja and Sameer see themselves 'on-screen' (6) and (7)]. Bollywood cinema mocks (perhaps even invalidates) its own form and conventions [amateur 60s/70s film set (8)] and the performativity and staged femininity of the Bollywood heroine is mocked [Pooja's exaggerated poses as a 90s film heroine (9)]. The levels of reality between Sameer and Pooja's world and the 'on-screen' world are now entirely fused. This final harmonisation of 'on-screen' fantasy and diegetic reality produces both audience pleasure and a kind of narrative or textual disorientation [Sameer and Pooja sing the final lines of the song to each other in the auditorium (10)]. We the audience are forced to register our own emotional investment, pleasure, and submersion in the film action as it is played out before us by our on-screen mirror doubles [the on-screen 'audience' start to dance to the music (11)]. The film inverts its own traditional conventions through paratextuality[16] and thus addresses its function as storyteller [at the end of the song sequence, the diegetic 'screen' reads *The Beginning* instead of *The End* to highlight the start of Sameer and Pooja's love story (12)]. Not only is the characters' fictionality being played with and exposed, but also the film world's fictionality (verisimilitude is explicitly denied), the performativity of the actors, Bollywood's film style, and the audience themselves who are receiving pleasure from watching at that moment.

DCH switches between the fantastical and the conventional, the diegetic and the extra-diegetic. It simultaneously identifies with and undermines its filmic conventions, its heritage, and its textuality, offering an altogether unique and innovative form of audience viewing pleasure. The film thus confirms Harries' earlier argument concerning film parody's potential to question and/or deconstruct established norms. Though it may be too harsh to declare Bollywood an elimination target for Akhtar in this film, the film crucially succeeds in pushing the cinema off a tangent and 'maiming it with a smile' (Harries: 123). As lead characters Akash, Sameer and Sid (somewhat ironically) exclaim in the film's opening song sequence: 'hum hai nahe, andaaz kyun ho purana?' [We are new, so why should our style be old?]. One answer to this question lies in the fact that Bollywood, in true postmodern style, has come to recognise its potential to break new ground, to be creative, and to innovate itself through recycling the past.

ACTION MOVIES, IDENTITY AND THE 'COOL' AESTHETIC IN *KAANTE*

The action movie genre has remained consistently popular in Bombay cinema, particularly since the 1970s, but it has also transformed significantly in the past decade (see Vitali, 2008). Increased film budgets have led to ever more daring stunts, giant rigged explosions and Bond-like gadgets, courtesy of the industry's financial structural shifts. Motivated by the increase in Indian computer effects studios and the industry's growing international exchanges, the cinema has begun to invest heavily in martial arts choreography training by Hong Kong experts (where stars are put under tougher fitness regimes) as well as digital pyrotechnics, wire-work and green screen technology – all of which have contributed to the cinema's aforementioned technorealism. However, as Valentina Vitali has noted in her study of changes in the contemporary Hindi action film, the predominance of modern technology in such films is rather redundant. Technology has a less functional purpose and instead is there to serve the aesthetics and *mise-en-scène*. Vitali also makes a similar point about the male body in these newer films, which is less 'acrobatic' and 'agile' than in earlier eras. Instead, the actor's body is 'representative' – its 'unreal plasticity' is now a 'symbol of luxury and leisure'. Vitali argues that technorealism has suppressed the acrobatics and energy of fight scenes. The action choreography is 'cut to the bone because each action sequence relies primarily on a combination of digital manipulation and jump-cuts' (240). As a result, physical movements of the actors are 'discontinuous' and 'reduced to a few crucial temporal fragments ... for the sake of brevity' while this technical style 'enhances the visual impressions of speed' and an 'emphatic, even aggressive mode of address' (241). The image sequences of these films are comparable with the sensory effects and subliminal techniques of advertising. The experience for spectators in such moments is thus a kind of 'sensory overload' resulting in a supposed anaesthesia (a numbing of the senses) towards the visual stimuli. Vitali's somewhat deterministic formulation of the contemporary Bollywood action film genre ultimately sees it as built around the luxury goods it advertises. So deeply is it driven by economic pressures that film sponsorship now dictates this cinema's modes of operation.

Having dispersed comfortably across a variety of masculine sub-genres (revenge, heist, gangster, thriller, adventure, sci-fi, war, buddy), the Bollywood action movie presents itself as perhaps the most faithful disciple of the Bollywood-Hollywood remake. Within the post-millennial decade, a significant portion of A-list action movies have been moulded around Hollywood films and conventions. Films such as the *Dhoom* franchise, *Main Hoon Na*, *Fight Club: Members Only*, *Kaante*, *Ek Ajnabee*, *Chocolate: Deep Dark Secrets*, *Dus*, *Zinda* and *Don: The Chase Begins* do not only have their popularity in common as major box-office releases, but also the fact that each of them has been created with a high concentration of Hollywood/foreign film aesthetics – in some cases abandoning traditional Bollywood conventions altogether. For example, in *Zinda* song sequences are absent and almost every frame set-up and camera shot endeavours to carefully duplicate the Korean original. As a result, the entire film text is edited and stitched together with an experimental style unfamiliar to popular Indian cinema. *Zinda*, as shot-for-shot remake,[17] is an extreme example of Bollywood cinema's gradual surrender to foreign cinematic styles and techniques at the expense of its own generic identity – an identity which is increasingly problematised and repeatedly put to question. When judged according to the generic definitions of Bollywood currently available to us (as discussed in Chapter 2), were it not for its Indian lead characters and Hindi dialogue, *Zinda* could cease to possess any of the traits allowing it to register as a conventional product of popular Indian cinema. Given that films such as *Zinda* do not openly acknowledge themselves as remakes, and since a large portion of the viewing public in India may have little or no knowledge of *Oldboy*'s existence, such films can easily pass off as products of a new style of contemporary Bollywood. As Andrew Willis has noted: 'the first thing we may watch will be the remake so the chronological wires are crossed. The remake is us taking a look at the original before we've seen it. Before we've seen it we are analysing it' (Willis, 2003: 147). Thus here, the styles and techniques of foreign cinema can become part of Indian cinema's own identity. For Bollywood and its audience, the cross-cultural remake can paradoxically be taken and used to indicate or advocate change, innovation, and progression within the Indian film industry. Furthermore, as the remake 'neutralises the otherness of the foreign film' (Willis: 149) and makes it culturally proximate, it estranges itself from its own conventions, creating an altogether unusual kind of hybrid text. But regardless of how much Bollywood remakes may 'steal' from outside sources or stray from their own conventions, they cannot be experienced or labelled as foreign, Western or non-Indian productions. Their methods of appropriation and resulting hybridity are still a product of (and tied to) Bollywood's unique film language. Current definitions of Bollywood cinema have yet to accommodate this particular variety of hybrid films, but a space and name for such films is imperative – particularly when we consider their normalisation, proliferation and increasing popularity with in-land audiences.

Bollywood-Hollywood remakes are schizophrenic by nature. They lack fixed identities, and this may explain why some viewers (possessing a certain level of global cultural capital) might find watching them an unsettling, even uncanny experience. In many cases, the effect of borrowing from Western cinematic conventions becomes an almost hostile act. Once these familiar traits have been used, exposed and exaggerated, they no longer remain pure. As with Benjamin's account of mechanical reproduction, the original loses its soul and even its affectivity in relation to its aesthetic allure. For example, in his remake of *Reservoir Dogs*, director Sanjay Gupta chooses to take an archetypal American low-budget independent film and present it as a Bollywood film through using stylistic techniques better accustomed to a Hollywood blockbuster. However, these Hollywood conventions are unable to function and achieve effect customarily when applied to a story originally presented as a low-key independent cult film and subjected to a semi-Bollywood regime of storytelling. Though the film still adheres to the song sequence formula, its musical sequences are distorted via the film's Western cinematic style. For example, the song 'Mahi Ve' [My Beloved] is sung in traditional Punjabi-Urdu style, yet presented in the manner of an MTV pop video (shot in an LA night club), thus somewhat contradicting and undermining the folk song music track it accompanies. In *Kaante*'s song sequences, conventional Bollywood shots of hip-swinging Indian women in traditional outfits are exchanged for close-up shots of the bottoms of multiracial dancers in tight hot pants, whilst images of women dancing sexually with other women or muscular black men almost subliminally flash onto the screen. The effect of merging traditional folk songs and Bollywood choreography with a glamorised, carefree and controversial American lifestyle (striptease and drinking culture) is extremely disorienting – producing a hybrid cinematic style that deviates from both Western and traditional Indian modes of filmmaking.

Kaante's opening title sequence also works to exploit certain cinematic conventions. The sequence resembles the famous *Reservoir Dogs* shot of a group of black suited men walking in slow motion – only this time the scene

Figure 7.3: Exploiting Hollywood conventions in the opening sequence of *Kaante* (Pritish Nandy Communications, 2002).

is further dramatised by large bold green title credits that flash onto the screen in Hollywood blockbuster style. A dramatic, fast paced action movie-style soundtrack is laid over the image of the protagonists who are dressed in designer sunglasses, suits and leather jackets, wearing twinkling gold jewellery, swinging chains, smoking cigarettes and chewing gum in slow motion. This two minute sequence uses the same shots repeatedly, to an extent that the scene eventually becomes almost monotonous. This moment of cinematic quotation can be read on two levels – firstly as an act of pastiche simply for the sake of heightening dramatic action via an aesthetic of 'American coolness', or secondly, as a moment of semi-parodic play (humour aside) with Hollywood's own forms of dramatic stylisation. I am not suggesting here that the postmodern appropriation in films such as *Kaante* actually impacts on or lessens the popularity of the original (*Reservoir Dogs* still maintains its status and retains its existing fans), but that this can lead some Bollywood audiences to view or reflect on the above Hollywood stylistic modes and conventions as more obviously constructed, if not contrived.

THE INDIAN 'COOL' AESTHETIC AS PROBLEMATIC

As I have already discussed with reference to the critical reception of 1990s Bollywood films, NRI and non-Indian audiences, as well as Western critics, have often found Bollywood's attempts to mimic Hollywood's American coolness difficult to accept, often rejecting them as cringeworthy and unconvincing. Admittedly, with its recent increase in film budgets and technical advancements, contemporary Bollywood's ability to appropriate this aspect of American cinema has somewhat improved. Nevertheless, even in later films there appears to be a major flaw in what I would call the 'Indian cool' aesthetic, which I think is largely a result of a fundamental clash or friction between the masculine representational codes used in Bollywood and Hollywood film texts. The appropriation of American 'coolness' in the contemporary Bollywood action film is perhaps the genre's most unflattering and off-putting attribute, particularly for some non-Indian spectators. There often seems to be an imbalance or inconsistency in the way the contemporary Bollywood text constructs its Hindi male leads as Hollywood-like heroes. On the one hand they are cigarette smoking, independent, free-spirited and indestructible individuals with a carefree attitude. They are kitted up on powerful motorbikes with their long hair and leather jacket blowing in the wind – yet they will also preach about religious superstitions, be tied to their family honour and culture, and sing, dance and go soft around women (see Unauthored, 2003a, in which *Kaante* is heavily criticised for its 'syrupy sentiment'). The problem thus lies with the masculine sensationalism of contemporary Bollywood cinema. Heroic men often express their emotions so extremely that they verge on melodrama and thus femininity, whether crying at the loss of a loved one, shouting with a vow for vengeance at an enemy, or getting carried away in a love song dance number. Of course, this has always to some extent been a difficulty with popular Hindi song and dance films (such as those of the 1970s Angry Man era), but I believe the problem has become more complex in post-millennium films which now heavily model themselves specifically on the testosterone-driven machismo of contemporary Hollywood cinema.

In the contemporary Bollywood-Hollywood remake it is often the technical style of a film (editing, *mise-en-scène*, music, song lyrics) that dictates the 'coolness' of a character to the audience rather than the narrative. For example, in both *Fight Club: Members Only* and *Dhoom*, the male lead's coolness is not so much constructed through witty dialogue, acts of bravery or narrative scenarios as through flashy title credits, dramatic music, MTV-style editing and a costume and make-up modelled on the persona of Tom Cruise in the *Mission: Impossible* trilogy. In some instances, such as in *Fight Club: Members Only*, there is very little narrative or contextual evidence of a character's masculine-heroic traits (such as bravery, strength, courage). We are instead left to acknowledge this purely through the character's visual style (leather jackets, designer clothes, sun glasses, oiled muscles) and the technical façade surrounding him (obtrusive electric guitar music and beating drums, excessive slow motion effects, frantic MTV cutting and repeated extreme close-ups). What is more, with regard to the use of dialogue, American lingo is often incorporated into the script to assist the film character's 'cool' image. However, when spoken by the male lead, American terms are often mispronounced with a noticeably Hindi accent or misplaced within the wrong context, almost to the effect of bad caricature (as most self-consciously demonstrated in films such as *Tashan* – see below). This issue of the 'Indian cool' aesthetic could therefore be seen as another key reason for Bollywood cinema's failure to attract international audiences as it mimics and *mutates* certain familiar Hollywood gender codes. Contemporary Bollywood produces an altogether confused and inconsistent form of masculinity because the Western modes of gender representation it chooses to pastiche fundamentally clash with or counteract its own cinematic language.

KAANTE: EXPOSING CONVENTIONS

Returning to my discussion of the Bollywood-Hollywood remake as a parodic exposé of Hollywood conventions, one can find further examples of how this is effectively achieved through *Kaante*. The very techniques that mainstream American films would use to disguise the text-as-construct (such as the effacement of the camera), *Kaante* uses to bring artistic construct to the fore. For example, the bank robbery shoot-out scene between the Indian criminal gang and the LA cops is shot in a style familiar to the Hollywood action blockbuster (slow-motion gun-play, loud, rapid gunfire, fast-paced action music, high-rigged explosions). However, each element of this style, from the sound of gunfire to explosions and plausibility of stunts, is exaggerated. At one point in the film, the audience is presented with an assortment of over thirty-five consecutive shots of guns being seamlessly loaded and fired at random. The bank shoot-out sequence is padded with repetitively recycled shots and sound effects lasting so long that the impact of the action sequence is almost lost and reduced to a parody of the style itself. What is more, the climactic scene of the bank robbery consists of cameras positioned everywhere but at eye level. Several different images overlap and occupy the frame at once. Diagonal tilts, rapid zooms and distorted camera angles are used to follow the action, as well as several shots taken at floor level, inviting characters to jump directly over the camera. Once again the effect is not of realism, but of a drawing attention to the stylistic techniques of the action movie. Furthermore, during a gang meeting on a building rooftop, the use of a handheld camera (a cinematic tool usually used to create a sense of realism) is instead seemingly deliberately used out of context and purely for aesthetic purposes. The scene lacks the tension or heightened action that would normally require such a shot; instead it is used to follow the six protagonists as they engage in friendly banter. The same can be said of the use of jump cuts when one of the lead characters, Andy, is taken into police custody at the start of the film. There are no narrative breaks created by such a technique to leave spectators in suspense. Instead, the scene (which in real time lasts under a minute) uses four jump cuts which interrupt the moment from Andy being held by the police to being pushed into a police car. Thus again this cinematic technique is used purely for figural effect. The use of slow motion shots, hand-held cameras and jump-cutting is often misplaced and so excessive that these techniques effectively assert the unreality of the text and create a distancing-like effect between spectator and text.

When viewed at surface level, *Kaante* can appear as merely a cheapened blank pastiche of its acclaimed pseudo-original (which is itself a remake of Ringo Lam's 1987 film *City on Fire*). But at a deeper level, one can also find opportunity for its critical appreciation. By playing with Quentin Tarantino's trademark 'coolness' in such a way, *Kaante* becomes a mocking caricature. As the film text magnifies and exploits its modes of presentation, it exposes itself as a cinematic construct for the sake of spectacle and sensationalism. In *Kaante* we witness independent American cinema collapse into Bollywood, which effectively collapses into Hollywood, until it soon becomes difficult to distinguish between the opposing styles. Once again, as argued in the case of *Abhay*, this film remake's subversive and hybrid tendencies make it difficult to simply shoehorn it into film categories bound by nation or status as run-of-the-mill conventional Indian cinema.

HIJACKING HOLLYWOOD: DISSOLVING AMERICAN IDENTITY AND REVERSE COLONIALISM

Kaante is also interesting with regard to how it constructs Western identity. Despite being entirely set in Los Angeles, the film appears to refuse any accurate portrayal of America. The LA portrayed in this Bollywood remake is an America without Americans. It is never quite allowed to represent itself as a 'real' place with 'real' American people. Cityscape shots of LA consist of empty skyscrapers and deserted office blocks. American extras often have their backs to the camera, are blurred out entirely, or appear as caricatures – such as a bald, fat, tattooed, thuggish American drug dealer with a comic moustache who appears at the start of the film. Ironically, despite this absence of White American characters, *Kaante* remains extremely Americanised through its Indian actors and lead protagonists who are set up to represent American-ness more genuinely in the film: they speak and dress American, they effortlessly occupy an American lifestyle, and in effect, they simultaneously *overwrite* authentic American-ness in the process.

Rather than Otherising the West and placing it in *opposition* to Indian-ness, in *Kaante* American identity and Hollywood are hijacked and swallowed up by Bollywood in a process of *reverse colonialism*. Through such films, India fulfils a secret fantasy of switching places with its 'white man' coloniser. In many contemporary Bollywood films, it is now often the Indians who teach the Westerners how to live, the Indians who represent and evoke the 'American cool', the Indians who run American businesses, and the Indians who are called to rescue the West from external threats. Cross-cultural copycatting allows Western power to be 'translated' or transferred into the Indian context (Dudrah, 2006: 144) and the sheer excess of appropriating Hollywood aesthetics in such a way can be a (perhaps naive) attempt to weaken their very impact and power. As Thomas Leitch comments: 'The true remake admires its original so much it wants to annihilate it' (Leitch, cited in Mazdon: 4).[18]

New Bollywood has continued to produce even more explicit examples of this simultaneous masquerading and mockery of Hollywood styles. In *Tashan* (2008), we are presented with characters who seemingly aspire to look and speak like Westerners. The film's villain Bhaiyyaji is an underworld Don who is pertinently first seen standing in front of a giant mural of the Mona Lisa, being fitted for a new outfit by a group of foreign tailors. He is eclectically dressed in a black and white polka dot waistcoat, matching necktie, and a clashing striped red and black velvet jacket which still reveals its tacking stitches. As the film progresses, Bhaiyyaji's hybridised transformation is completed as he is also tutored to speak English. However, in a peculiar speech recital (a rendition of dialogue from cult Hindi film *Deewar* which is awkwardly translated into English) the end result is far from glamorous and his anglicised diction appears somewhat unsophisticated and ridiculous. Similarly, in the song 'Dil Dance Maare' we see the films' lead actors dressed almost in Western drag (Kareena Kapoor sponsoring a short tight PVC dress and blonde wig, Saif Ali Khan in a headband and spiked mullet, and Akshay Kumar in a ginger wig) as they literally sing about 'white white faces'. The sequence appears to simultaneously appropriate and ridicule Western dress codes, iconography, mannerisms and even dance styles.

Some have argued that films like *Kaante* and *Tashan* mark the end of Bollywood, claiming that the cinema has sold itself to the West through such modes of appropriation. However, I believe the cinema's shift is not towards Hollywood but towards a new globalised postmodern cinema aesthetic. Such films belong to a cinema that is not quite itself (Indian) or its Other (Western). Thus the Bollywood-Hollywood remake, with its lost or fragmented identity, becomes a classic case of what Ross Chambers (1990) describes as the 'remake alter-ego':

> The [remake] text defines itself by defining an intertext as that which it is not; and the text defines itself as 'text', in similarly negative fashion,

Figure 7.4: Bhaiyyaji's postmodern-esque makeover in *Tashan* (Yash Raj Films, 2008).

against its own discourse, with which it should not be identified. In each case then, no positive term can be identified: we can say only that the text is not its 'alter-ego', it is *not not-I*, whether 'not-I' is the intertext against which the text is defining itself, or the discourse that traverses it and from which it is 'distanced'. (143)

Kaante's cross-cultural referencing is an example of Bollywood endorsing the 'naïve confusion' of American culture as a universal concern (Forrest and Koos, 2002: 28). However, as Richard Dyer notes with regard to cinematic pastiche: 'Closeness to the forms of the colonising culture may feel perilously like voluntarily ceding to its previously imposed authority, yet the act of pastiching is also always an affirmation of the position of the pasticheur ... it may form part of a politics of undermining and overthrow or also one of consolation' (Dyer, 2006: 157). McFarlane and Dudrah have both also attempted to determine the outcome of this remake rhetoric. From McFarlane's perspective, the sheer excess of appropriating Hollywood/American aesthetics in this way concurrently weakens their impact, influence and power (McFarlane: 145), while for Dudrah, Homi Bhabha's notion of cultural mimicry can be applied to further explain Bollywood's critical engagement with Western mainstream modes of filmmaking. In mimicking the Western-Other, the Other's colonial authority is visualised, disrupted and unmasked. Dudrah sees this act of copycatting as a strategy in which Western difference and power can be 'translated' into the Indian context (Dudrah, 2006: 144). In *Kaante*, the Indian film industry's fantasy of 'being like Hollywood' is realised in order to dislodge, if not eliminate its Western superior.[19] This form of mimicry is thus a symptom of the remake's ambivalent feelings of adoration and abhorrence towards its predecessor – its intimacy and distantiation, valorisation and denial, and ultimately, its *disavowal* of its counterpart (see Leitch in Forrest and Koos: 53).

Bollywood has indeed been influenced by American mainstream cinema, but such an 'effectively indigenised form [also] functions on its own terms, continuing to absorb and *transform* the foreign fertilizer fed to it' (Binford, 1998: 82, emphasis added). *Kaante* becomes one of the best examples of a postmodern Bollywood cinematic movement which 'interrogates the status quo of cinema' (Virdi, 2003: 211). The film illustrates contemporary Bollywood's potential to be critically evaluative not only of itself, but also other forms of dominant cinema. Ironically it seems that the very cinema which Western critics and audiences still consider to be too exclusive or different can in fact provide an interesting commentary on universalised modes of cinematic presentation. By studying hybrid remakes like *Kaante*, we can think beyond criticisms of contemporary Bollywood texts as simply 'flawed' filmmaking and instead embrace this fragmented mess of texts as enabling us to view Hollywood (and Bollywood) cinematic techniques in a new and *critical* light.

CONCLUSION

Through this study of Bollywood remakes, I have shown how intrinsic remaking, repetition, intertextuality and reflexivity are to Indian filmmaking, and therefore why they require more critical attention in Indian film studies. Popular Indian cinema has always been engaged in cultural borrowing and textual appropriation. However, through my analysis of newer Bollywood texts, we can see that contemporary Bollywood is utilising these strategies more consciously, critically and progressively. Remaking and intertextuality (in their many forms) have moved from being occasional devices used intermittently for the sake of novelty, and instead now serve as signature characteristics of Bollywood filmmaking in the twenty-first century (prevalent, though by no means ubiquitous). Remaking is without doubt a dominant phenomenon of contemporary Bollywood cinema.

The very fact that Bollywood is not successfully held back by copyright laws has allowed the remake and cross-cultural referencing to flourish in India. Copyright laws do exist and apply to the industry, but the legal proceedings against Bollywood films copying foreign texts are still rare, often inconclusive, or ineffective (see Raghavendra [2002] and Govil et al. [2005]).[20] The attraction to cross-cultural referencing has increased as a result of the Indian consumer and film industry becoming more globalised. The majority of film remakes I have identified through my research appear post-millennium and have been produced as high-concept productions with A-list stars and generous financial backing. Many of these films have been promoted and distributed through global marketing and, at the very least, produced with the *expectation* of high box-office returns.

There are so many arbitrary moments of remaking within contemporary Indian cinema that it is difficult to account for all of these myriad processes here. Furthermore, the degree to which a text borrows and remakes another will vary from film to film. Nevertheless, it is clear from the selection of remakes I have explored that many of these newer films have an affinity towards certain modes of referencing. Pre-2000 Bollywood-Hollywood remakes may have predominantly tended to borrow and '(H)Indianise' elements of the narrative, plot and storyline of the original work (as noted by Nayar and Ganti, and as seen in the earlier films of Vikram Bhatt) but those of the 2000 decade are more so inclined towards pastiche, parody and mimicking the visual style of other texts. Even if its story may remain more or less intact when remade, the foreign-original text may now alter or readjust the visual dynamics of Hindi film. A Bollywood film may have an original script, yet still blatantly evoke films like *The Matrix* or *Mission: Impossible* through its visual iconography and coding.

Bollywood's recent urge to remake films can primarily be explained through issues of accessibility and translation. As Bazin explains, the adaptation text as 'digest' makes its original more accessible to its audience not by simplifying it, but by presenting it through a different mode of expression. In Bollywood's case, the remake text alters the film lingo to better suit the Indian audience. It is, as Bazin crudely describes the process of adaptation, 'as if the aesthetic fat, differently emulsified, were better tolerated by the consumer's mind' (Bazin: 26). But it is not enough to assume that this need for the 'digestion' of Western texts by Bollywood is a simple issue of language barriers or cultural incoherences. Rather, I believe that these Bollywood remakes have sprung from the Indian audience's need for different methods of enunciation; that is, figural excess providing greater levels of emotion and sensation, as well as their growing demand for novelty. In the case of the former, there appears to be a need to transfer what is literal into the figural as images and symbolism elicit more pleasure than merely discursive storytelling. In the case of the latter, the experimentalism and commercial success of new remakes may be a sign of the coming-of-age of the modernised, globalised, multiplex-going Indian cinema audience. Filmmakers have begun to realise that their audience is becoming more tolerant of (or attracted by) Westernised iconography and conventions,[21] unlike in the past where these would be the first things to be changed and considered alienating and inappropriate (see Ganti, 2002). I would therefore assert that foreign texts are now less in need of '(H)Indianization' in the way that Ganti suggested of 1990s Bollywood cinema. Rather than seeing remaking as purely a process of reactionary filmmaking (keeping it all 'Indian'), I suggest that it can also doubly serve as a way of *liberating* Bollywood cinema and its audiences.

Of course, adjustments to an original text's storyline do still occur and often in order to accommodate Indian ethics and censorship (for example, as in the case of *Zinda*, where the oedipal-twist ending of *Oldboy*, seen as too problematic, is replaced with a portrayal of the 'immoral' Bangkok virgin sex trade). In some senses, Bollywood can never justifiably reproduce other foreign texts owing to its deep rooted differences in terms of its film language, but this goes even further to support the fact that these films should rarely be seen as plagiarisms but rather reinventions. One could argue that a film such as Arthur Penn's *Bonnie and Clyde* can never be remade in Bollywood owing to the fundamental sensibilities which Indian cinema and its audience rely upon: the film cannot be without colour, dishonest and sinful heroes must repent, even the anti-heroes' motives must be morally justified, and the favoured protagonists must live. Thus, in *Bunty aur Babli*, the realist and gritty style that lay at Penn's original text's core is transformed into a colourful tongue-in-cheek rom-com caper, to the extent at that the film bears little or no resemblance to its original and becomes an as-good-as-original in its own right. As Horton and McDougal observe, film remakes 'constitute a particular territory existing somewhere between unabashed larceny and subtle originality' and even 'problematize the very notion of originality' (Horton and McDougal: 4). With this in mind, there is *always* a sense of failure that accompanies the Bollywood-Hollywood remake.

Looking over my list of contemporary Bollywood remakes, we can see a pattern of key attributes that provide further reasons for the recent boom in cross-cultural remakes in addition to those mentioned above. Many of the original films carry some form of critical credibility in the West, either as award winners (*Reservoir Dogs*, *Oldboy*, *The Miracle Worker*, *The Godfather*) or much talked about repeat-view-friendly cult movies (*Fight Club*). Many of the referenced texts have also been celebrated for their shock plot-twists (*The Usual Suspects*, *What Lies Beneath*, *Matchstick Men*, *U-Turn*, *The Gift*). These are all features in short supply in an industry that has a reputation for struggling to commit to pre-scripted film production. Furthermore, many of these remade films borrow from supernatural thrillers (*Powder*, *The Gift*), Horrors (*The Ring*, *The Eye*) or the sci-fi superhero film (*E.T.*, *Superman*, *The Matrix*, *Daredevil*), suggesting that Bollywood is using remaking as a way of pushing itself towards catering for genres that are not as readily or easily produced through its traditional filmmaking formula. As such, this remaking has possibly led to an increase in murder-mystery films (*36 China Town* and *Murder*) and disability-dramas such as *Black* and *Main Aisa Hi Hoon*. I have also discussed how another attraction to sourcing Hollywood texts lies in the masculine-oriented stories and perspectives they offer, which perhaps the usual masala melodrama cannot fulfil. Film remakes like *Kaante*, *Fight Club: Members Only*, *Zinda*, *Ek Ajnabee* and *Sarkar* all borrow from texts which focus on male characters. Each of these films evoke masculine styles and sensibilities and more noticeably have absent or redundant female characters. Male camaraderie, machismo, revenge, repentance, alcoholism, patriarchal politics, danger, daringness, father–son relationships and betrayal are the more central themes of these films. This is not to suggest that movie remaking is purely a masculine field in Bollywood (there has also been a series of romantic movies and 'chick-flick' remakes during this period including *My Best Friend's Wedding*, *Heartbreakers* and *Meet John Doe*) but that it is used in abundance when producing male-oriented genres.

There is also a particular pleasure and gratification to be found in the act or experience of cross-cultural translation itself. This unique pleasure is exemplified through the prior examples of reverse colonialism via cultural mimicry, and through the fact that Indian audiences thrive on seeing Bollywood film personae hybridise with those in the West. They enjoy seeing Amitabh Bachchan as Marlon Brando (*Sarkar*), Shah Rukh Khan as Tom Cruise (*Main Hoon Na*), or Hrithik Roshan as Batman (*Krrish*). Just as Western spectators superimpose their faces onto their on-screen heroes in the theatre auditorium, Indian audiences doubly enjoy viewing the superimposition of their national heroes onto global iconic heroes. Given this form of cinematic hybridisation, it is clear that the Hindi remake text offers its audiences a unique pleasure that it could not produce, were it an original.

The Bollywood remake texts explored above offer us insight into how cross-cultural referencing can impact upon genre, film form, and audiences. They demonstrate how the term 'remake' is in fact a complex variable, and as such, cannot be exclusively detained within a dogma of crystal-clear authorial intent and institutional endorsement. As to whether these films should be regarded as quotation or plagiarism, I would argue that they are at once both and neither. A postmodern perspective would suggest that they enter as plagiarism, but once engaged with they become quotations, if not *reinventions*. As seen in the case of *DCH*, contemporary Bollywood cinema, in appropriating its own past cinematic styles, will sometimes mock or critique its traditional conventions in order to differentiate itself. This pastiche is its way of distancing itself from the very past conventions it continues to remain trapped within. It utilises postmodern methods in order to strive to say something new within a vernacular of the old.

It is clear from the range of texts discussed in this book that the level of recognition or acknowledgement of a film remake is particular to each film. In some cases a spectator may be forced to recognise a momentary reference (such as the rickshaw sequence in *Main Hoon Na*). In others, a blatant remake can pass unnoticed owing to the obscurity or lack of exposure and circulation of the original (*Zinda*), and in the case of texts which borrow *style* rather than narrative (such as *Dhoom*), the recognition of a film's original influence is subconscious. Many would argue that the average film-illiterate cinemagoer in India remains oblivious to the complexity of film referencing present in the contemporary Indian cross-cultural remake. However, I would argue that as film consumption in India moves towards the multiplexes, and as Indian cinema itself becomes more sophisticated and experimental in its pursuit of international success, this may not necessarily be the case for long. Even if the film remakes mentioned are produced with naivety and no active intent for conscious cross-cultural critique, and even if these texts are anticipated as unacknowledged references for the sake of simple pastiche or fast-track film-making, there is still potential for a writerly reading by an active spectator. At the very least, for its globalised multiplex audience (those with access to a broad consumption of different cinematic products), the Bollywood remake offers a schizophrenic reading experience and two kinds of viewing pleasure: that which comes through a position of voluntary suspension of disbelief, and that which comes through witnessing and indulging in the cross-cultural collision of multifarious cinematic forms.

Remaking is widespread in contemporary Bollywood cinema and yet it still requires affirmation as it does not quite fit into the remake categories currently available to us. So what existing adaptation categories does the Bollywood remake genre most closely fall into? Geoffrey Wagner's three categorisations accounting for the different forms of adaptation are useful here. Certainly, the Indian remake can never fit his first category of 'transposition', which involves a direct transposition with minimal interference (Wagner, cited in McFarlane: 10). With the Indian remake, there is always a distinctive difference from its foreign original (especially in terms of affect), even when things seem almost identical (such as the shot-for-shot replication in *Zinda*). With regard to his second category of 'commentary' – where the original is purposely altered or 'violated' for the filmmakers' different agenda (ibid.) – Bollywood remakes clearly lack the required level of subversive intent to be regarded as social commentary. However, if we interpret this category to concern not social reform, but rather a politics of representation, then it becomes possible to view these remakes as a form of *discourse* (Andrew: 37), regardless of whether their message arrives through intention or interpretation. Wagner's third category concerning a textual adaptation's departure from its original 'for the sake of art' is perhaps closest to the real agenda. But yet again this notion is problematic if the kind of artistic integrity referred to here is restricted to traditional Western perceptions of art. Ultimately, it seems that the Bollywood remake's agenda sits and shifts simultaneously between profit and capital, exploitation, cultural-political commentary, a postmodern art-for-art's sake sensibility, and *accident*.

Although the current output of remakes may be masterful in their visual design and effects, there appears to be something deeper rooted in the films' style and semiotics that may further repel and alienate the Western eye. Perhaps, as suggested with *Devdas*, some cannot endure the emotional voltage of the cinema and its increasingly exposed stylisation. Perhaps some audiences, who are more favourable towards familiar cinematic representations of realism, are unable to stomach fantasy unless it is situated in some form of simulated logic or reality. They may struggle to be persuaded by the Indian-cool aesthetic. Their ability to engage with the text may become difficult when the visual cues on offer and the reading-logic required for the Bollywood text contradict or clash with their own. Even in cases where a film such as *Zinda* adopts a seemingly identical story and visual set-up, Bollywood still produces divergent levels of emotion, tone, narrative pacing and story chronology which may alienate Western audiences.[22] The resemblance of the Indian remake to its original is often uncanny – familiar yet very different. This uncanniness makes the Bollywood remake all the more unsettling and may contribute to the ongoing negative reactions by some non-indigenous audiences to this particular mode of filmmaking. With this in mind, there is clearly value in Indian film studies investigating non-Indian spectators' responses to Bollywood cinema – particularly towards those texts which are remakes of films that they have previously enjoyed or held in high regard. It would also be interesting to investigate what would need to be changed in order for a Bollywood original to be suitably remade or officially franchised for Western audiences – particularly if the Bollywood product offers differentiation more through genre or style rather than narrative content. Although this kind of remake has yet to manifest, there is evidence of interest: for example, Twentieth Century Fox's 2005 purchase of the Bollywood film script for *Munna Bhai MBBS* may eventually see the West conversely adapting an Indian text into a Hollywood comedy.[23] These kinds of further studies can help us better understand the barriers and differences in Bollywood and Hollywood filmmaking and such a polarisation of audience viewing processes.

Devaluations of Bollywood remakes as 'rip-offs' and 'cheap imitations' carry with them a certain level of ignorance. These negative stigmatisations are 'loaded with Western signs and meanings of power' and can be seen to imperialistically mark 'Other' cultures as 'inferior' (Dudrah, 2006: 142). Indeed, there is a certain level of threat involved here, particularly due to the inability to police Indian cinema's level of appropriation or prevent Bollywood texts from presenting their borrowed material as organic or indigenous elements of the cinema. Furthermore, as I have suggested, once films such as *The Matrix*, *Mission: Impossible 2* and *Reservoir Dogs* have been manipulated, mutated and exposed through Bollywood remaking, a certain level of lost aura (an original text's authenticity and distinctiveness) can take place as a consequence. For some Indian spectators, Hollywood codes, once consumed through parody or pastiche, may no longer be as monolithic. Tarantino's cool aesthetic may no longer retain the same level of wonder once seen in exaggerated form in an indigenous film like *Kaante*. Worton and Still have commented on the remake's simultaneous eroticism and violence, stating that 'the object of an act of influence . . . does not receive or perceive that pressure as neutral' (2). In the contemporary Bollywood remake intertextuality is at once seductive and destructive, appealing and repulsive, and the text aims to both appropriate and *resist* its indigenised style.

The remake phenomenon has also caused Bollywood to lose its own identity in terms of its traditional formal style and conventions. The lack of controlling or successfully sanctioning appropriation in Indian films has led remaking to proliferate so much that it now forms part of Bollywood cinema's generic identity. It has become increasingly difficult to separate and distinguish borrowed foreign styles and techniques from the normative style of contemporary Bollywood texts. Bollywood mainstream cinema is in a state of flux where a *bricolage* of multiple genres, styles and conventions continue to cancel out or invalidate one another. The remake is the prime example of the current identity collapse of Bollywood cinema; however, it also paradoxically signals the beginnings of a new form of cinema.

Although the above remake films may at times question the integrity of contemporary Bollywood films and (perhaps naively) pose a threat to Hollywood, the postmodern Bollywood cross-cultural remake nevertheless offers us new ways of investigating our own familiar positions of spectatorship and our own modes of filmmaking:

> . . . a postmodern artist has no other way to 'interview' reality but through an interpreter of another culture . . . the cultures must vary . . . [but] in any case, the remake remains a metacultural medium that has to cross borders, temporal or spatial in order to connect. (Brashinsky, 1998: 169–70)

The film remake should not be underestimated, for it too is a 'species of interpretation' (Braudy, 1998: 327), and it is only in its self-destructive state (as a remake) that the Bollywood text can begin to critically pull apart not only its own, but other more universalised cinematic techniques, such as those of Hollywood. In contemporary Bollywood, Hollywood cinema is 'recast to fit the nuances and developments in the cultural landscape of popular Hindi cinema's audiences' (Dudrah, 2006: 146). However, simultaneously, Bollywood too is being recast and remoulded to fit the international market. This circular process has resulted in the production of an ultimately confused, fragmented, schizophrenic, postmodern-esque form of self-destructive Indian cinema. Ironically, despite their countless moments of borrowing, intertextual referencing and blatant plagiarism, these contemporary cross-cultural remakes serve as examples of Bollywood filmmaking at its most inventive and innovative – a classic case of art renewing itself through creative mistranslation (Stam: 62).

NOTES

1. Although several filmic versions preceded Roy's film, the success and critical acclaim of this particular remake heralded it as a 'classic', and the film is often regarded by many as the Indian film industry's original adaptation of Saratchandra Chattopadhyaya's 1917 novel (Chattopadhyaya, 1917).
2. The term refers to social realism in Indian cinema, encompassing films which depicted the harsh realities of urban life, such as poverty and famine, and the feudal roots of India's patriarchal society.
3. See reviews of the film in *Sight and Sound* (Ramachandran, 2002), *Screen International* (Johnston, 2002), *Variety* (Elley, 2002) and India's *Trade Guide* (Unauthored, 2002). See also Freer (2002), Laight (2002), Lall (2002), Nair (2002), Singhal (2002).
4. Dwyer goes on to complain of the way in which Hungary is used as a location replacement for Italy in the film, without any attempt to conceal or disguise its characteristic scenery or landmarks.
5. These terms feature significantly in the film's 'curtain edition' DVD and vox pops taken from audiences after viewing the film at the Cannes Film Festival (DVD special feature: 'World premiere at Cannes').
6. Indeed, the notion of a figural cinema is not a new one, but Lash explains how the function and authority of images are amplified in peculiar ways in postmodern films.
7. Lash identifies this shift to a postmodern cinema of spectacle as beginning with the commercial cinema of the late 1960s, although his article largely focuses on Hollywood films from the 1980s.
8. Indeed, one could take this aesthetic excess as a clear opening statement of intent that the film will not be faithful to its original.
9. As noted in 'The making of *Devdas*' note on the film's official website (devdas.indiatimes.com).
10. The film's abundant use of echoes and surround sound could also be seen to assist this excess, giving a sense of the grand scope and scale of the film's wide narrative space (Sergi: 147).
11. From 'An interview with Dilip Kumar' in the DVD of Bimal Roy's *Devdas* (1955).
12. A traditional sarong-like men's garment consisting of a piece of fabric that is wrapped around the waist and legs.
13. Contemporary Bollywood's investment in stereoscopic 3D cinema began with *Haunted 3D* (2011) and has continued with the releases of *Don 2* (2011), *Ra.One* (2011), *Raaz 3* (2012), *Dangerous Issqh* (2012), *Bhoot Returns* (2012), animation film *Delhi Safari* (2012) and a digitally altered rerelease of cult classic *Sholay* (2014).
14. Some of Varma's reflexive work that I have listed here precedes the contemporary period I am investigating, and it is clear that certain kinds of self-reflexivity manifest earlier on in Bollywood's film history. However, again, what I wish to stress here is that there is a significantly heightened and concentrated use of self-reflexive devices in the film industry's post-millennium era.
15. These subtle hints at Khan's iconic celebrity status are clearly abundant as demonstrated in *Om Shanti Om* and discussed further in the following chapter.

16. The term refers to intertextual referencing via a film's graphic or title credits (see Genette, 1982).
17. It is important to stress here that *Zinda* does not mirror the camera work of its original as perfectly as, for example, Gus Van Sant's 1998 remake of Alfred Hitchcock's *Psycho*. What is more, even in its moments of closest replication there is an irrefutable difference in emotional tone and pacing – something which I address at the end of the chapter.
18. The intent and process here are almost counter-cinematic, but unlike the avant-garde work of Jean-Luc Godard (Wollen, 1986), such a technique is not intended to be as destructive or dissatisfying for the audience (and is therefore relatively unnoticed and under-appreciated).
19. To clarify, this attempted overshadowing occurs at a textual level. I describe this as a fantasy as I do not wish to suggest that Bollywood actually achieves global dominance in reality. But as I explain, there may be an eventual impact in terms of the way some Bollywood audiences perceive or decode Hollywood aesthetics.
20. However, Twentieth Century Fox's 2009 $200,000 court settlement for a Bollywood plagiarisation of *My Cousin Vinny* has suggested that this situation is slowly changing (see Wax, 2009) and that more Bollywood filmmakers are opting to buy rights for Hollywood films (see Bhatti, 2010).
21. The fact that Bollywood films now incorporate non-chronological narratives, as in box-office hits like *Chocolate: Deep Dark Secrets*, *Saatiya* and *Ghajini*, further confirms this new level of tolerance.
22. We have yet to develop appropriate strategies to help us adequately measure, analyse and illustrate the differences in variables such as tone and pace in cross-cultural remaking.
23. The film was to be remade as Hollywood production *Gangsta M.D.*, starring Chris Tucker and directed by Mira Nair, but the project was subsequently abandoned.

CHAPTER 8

Conclusion: A Bollywood Renaissance?

Throughout this book, I have aimed to demonstrate some of the fundamental and peculiar ways in which Bollywood cinema has formally changed after its economic liberalisation at the turn of the twenty-first century. All the film texts I have analysed, which spring from this millennium period, incorporate some form of aesthetic enterprise serving the principles and traits of the postmodern. My case studies have verified that Bollywood, as well as being global and transnational, has reached a postmodern stage and that this postmodern tendency has enabled the cinema to adopt new critical tools (such as self-critique and dismantling the authority of other dominant cinematic forms), thereby offering up new ways of reading Bollywood.

We have explored how certain aspects of Bollywood filmmaking, previously regarded as primitive, formulaic or mediocre, have become the very attributes fuelling Bollywood's creativity and artistic experimentation today. Figural excess and hyperrealism are two such devices at the core of New Bollywood's unique cinematic language, which enable the cinema to operate differently as an art form and film language. I have elaborated on how these rather complex traits function to provide a particular kind of pleasure and experience for their audiences, such as offering access to sublime emotions, a greater level of submersion in the text, multi-dimensional perspectives and synaesthesia, whilst also demonstrating how these traits may be the very aspects of Bollywood cinema that lead to increased displeasure for the Western critic or spectator, and ultimately obstruct the cinema's ability to perform well critically or commercially in other parts of the world.

This book has also challenged the common assumption that contemporary Bollywood cinema still works to maintain and preserve a pure sense of Indian national identity and cultural tradition by having these conflict with and prevail over representations of the 'modern' and the 'West' as Other. I have demonstrated how, in newer films, clear distinctions between modern/

traditional, East/West and Western/Indian no longer stand. Bollywood films no longer exclusively work to unambiguously serve certain socio-political or nationalist sentiments. Instead, they now actively seek to blur or intersect these binaries in order to produce an altogether fragmented, dismantled and often contradictory representation of global Indian identity.

Further to the above, I have also revealed how these post-millennial films embrace a dissolving of distinctions between, and an alignment of, Hollywood and Bollywood formal aesthetics. Particularly in the case of films such as *Kaante*, these two cinemas' filmic conventions overlap and almost cancel one another out, often with the intended effect of depriving Hollywood of its lustre. American cinema may lose its brilliance once Indian viewers witness a dimming of the effect of its most revered conventions, such as its Tarantino-esque masculine 'cool' aesthetic, its cutting-edge special effects, its fast-paced dramatic editing techniques, or its verisimilitude. By appropriating, mimicking, parodying, pastiching and dismantling these characteristics, Bollywood endeavours to overshadow the significance of Hollywood, attempting to block out its global dominance – a process which I have described as a kind of cinematic *reverse colonialism*.

This book has given much attention to the process of remaking – a signature characteristic of noughties Bollywood that continues to receive much international criticism. In analysing the diverse ways in which Bollywood remakes reference other material, I have argued against the claim that remaking is purely a means of plagiarism in Bollywood, and therefore something to be expelled from 'faithful' definitions of the cinema. My case studies have instead presented remaking as contemporary Bollywood's most significant and effective means of achieving creative innovation. Remaking has been a prevailing feature of Bollywood cinema in the noughties, so much so that it has operated as a genre in its own right. Textual recycling in Bollywood does not work as before, but has evolved. It is now being used as a self-reflexive device, an indicator of Bollywood's current situation as a cinema at once escaping from and imprisoned by its formulaic roots (as exemplified most explicitly in the case of *Om Shanti Om*). In postmodern fashion, film remakes paradoxically allow Bollywood to achieve change and progress via repetition and the past. Remaking thus proves to have both creative and destructive implications for Bollywood, on the one hand assisting creativity (and offering audiences a unique kind of reading and viewing pleasure), and on the other, self-destructively marking the cinema's loss of authentic originality and distinctive identity as it shifts to a new era of endless postmodern parodic production.

As with other established postmodern texts, parodic reflexivity in newer Bollywood films 'becomes the way – possibly the only way – to inform contemporary creativity' (Degli-Eposti, 10). Particularly with regard to its remake phenomenon, Bollywood's 'activities of replication . . . have turned into a real "pleasure of repetition" for which everyone can enjoy a different kind of experience where the practice of replication melts into a multiplicity of signifying worlds' (ibid.: 13). Thus it seems that, to paraphrase an important point made by Lyotard, contemporary Bollywood too can only be modern by first being postmodern. It has become a cinema which accesses the new and modern by creatively pastiching, borrowing, recycling and *reworking* rather than by inventing something wholly original.

USING POSTMODERNISM TO UNDERSTAND CONTEMPORARY INDIAN CINEMA

My investigation has highlighted several problems with regard to prevalent attitudes towards and perceptions of contemporary Bollywood. The cinema's recent global shift may have brought a rise in its international profile, but this has also resulted in a diminishing of its artistic reputation. I have explained how many critics and scholars of Indian cinema have viewed its current phase as its downfall, marking a decline in the cinema's production of sophisticated and original films in favour of mass-produced, sensationalist and trivial reproductions. Bollywood's global economic restructuring has been accused of obscuring, darkening or extinguishing the credibility of Indian cinema, so much that it has sometimes been described in extreme terms as having run out of ideas and as a cinema at its end. There is indeed something affecting Bollywood cinema in a way that causes it temporarily to lose its grasp of 'authentic' Indian-ness and traditionalist modes of representation. However, as I have argued, this postmodern veil that has been cast over the film industry has obscured our understanding of popular Indian cinema, but as such, it works refreshingly to obstruct (and challenge) older models of Indian film criticism, instead encouraging us to seek and offer new perspectives, definitions and approaches to the cinema.

As Degli-Esposti has duly noted, there are multiple ways in which images can be perceived as postmodern, and many 'different perspectives on what can be defined as postmodern filmic expression' (14). My investigation into contemporary Bollywood cinema has helped to illustrate the fact that postmodernism is not simply a predicament of Euro-American and First World high-tech Asian societies, but a *global* phenomenon that can be applied to less developed non-Western cultures. (Ultimately, postmodernism cannot be constrained by its West-centric, capitalism-driven definitions as this defeats the very concept of border crossing on which it depends.) Through this global prism, we are able to witness postmodern art's dissolving of grand narratives and binaries on an escalated scale. Postmodern films are not purely a marginal phenomenon produced by a small selection of surrealist mainstream *auteurs*.

Rather, I have revealed how postmodernism has come to shape the fundamental characteristics of an entirely new genus of popular cinema consumed by millions worldwide. In India, postmodern aesthetics are being used to facilitate global and cultural exchange and have become part of the film industry's international economic operations. Postmodernism is thus by no means an exhausted concept. It can be viewed in new contexts as something that is always evolving and diversifying in both form and application.

We need to consider more seriously the value of using postmodern theory to study contemporary shifts in Indian popular cinema, particularly its potential to help broaden the cinema's definitions, accessibility and applicability in Western academic film studies programmes. Instead of leaving students with an acute, outmoded or pessimistic understanding of global Bollywood cinema, postmodern analysis may help illuminate how and why Indian cinema aesthetics choose to operate and provide pleasure in ways that may at first seem vulgar or insincere. As I have shown, this postmodern perspective helps us to view the effectiveness of Indian popular cinema through its aesthetic dimensions, rather than simply through its discursive frameworks and socio-political rationale – allowing us to appreciate Bollywood as an art form in its own right. A heightened appreciation of the artistic practices of New Bollywood also calls us to rethink or reconfigure the universal discourses and processes we would normally use to value 'good' cinema, as they now appear problematic, particularly as regards their overvalued obsession with cultural authenticity.

As I have sought to show, the level of postmodern sensibilities in Bollywood varies from text to text. In some situations it is a case of actively applying a postmodern reading strategy to a text in order to speculate on the transgressive potential a certain film may have if read by particular audiences in particular ways in specific contexts, whilst in others it is filmmakers themselves (such as Farah Khan) who are *intentionally* seeking to achieve postmodern ends. Naturally, there are always problems when applying any Western-born condition to a non-Western culture, and in the case of postmodernism a certain level of resistance comes with the territory. Many will continue to find my postmodern application objectionable for its danger of making Western values appear universally applicable. Comparisons between Hollywood and Bollywood are particularly prone to this kind of criticism, although simply denying the cross-cultural exchange going on between these cinemas is not an ideal solution either. Certainly, if the aesthetic conventions of Hollywood are being 'normalised' by Bollywood, these cinemas may also begin to overlap in terms of their intentions, effects, goals and agendas. This normalisation of foreign conventions may even eventually start to have financial implications for Hollywood films in India as the elements of American cinema, which would normally offer product differentiation in order to attract Indian multiplex audiences, are already being appropriated and supplied by Bollywood films (if in somewhat subversive ways). Such a process also has cultural and political implications. In these hybrid productions, Indian-ness is displaced as the visual and stylistic codes that would normally mark cultural distinctions between 'American' and 'Indian' are merged, confused and broken down. The inclusion and indigenisation of Hollywood stylistic traits in Indian films is also a political act on Bollywood's part to critique American filmmaking practices and attempt to overshadow this hegemonic Western cinema. Through this process of cultural appropriation, Bollywood instead asserts its own (imagined) authority as a globally dominant cinema.

The Bollywood features I have identified as postmodern are such because they share certain intentions and purposes associated with other postmodern (Western) texts, but that is not to say that these intentions do not also serve other purposes specific to Indian cinema. In the films I have analysed, these postmodern devices have the effect of questioning modes of representation (reality, identity) and dismantling or obscuring grand narratives like religion, science, nation, Indian-ness and Hollywood. The films openly address and draw attention to their own textuality and thus their status as mass produced, manufactured commodities. They help provide a commentary on how Bollywood cinema is trapped in a cycle of repetition, unable to be authentic, original or novel in the purest sense. They help celebrate and stage the saturation and circulation of images in Indian society. They reinforce the dominance of the figural and the redundancy of the discursive. They take acclaimed 'artistic' works and turn them into profit-and-capital commodities (mainly through remaking) and in doing so cause us to question institutionalised, universalised value judgements regarding cinematic art. They retaliate against fixed categories and identities, instead presenting more fragmented versions of the self which perhaps better account for Indians' experiences in the current global consumer climate.

REDEFINING CONTEMPORARY BOLLYWOOD

I have examined how and why Bollywood filmmaking in the first decade of the twenty-first century needs to be differentiated from previous eras. Both filmmakers and audiences have become much more open to novelty and aesthetic experimentation, though not entirely in a way that does away with past conventions and formulas. There may no longer be a prominent parallel or alternative art cinema in India, but I have explained how there is nevertheless a different kind of challenging, radical experimentation and disruptive playfulness being generated from within mainstream Indian cinema itself. Popular Indian films too have the ability to question and unveil established modes of cinematic presentation. By dismantling formulas and conventions, and by adopting inventive avant-garde techniques, they are able to render authenticity and the 'real' suspect. Often consciously inauthentic (particularly through their abundant appetite for appropriation), they can take a more ambiguous approach to Indian culture, tradition, identity and the past. Contemporary Bollywood texts are also often self-critical, mocking their own fictional customs while simultaneously exploiting them for profit – thus drawing attention to themselves as manufactured commercial commodities.

On the basis of this book's investigation, we can reformulate our understanding and description of contemporary popular Indian filmmaking as follows. Post-millennial Bollywood films are often marked by a highly cosmetic visual set-up, fetishised supermodel film stars, and a visceral, excessively figural style – including ornamented frames, image-layering techniques (that sometimes dispense with perspective), and a vivid, saturated use of colour. More is conveyed through images and synaesthesia than through discursive devices such as story or dialogue. The kind of picturesque imagery previously reserved for song sequences (which are now sometimes absent from the text) now features throughout the film, irrespective of the situation or context of a scene. Through this figural excess, Bollywood films achieve a kind of hyper-realism which conveys sublime experiences and emotions that realist or traditional cinematic modes of presentation fail to provide. New Bollywood films also exhibit a heightened interest in self-conscious technical experimentation, drawing attention to their use of special effects, CGI, animation, fluid camera work, rapid editing, dramatic lighting and sound design. These films also mark a departure from masala filmmaking in favour of packaging into blatant genre categories familiar to the West: science-fiction, the gangster film, the heist film, the horror film, the action movie. However, even within these genre categories, Bollywood still maintains a kind of eclecticism, particularly by utilising *bricolage*, a schizophrenic style, and modes of presentation which may depart from generic labelling.

Contemporary Bollywood is also marked by its increased production of film remakes, which are so abundant that they occupy a genre all on their own. This remake genre indulges a distinct kind of audience pleasure (cinephilia) and employs a broad yet distinctive set of appropriation techniques. Contemporary Bollywood's remakes engage in a dialogue with (and investigate) both foreign and the Indian film industry's own cinematic histories, and it is evident that Bollywood has used its remakes as a means of constructing its own mythic film canon.

The above changes all go hand in hand with the cinema's recent increased sexual openness, its penchant for big-budget wealth and luxury, and its trend for global travelling, as discussed by scholars who have already published on this latest phase of filmmaking. In the case of the first of these, we need only look at Bipasha Basu's bikinis and transparent outfits in *Dhoom* and *Body*

Heat/Double Indemnity remake *Jism*, Aishwarya Rai's dominatrix persona in *Dhoom 2*,[1] Shah Rukh Khan's satirical wet dream in *Om Shanti Om*, and the topicality of sex before marriage, homosexuality, divorce and adultery in *Salaam Namaste*, *Dostana*, *KANK* and *Murder* respectively, to see that films have become more sexually charged and risqué. However, in the case of the travelling global Indian trait (usually explored academically in the form of the diasporic hero) I would add that New Bollywood no longer purely focuses its attention on the NRI. Given the aforementioned aspirations and empowering motives of the Bollywood-backed India Poised campaign, the notable indigenisation and normalisation of Hollywood conventions, and the fragmented identities offered in contemporary films, it is clear that the industry's audience targets are no longer primarily fixated on the diaspora. New Bollywood also draws attention to the fragmented, modernised Indian in India. Since India is now often presented as modern and urbanised, and the West is represented by Indians (albeit in Western drag), our existing ideas of how the Indian, the NRI, the Western, the modern, and the traditional present themselves in contemporary Indian films need to be reviewed once more. Postmodern Bollywood texts enable us to move beyond the near-exhaustive post-1990s discussions surrounding Bollywood's fascination with national identity preservation and diaspora.

The post-millennium decade could be described as a renaissance period for popular Indian cinema – an apt term, given how this change has been achieved partly through the rebirth of old styles, the reincarnation of other texts, and the reinvention of past conventions. Indeed, this aesthetic shift cannot wholly help Bollywood finally break free of its formulaic trappings and achieve total modernisation and international success, particularly as it simultaneously dismantles the authenticity, individuality and identity of its cinema. Nevertheless, films such as those discussed in this book should be given more critical attention, as they can reveal much about how global Bollywood is currently in a state of crisis. What we need to decide is whether we want to see this period of film production, as many Indian film scholars do, as the end or 'fall' of Indian cinema, or whether we want to see it as the rebirth of a strange new era of Bollywood filmmaking which we might call postmodern.

THE FUTURE OF BOLLYWOOD

In July 2009, as millions of Indians prepared to watch a total solar eclipse through high-tech solar viewers (or to lock themselves away from it out of superstitious fear), Bollywood – an industry that had experienced its own kind of eclipse over the past decade – was attempting to recover from a recession-related mass strike which had its producers boycotting multiplex theatres in a stand-off dispute over box-office takings. The strike was the result of film producers wanting a higher share of the multiplex owners' revenues. It lasted two months, from April to June 2009, with multiple theatres shutting down and films ceasing to be screened. The boycott resulted in a Rs 250 crore loss for multiplex owners and a Rs 100 crore loss for producers in interest costs (see Bamzai, 2009). Although by this time a settlement had been reached, the film industry was nevertheless left with a traffic jam of films awaiting release, as well as numerous stalled productions, delayed film premieres, major film projects struggling for buyers, a huge dip in star salaries, a loss of satellite and music rights and a series of non-profiting 'flop' releases. In the light of this event, it became unclear whether the kind of cinema dominant in the noughties would continue to prevail, and thus whether the postmodern traits investigated in this book were to characterise only a single decade. Responses from Bollywood's biggest moguls suggested the latter. For example, Mahesh Bhatt stated that the strike was a sign that 'Bollywood cannot afford to make bad, expensive films any more. It has to get *real*' (Bhatt, cited in Bamzai, 2009: 4, emphasis added).

Some argue that such a change and realism have already arrived in the form of *Hatke* ('different', 'eccentric' or 'offbeat') films. This form of cinema, targeted at inland young cosmopolitan and middle-class audiences, and often exhibited on the smaller screens of metropolitan multiplex theatres, emerged sporadically in films such as Nagesh Kukunoor's *Hyderabad Blues* (1998) and has flourished since the mid-2000s. Although still commercial, *Hatke* films are distinct from films in the formulaic and melodramatic Bollywood style, being generally lower in budget and tackling bolder or unconventional themes and storylines (for example: sperm donation, sexual privacy and land-grabbing). Formally, they incorporate television aesthetics and show a preference for independent music and sound design that is more integrated in the diegesis. These films strive to capture Indian life more authentically, setting themselves apart from Bollywood's postmodern aesthetic style. They offer realism by shooting in real locations (particularly portraying the landscape of cities such as Delhi and Mumbai) and by casting lesser-known stars. However, *Hatke* films too are known to occasionally break with realism in order to parody the very Bollywood cinema they are pitted against (see Rachel Dwyer's discussion of pastiche in *Dev D*, *Love, Sex Aur Dhokha*, *Oye Lucky! Lucky Oye!* and *Main, Meri Patni . . . Aur Woh!* [2011: 198]).

As has been discussed above, Sangita Gopal has regarded *Hatke* films as the real indicator of change and innovation in the industry, asserting that whereas contemporary Bollywood 'invents a new relation to the old', *Hatke* films are marked by an 'addiction to the new' (Gopal, 2011: 34). As *Hatke* involves a merging of mainstream and realist aesthetics, there is a feeling that this genre may eventually replace the dominance of Bollywood's figural aesthetics. Gopal suggests that this has already happened in the form of audiences 'overdosing' on the exoticism and lengthy excess of big-budget Bollywood films (2011: 192). However, it is still debatable what exactly qualifies as a *Hatke* film, and many films fall between Bollywood and *Hatke*, or under a different classification as 'multiplex cinema' (see Dwyer [2011] for details of the subtle differences between these otherwise overlapping genres). Rachel Dwyer and Jerry Pinto's (2011) attempt to confirm its existence reveals reluctance even on the part of the central actors associated with the *Hatke* genre. For example, when interviewed about *Hatke*, Abhay Deol argues against the label in a statement with strikingly postmodern undertones: 'I'm not sure if it exists. If you produce a film, that's art. It can be good art, or bad art but it is still art' (Dwyer and Pinto: 257).

Despite Bhatt's call for Bollywood to redirect itself in light of the recession and the successful emergence of *Hatke* cinema, when one looks at current film releases and upcoming film projects, it does not seem that things are about to change in a hurry. Since 2009, Bollywood has continued to produce visually excessive, generically diverse blockbusters and churn out remakes and sequels. The industry has had more special effects and science-fiction films in production, such as Vikram Bhatt's 3D monster movie *Creature 3D*, Shekhar Kapur's dystopia-set *Paani*, and indigenous superhero films *Prince Vali* and *Doga*.[2] Different varieties of cross-cultural remakes have continued to emerge in the 2010s: *We Are Family* (2010) [*Stepmom*, 1998], *Milenge Milenge* (2010) [*Serendipity*, 2001], *Players* (2011) [*The Italian Job*, 1969], *Son of Sardaar* (2012) [*Our Hospitality*, 1923], *Bang Bang* (2014) [*Knight and Day*, 2010]; self-remakes in the form of *Bol Bachchan* (2012) [*Gol Maal*, 1979], *Agneepath* (2012/1990), *Zanjeer* (2013/1973), *Chashme Baddoor* (2013/1981), *Himmatwala* (2013/1983); and numerous South Indian film remakes – all demonstrating that this impulse for recycling texts is no temporary short-term fad.

The landscape of Bollywood is also becoming ever more transnational as the 2010s have seen a continuation in global casting. To an even greater extent than foreign stars have been attracted to India (see Ben Kingsley in *Teen Patti* and Barbara Mori's appearance as Hrithik Roshan's love interest in the 2010 Bollywood-Telenovla hybrid *Kites*), in recent years Bollywood actors have increasingly ventured West. Examples are Anupam Kher in *Silver Linings Playbook* (2012), Irfan Khan in *The Amazing Spider-Man* and *Life of Pi* (2012), Amitabh Bachchan's brief yet memorable appearance in *The Great Gatsby* (2013), and Bipasha Basu's pairing with Josh Hartnett for the transnational production *Singularity* (forthcoming). Bollywood's increased interest in foreign production has also seen an agenda-shift in the form of a moving away from Indian content altogether. The Indian-owned media conglomerate Reliance Big Entertainment (one of the corporations responsible for dropping

CONCLUSION: A BOLLYWOOD RENAISSANCE? 199

Figure 8.1: Shah Rukh Khan's self-simulation in *Billu Barber* (Red Chillies Entertainment, 2009).

several forthcoming Bollywood productions in the aforementioned strike) reportedly invested 10 billion dollars in producing ten Hollywood films starring top American stars such as Brad Pitt, Jim Carrey, Tom Hanks and George Clooney (Alberge, 2008) and recently financed major Hollywood releases, including *Dredd* (2012) and *Walking with Dinosaurs 3D* (2013).

Whatever the result of the above projects may be, it is clear that India's transnational and postmodern-esque productions have proliferated since the 2000s, and that they have been marked by a (perhaps desperate) call for experimentation. Interestingly, whereas in the West postmodernism was often regarded as marking the *end* of the new (we can only go backwards as we have exhausted everything new, modern and original), India's Bollywood cinema – which has always fundamentally worked through some form of repetition – proves to surprise us and provide us with something altogether strangely refreshing.

The crisis of postmodernism (the loss of authenticity and global commodification) in Bollywood is perhaps best exemplified by film stars such as Shah Rukh Khan, who now openly acknowledge and advocate their own status as postmodern commodities. Khan, in particular, has seen postmodern techniques such as self-reflexivity, replication, pastiche and intertextuality as an opportunity to manufacture, saturate the media with, and comment on his own star image – whether this be achieved by unveiling a wax replica of himself at Madame Tussauds museum in London, producing collectable lifelike Shah Rukh dolls,[3] or by appearing as pastiched or parodic versions of himself in films such as *Om Shanti Om*, *Billu Barber*, *Rab Ne Bana Di Jodi* and *Luck by Chance*. Although Khan emulates or appears as a Bollywood film star in each of these films, *Billu Barber* is a particularly interesting example. In this film, not only does Khan play Bollywood film star Sahir Khan (whose persona bears a striking resemblance to the actor in real life), but in the song 'Ae Aa O' the sequence is flooded with numerous inserts from Khan's previous films. The screen rapidly flashes with images of him in his most iconic film roles, which span his entire career. The postmodern replication of Khan's star persona in his recent films is perhaps the most pertinent and iconic example of how Bollywood cinema has become lost in its own circle of images, or how it self-reflexively responds to (and is capitalising on) a postmodern world by giving it what it wants – copies of copies. These recycled images have assisted Bollywood in the branding, mass production, marketing and dissemination of its cinema across the globe. The success of Khan's image-recycling in India (all of his above-mentioned films were commercially successful) confirms that the Indian public too has surrendered to postmodern image consumption. Given this fully-fledged investment in the postmodern, one wonders if the Bollywood film industry will ever produce another truly 'authentic' text. The cinema, its filmmakers, its film stars and its audience have become caught up in a playful game of inauthentic reproduction, intertextual referencing and cultural appropriation. Bollywood is lost in its own simulacrum. It is no wonder that Khan, when asked about his status in contemporary Bollywood and the world, commented: 'I live in an unreal world, my persona is unreal, I myself am unreal.'[4]

NOTES

1. In the song 'Crazy Kiya Re' [You Made Me Crazy], Rai's tight black leather corset and whipping and slapping dance movements connote the bondage and disciplinary sexuality of a dominatrix.
2. Forthcoming at the time of writing.
3. The 'Bollywood Legends' Shah Rukh Khan doll was one of four Indian star-based toys produced by India's leading toy manufacturer, Funskool. The dolls were launched in 2006.
4. Shah Rukh Khan, cited in Chopra (2007: 221–2).

Bibliography

BOOKS AND ARTICLES

Abbas, Kwaja Ahmad (1949) 'Contemporary Indian Films for International Understanding', *UNESCO Courier Supplement*, vol 2, no. 4, May, p. 8.

Aftab, Kaleem (2002) 'Brown: The New Black! Bollywood in Britain', *Critical Quarterly*, vol. 44, no. 3, pp. 88–98.

Alberge, Dalya (2008) 'Indian Billions Tie Bollywood to Hollywood at Cannes', *Times Online*, 20 May, <:http://entertainment.timesonline.co.uk/tol/arts_and_entertainment/film/cannes/article3965523.ece> (last accessed 30 July 2009).

Alessio, Dominic and Jessica Langer (2007) 'Nationalism and Postcolonialism in Indian Science Fiction: Bollywood's *Koi . . . Mil Gaya*', *New Cinemas: Journal of Contemporary Film*, vol. 5 no. 3, pp. 217–19.

Andrew, Dudley (2000) 'Adaptation', in James Naremore (ed.), *Film Adaptation*, London: Athlone Press, pp. 28–37.

Appiah, Kwame Anthony (1991) 'Is the Post- in Postmodernism the Post- in Postcolonial?', *Critical Inquiry*, vol. 17, no. 2, winter, pp. 336–57.

Ashcroft, Bill, Gareth Griffins and Helen Tiffin (2002) *The Empire Writes Back: Theory and Practice in Post-Colonial Literatures*, 2nd edn, London and New York: Routledge.

Athique, Adrian M. (2008) 'The "Crossover" Audience: Mediated Multiculturalism and the Indian Film', *Continuum*, vol. 22, no. 3, pp. 299–311.

Athique, Adrian M. (2012) 'Bollywood, Brand India and Soft Power', in *Indian Media*, Cambridge and Malden, MA: Polity Press, pp. 111–30.

Aufderheide, Patricia (1998) 'Made in Hong Kong: Translation and Transmutation', in Andrew Horton and Stuart McDougal (eds), *Play It Again, Sam: Retakes on Remakes*, Berkeley, CA and London: University of California Press, pp. 191–9.

Bamzai, Kaveree (2009) 'Bollywood's Worst Season', *Indian Today*, 15 June, India: Living India Media.

Banerjee, Kanchana (2003) 'Cloning Hollywood', *The Hindu Online*, 3 August, <http://www.hindu.com/thehindu/mag/2003/08/03/stories/2003080300090400.htm> (last accessed 20 June 2006).

Barthes, Roland (1975) *S/Z*, trans. R. Miller, London: Cape.

Barthes, Roland (1977) 'Death of the Author', *Image, Music, Text*, trans. Stephen Heath, London: Fontana.

Baudrillard, Jean (1983) 'The Evil Demon of Images/The Precession of Simulacra', *Simulations*, New York: Semiotext(e).
Bazin, André (2000 [1948]) 'Adaptation, or the Cinema as Digest', *Film Adaptation*, London: Athlone Press.
Benjamin, Walter (1999) 'The Work of Art in the Age of Mechanical Reproduction', in Hannah Arendt (ed.), *Illuminations*, London: Pimlico, pp. 211–44.
Bertens, Hans (1986) 'The Postmodern *Weltanschauung* and its Relation to Modernism: An Introductory Survey', in Linda Hutcheon and Joseph Natoli (eds), *A Postmodern Reader*, 1993, Albany: State University of New York Press, pp. 25–70.
Bertens, Hans (1997) 'The Debate on Postmodernism', in Hans Bertens and Douwe Fokkema (eds), *International Postmodernism: Theory and Literary Practice*, Amsterdam: John Benjamins, pp. 3–14.
Bertens, Hans and Douwe Fokkema (1997) *International Postmodernism: Theory and Literary Practice*, Amsterdam: John Benjamins.
Bhabha, Homi (1984) 'Of Mimicry and Man: The Ambivalence of Colonial Discourse', *October*, vol. 28, spring, pp. 125–33.
Bhattacharya, Nandini (2005) 'Annu Palakunnathu Matthew's Alien: Copy with a Difference', *Meridians: Feminism, Race, Transnationalism*, vol. 6, no. 1, pp. 82–110.
Bhatti, Sharin (2010) 'Bollywood now lawfully producing remakes', *Hindustan Times*, 23 May, < http://www.hindustantimes.com/news-feed/entertainment/bollywood-now-lawfully-producing-remakes/article1-545592.aspx> (last accessed 24 March 2014).
Bhaumik, Kaushik (2006) 'Consuming "Bollywood" in the Global Age: The Strange Case of an "Unfine" World Cinema', in Stephanie Dennison and Song Hwee Li (eds), *Remapping World Cinema: Identity, Culture and Politics in Film*, London: Wallflower Press, pp. 188–98.
Bhaumik, Kaushik (2007) 'Lost in Translation: A Few Vagaries of the Alphabet Game Played Between Bombay Cinema and Hollywood', in Paul Cooke (ed.), *World Cinema 'Dialogues' with Hollywood*, Basingstoke and New York: Palgrave Macmillan, pp. 201–17.
Binford, Mira Reym (1988) 'Innovation and Imitation in the Contemporary Indian Cinema', in Wimal Dissanayake (ed.), *Cinema and Cultural Identity: Reflections on Films from Japan, India and China*, Lanham: University Press of America, pp. 77–106.
Bordwell, David (2000) 'Hong Kong and/as/or Hollywood', in *Planet Hong Kong: Popular Cinema and the Art of Entertainment*, Cambridge, MA: Harvard University Press, pp. 18–25.
Bose, Derek (2006) *Brand Bollywood: A New Global Entertainment Order*, London, New Delhi and Thousand Oaks: Sage.
Bose, Mihir (2007) *Bollywood: A History*, Stroud: Tempus.
Brashinsky, Michael (1998) 'Virgin Spring and Last House on the Left', in Andrew Horton and Stuart McDougal (eds), *Play It Again, Sam: Retakes on Remakes*, Berkeley, CA and London: University of California Press, pp. 162–71.
Braudy, Leo (1998) 'Afterword: Rethinking Remakes', in Andrew Horton and Stuart McDougal (eds), *Play It Again, Sam: Retakes on Remakes*, Berkeley, CA and London: University of California Press, pp. 327–33.
Brooker, M. Keith (2007) *Postmodern Hollywood: What's New in Film and Why It Makes Us Feel So Strange*, Westport, CT and London: Praeger.
Brooker, Peter and Will Brooker (1997a) *Postmodern After-Images: A Reader in Film Television and Video*, London, New York, Sydney and Auckland: Arnold.
Brooker, Peter and Will Brooker (1997b) 'Pulp Modernism: Tarantino's Affirmative Action', in *Postmodern After-Images: A Reader in Film Television and Video*, London, New York, Sydney and Auckland: Arnold, pp. 89–100.
Burger, Peter (1984) *Theory of the Avant-Garde*, Manchester: Manchester University Press.

Chakravarty, Sumita (2007) 'Teaching Indian Cinema', *Cinema Journal*, vol. 47, no. 1, Fall, pp. 105–8.
Chakraverty, Anjan (1996) *Indian Miniature Painting*, New Delhi: Lustra Press.
Chambers, Ross (1990) 'Alter Ego: Intertextuality, Irony and the Politics of Reading', in *Intertextuality: Theories and Practices*, Manchester: Manchester University Press.
Chanderohri, Vishwa (2001) *The Technique of the Pahari Painting: An Inquiry into Aspects of Materials, Methods and History*, New Delhi: Aryan Books International.
Chapman, James (2003) 'Film History: Sources, Methods, Approaches', *Cinemas of the World: Film and Society from 1895 to the Present*, London: Reaktion.
Chattopadhyaya, Saratchandra (2002 [1917]) *Devdas*, New Delhi: Penguin Books India.
Chattopadhyaya, Saratchandra (2005) *Parineeta*, trans. Malobika Chaudhuri, New Delhi: Penguin Books India.
Chaudhuri, Shohini (2005) *Contemporary World Cinema: Europe, The Middle East, East Asia and South Asia*, Edinburgh: Edinburgh University Press.
Chitrapu, Sunitha (2012) 'The Big Stick behind "Soft Power"? The Case of Indian Films in International Markets', in David J. Scheafer and Kavita Karan (eds), *Bollywood and Globalization: The Global Power of Popular Hindi Cinema*, London: Routledge.
Chopra, Anupama (2007) *King of Bollywood: Shah Rukh Khan and the Seductive World of Indian Cinema*, New York: Grand Central Publishing.
Choudhuri, Indra Nath (1997) 'Facets of Postmodernism: A Search for Roots. The Indian Literacy Scene', in Hans Bertens and Douwe Fokkema (eds), *International Postmodernism: Theory and Literary Practice*, Amsterdam: John Benjamins, pp. 491–7.
Choudhury, Malay Roy (2001) *Postmodern Bangla Short Stories: An Overview*, Calcutta: Haowa49.
Ciecko, Anne Tereska (2006) 'Theorising Asian Cinema(s)', *Contemporary Asian Cinema*, Oxford and New York: Berg, pp. 3–31.
Coleridge, Samuel Taylor (1909 [1817]) *Biographia Literaria*, London: Dent.
Comolli, Jean-Luc and Jean Narboni (2004 [1969]) 'Cinema/Ideology/Criticism', in Leo Braudy and Marshall Cohen (eds), *Film Theory and Criticism*, 6th edn, New York and Oxford: Oxford University Press pp. 812–19.
Connor, Steven (1989) 'Postmodern TV, Video and Film', *Postmodernist Culture: An Introduction to Theories of the Contemporary*, Oxford: Blackwell.
Constable, Catherine (2005) 'Postmodernism and Film', in Steven Connor (ed.), *A Cambridge Companion to Postmodernism*, Cambridge: Cambridge University Press, pp. 43–61.
Cousins, Mark (2009) 'Widescreen: Indian Cinema Rising', in *Prospect*, March, London, p. 81.
Creekmur, Corey (2007) 'Remembering, Repeating and Working Through *Devdas*', in Heidi Pauwels (ed.), *Indian Literature and Popular Cinema: Recasting the Classics*, London and New York: Routledge, pp. 173–202.
Das, Bijay Kumar (2007) *Postmodern Indian English Literature*, New Delhi: Atlantic Publishers.
Degli-Eposti, Christine (1998) 'Introduction', *Postmodernism in the Cinema*, New York and Oxford: Berghahn.
Denzin, Norman K. (1991) *Images of Postmodern Society: Social Theory and Contemporary Cinema*, London, Newbury Park and New Delhi: Sage.
Desai, Jigna (2004) *Beyond Bollywood: The Cultural Politics of South Asian Diasporic Film*, New York and London: Routledge.
Dewey, Susan (2007) 'Doing Bombay Darshan: The IMF Structural Adjustment and National Identity in the Hindi Film Industry', in Gurbir Jolly, Zenia Wahwani and Deborah Barretto (eds), *Once Upon a Time in Bollywood: The Global Swing in Hindi Cinema*, Ontario: TSAR publications, pp. 1–19.

Dika, Vera (2003) *Recycled Culture in Contemporary Art and Film: The Uses of Nostalgia*, Cambridge: Cambridge University Press.
Dirlik, Arif and Xudong Zhang (2000) *Postmodernism and China*, Durham, NC and London: Duke University Press.
Dissanayake, Wimal (1988) *Cinema and Cultural Identity: Reflections on Films from Japan, India and China*, Lanham: University Press of America.
Dissanayake, Wimal and K. Moti Gokulsing (1998) *Indian Popular Cinema: A Narrative of Cultural Change*, Stoke-on-Trent: Trentham.
Dissanayake, Wimal and K. Moti Gokulsing (2004) *Indian Popular Cinema: A Narrative of Cultural Change*, 2nd edn, Stoke-on-Trent: Trentham.
Dostoevsky, Fyodor (2012 [1848]) *White Nights and Other Stories*, ed. Max Bollinger, London: Sovereign.
Druxman, Michael B. (1975) *Make It Again Sam: A Survey of Movie Remakes*, Cranbury, NJ: Barnes.
Dudrah, Rajinder (2006) *Bollywood: Sociology Goes to the Movies*, New Delhi, Thousand Oaks and London: Sage.
Dudrah, Rajinder (2012) *Bollywood Travels: Culture, Diaspora and Border Crossings in Popular Hindi Cinema*, London and New York: Routledge.
During, Simon (1998) 'Postcolonialism and Globalisation: A Dialectical Relation After All?', *Postcolonial Studies*, vol. 1, no. 1, pp. 31–47.
Dwyer, Rachel (2005) *100 Bollywood Films*, London: BFI Publishing.
Dwyer, Rachel (2011) 'Zara Hatke!: The New Middle Classes and the Segmentation of Hindi Cinema', in *Being Middle-Class in India: A Way of Life*, ed. Henrike Donner, London and New York: Routledge, pp. 184–208.
Dwyer, Rachel and Divya Patel (2002) *Cinema India: The Visual Culture of Hindi Film*, London: Reaktion, 2002.
Dwyer, Rachel and Jerry Pinto (2011) *Beyond the Boundaries of Bollywood: The Many Forms of Hindi Cinema*, Oxford: Oxford University Press.
Dyer, Richard (2004) *Heavenly Bodies: Film Stars and Society*, London: Routledge.
Dyer, Richard (2006) *Pastiche*, London: Routledge.
Dyer, Richard and Paul McDonald (1997) *Stars*, 2nd edn, London: British Film Institute.
Eagleton, Terry (1986) 'Capitalism, Modernism and Postmodernism', in *Against the Grain*, London: Verso, pp. 131–48.
Eberwein, Robert (1998) 'Remakes and Cultural Studies', in Andrew Horton and Stuart McDougal (eds), *Play It Again, Sam: Retakes on Remakes*, Berkeley, CA and London: University of California Press, pp. 15–33.
Elley, Derek (2002) 'Film Reviews: Devdas', *Variety*, 17 June, pp. 24–5.
Ende, Michael (1985 [1979]) *Die Unendliche Geschichte*, trans. R. Manheim, Harmondsworth: Puffin.
Forrest, Jennifer and Leonard Koos (2002) 'Reviewing Remakes: An Introduction', in Jennifer Forrest and Leonard Koos (eds), *Dead Ringers: The Remake in Theory and Practice*, Albany: State University of New York Press, pp. 1–36.
Freer, Ian (2002) 'Devdas', *Empire*, no. 158, 1 August, p. 123.
Friedberg, Anne (1994) 'The End of Modernity: Where Is Your Rupture?', *Window Shopping: Cinema and the Postmodern*, London: University of California Press, pp. 157–80.
Ganti, Tejaswini (2002) '"And Yet My Heart Is Still Indian": The Bombay Film Industry and the (H)Indianization of Hollywood', in Faye Ginsburg, Lila Abu-Lughod and Brian Larkin (eds), *Media Worlds: Anthropology on New Terrain*, London: University of California Press, pp. 281–300.

Ganti, Tejaswini (2004) *Bollywood: A Guidebook to Popular Hindi Cinema*, New York and London: Routledge.
Ganti, Tejaswini (2008) 'Mumbai Versus Bollywood: The Hindi Film Industry and the Politics of Cultural Heritage in Contemporary India', in Anandam P. Kavoori and Aswin Punathambekar (eds), *Global Bollywood*, New York and London: New York University Press, pp. 52–78.
Garwood, Ian (2006) 'The Songless Bollywood Film', *South Asian Popular Culture*, vol. 4, no. 2, pp. 169–83.
Gateward, Frances and David Desser (2006) 'Introduction: Indian Cinema and Film Studies', *Post Script* (special: Indian Cinema), vol. 25, no. 3, summer, pp. 3–6.
Gehlawat, Ajay (2010) *Reframing Bollywood: Theories of Popular Hindi Cinema*, New Delhi: Sage.
Genette, Gerard (1982) *Palimpsests: Literature in the Second Degree*, trans. Channa Newman and Claude Doubinsky, London and Lincoln, NE: University of Nebraska Press, 1997.
Gopal, Sangita (2011) *Conjugations: Marriage and Form in New Bollywood Cinema*, Chicago and London: University of Chicago Press.
Gopal, Sangita and Sujata Moorti (2008) *Global Bollywood: Travels of Hindi Song and Dance*, Bristol: University of Minnesota Press.
Gopalan, Lalitha (2002) *Cinema of Interruptions: Action Genres in Contemporary Indian Cinema*, London: BFI.
Gordon, Andrew (2008) 'E.T. (1982) as Fairytale', in *Empire of Dreams: The Science Fiction and Fantasy Films of Steven Spielberg*, USA: Rowman & Littlefield, pp. 75–92.
Govil, Nitin (2005) 'Hollywood's Effects, Bollywood FX', in Greg Elmer and Mike Gasher (eds), *Contracting Out Hollywood: Runaway Productions and Foreign Location Shooting*, Lanham, Boulder, New York, Toronto and Oxford: Rowman & Littlefield, pp. 92–116.
Govil, Nitin and Toby Miller, John McMurria, Richard Maxwell and Ting Wang (2005) 'Hollywood's Global Rights', *Global Hollywood 2*, London: BFI, pp. 213–58.
Gunning, Tom (1990) 'The Cinema of Attractions: Early Film, Its Spectator and the Avant-Garde', in Thomas Elsaesser and Adam Baker (eds), *Early Cinema: Space, Frame, Narrative*, London: BFI, pp. 56–62.
Gupta, Chidananda Das (1991) *The Painted Face: Studies in India's Popular Cinema*, New Delhi: Roli Books.
Hansen, Miriam (1991) 'Male Star, Female Fans', *Babel and Babylon: Spectatorship in American Silent Film*, Cambridge, MA and London: Harvard University Press, pp. 245–68.
Hardy, Justine (2002) 'Welcome to the Fantasy Factory', *Vanity Fair Salutes Bollywood* [in association with Selfridges], London: Condé Nast, pp. 12–13.
Harootunian, Harry D. and Masao Miyoshi (1994) *Postmodernism and Japan*, Durham, NC and London: Duke University Press.
Harries, Dan (2000) *Film Parody*, London: BFI.
Harvey, David (1990) 'Time and Space in the Postmodern Cinema', *The Condition of Postmodernity: An Enquiry Into the Origins of Cultural Change*, Malden, MA: Blackwell.
Hegel, G. W. F. (1975) *Aesthetics: Lectures on Fine Art*, trans. T. M. Knox, Oxford: Clarendon.
Hill, John (1998) 'Film and Postmodernism', in John Hill and Pamela Church Gibson (eds), *The Oxford Guide to Film Studies*, Oxford: Oxford University Press, pp. 96–105.
Hogan, Patrick Colm (2008) *Understanding Indian Movies*, Austin, TX: University of Texas Press.
Hooks, Bell (1991) 'Postmodern Blackness', in *Yearning: Race, Gender and Cultural Politics*, London: Turnaround, pp. 23–31.

Horton, Andrew (1998) 'Cinematic Makeovers and Cultural Border Crossings: Kusturica's *Time of the Gypsies* and Coppola's *Godfather* and *Godfather 2*', in Andrew Horton and Stuart McDougal (eds), *Play It Again, Sam: Retakes on Remakes*, Berkeley, CA and London: University of California Press, pp. 172–90.

Horton, Andrew and Stuart Y. McDougal (1998) *Play It Again, Sam: Retakes on Remakes*, Berkeley, CA and London: University of California Press.

Hsiao-peng Lu, Sheldon (2000) 'Global POSTmodernIZATION: The Intellectual, the Artist and China's Condition', in Arif Dirlik and Xudong Zhang (eds), *Postmodernism and China*, Durham, NC and London: Duke University Press, pp. 145–74.

Hutcheon, Linda (1985) *A Theory of Parody: The Teachings of Twentieth Century Art-Forms*, London: Methuen.

Hutcheon, Linda (1988) 'Theorising the Postmodern: Towards a Poetics', *A Poetics of Postmodernism: History, Theory, Fiction*, London: Methuen, pp. 1–21.

Hutcheon, Linda (1989) *The Politics of Postmodernism*, London: Routledge.

Hutcheon, Linda (2002) *The Politics of Postmodernism*, 2nd edn, London and New York: Routledge.

Hutcheon, Linda and Joseph Natoli (1993) *A Postmodern Reader*, Albany: State University of New York Press.

IANS (2012) 'Devdas Is Apt for 3D Says Sanjay Leela Bhansali', *India Today*, 1 June, <http://indiatoday.intoday.in/story/devdas-is-apt-for-3d-says-sanjay-leela-bhansali/1/198575.html> (last accessed 17 March 2014).

Iyer, Sandhya (2002) 'National Anthem in Theatres: Good, Bad or Unnecessary?', *Times of India Online*, 1 December, <http://timesofindia.indiatimes.com/articleshow/29982702.cms> (last accessed 3 October 2008).

Jameson, Fredric (1991) *Postmodernism, or, The Cultural Logic of Late Capitalism*, London: Verso.

Jess-Cooke, Carolyn (2009) *Film Sequels: Theory and Practice from Hollywood to Bollywood*, Edinburgh: Edinburgh University Press.

Jha, Priya (2003) 'Lyric Nationalism: Gender, Friendship and Excess in 1970s Hindi Cinema', *The Velvet Light Trap*, no. 51, spring, pp. 43–53.

Johnston, Sheila (2002) 'Visual Space Overwhelms Slim Story: Devdas', *Screen International*, no. 1,363, 12 July, pp. 17, 20.

Jolly, Gurbir (2007) 'Globalization: The Musical', in Gurbir Jolly, Zenia Wahwani and Deborah Barretto (eds), *Once Upon a Time in Bollywood: The Global Swing in Hindi Cinema*, Ontario: TSAR Publications, pp. vii–xiv.

Jolly, Gurbir, Zenia Wahwani and Deborah Barretto (2007) *Once Upon a Time in Bollywood: The Global Swing in Hindi Cinema*, Ontario: TSAR Publications.

Kapur, Geeta (2000) *When Was Modernism: Essays on Contemporary Cultural Practice in India*, New Delhi: Tulika Books.

Kapur, Geeta (2001) 'Visual Culture in the Indian Metropolis: Critical Intervention through Art', *Asia Art Archive*, <http://www.aaa.org.hk/Collection/CollectionOnline/SpecialCollectionItem/2992> (last accessed 17 February 2014).

Karan, Kavita and David J. Schaefer (2013) *Bollywood and Globalization: The Global Power of Popular Hindi Cinema*, London: Routledge.

Kaur, Raminder (2005) 'Cruising on the *Vilayeti* Bandwagon: Diasporic Representations and Reception of Popular Indian Movies', in Raminder Kaur and Ajay J. Sinha (eds), *Bollyworld: Popular Indian Cinema through a Transnational Lens*, New Delhi, Thousand Oaks and London: Sage, pp. 309–29.

Kaur, Raminder and Ajay J. Sinha (2005) *Bollyworld: Popular Indian Cinema through a Transnational Lens*, New Delhi, Thousand Oaks and London: Sage.

Kavoori, Anandam P. and Aswin Punathambekar (2008) *Global Bollywood*, New York and London: New York University Press.
Keating H. R. F. (1976) *Filmi, Filmi, Inspector Ghote*, London: Collins.
King, Geoff (2002) 'Narrative Vs. Spectacle in the Contemporary Blockbuster', *New Hollywood Cinema: An Introduction*, London: I. B. Tauris.
Kramer, Lucia (2008) 'Bollywood in the Classrooms: Opportunities and Problems of Teaching Popular Indian Cinema', *Teaching India*, Anglistik and Englischunterricht, Universitätsverlag, Winter Heidelberg, Band 72, pp. 107–24.
Lacan, Jacques (1977) 'The Mirror Stage as Formative of the Function of the I as Revealed in Psychoanalytic Experience', *Écrits: A Selection*, London: Tavistock, pp. 1–7.
Laight, Rupert (2002) 'Devdas', *Film Review*, no. 621, 1 August, p. 83.
Lal, Vinay (1998) 'The Impossibility of the Outsider in Modern Hindi Film', in Ashis Nandy (ed.), *The Secret Politics of Our Desires: Innocence, Culpability and Indian Popular Cinema*, London: Zed Books, pp. 228–59.
Lall, Bhuvan (2002) 'India Pins BO Hopes on Devdas', *Screen International*, no. 1,362, 5 July, pp. 1, 4.
Lash, Scott (1988) 'Discourse or Figure? Postmodernism as a "Regime of Signification"', in *Theory, Culture and Society*, vol. 5, London, Newbury Park, Beverley Hills and New Delhi: Sage, pp. 311–36.
Leitch, Thomas (2002) 'Twice-Told Tales: Disavowal and the Rhetoric of the Remake', in Jennifer Forrest and Leonard Koos (eds), *Dead Ringers: The Remake in Theory and Practice*, Albany: State University of New York Press, pp. 37–62.
Lyotard, Jean-François (1992) 'Note on the Meaning of Post', *The Post Modern Explained to Children: Correspondence 1982–1985*, London: Turnaround.
Malcolm, Derek (2002) 'To Bollywood and Beyond', *Vanity Fair Salutes Bollywood* [in association with Selfridges] London: Condé Nast, pp. 3–4.
Marks, Laura (2000) *The Skin of the Film: Intercultural Cinema, Embodiment, and the Senses*, Durham, NC and London: Duke University Press.
Mazdon, Lucy (2000) *Encore Hollywood: Remaking French Cinema*, London: BFI.
Mazumdar, Ranjani (2007) 'Gangland Bombay', in *Bombay Cinema: An Archive of the City*, Minneapolis, MN and London: University of Minnesota Press, pp. 149–96.
McFarlane, Brian (1996) *Novel to Film: An Introduction to the Theory of Adaptation*, Oxford: Clarendon Press.
Mehta, Ankita (2013) 'Dilwale Dulhania Le Jayenge Completes Historic 900 Weeks at Maratha Mandir', *International Business Times*, 12 January, <http://www.ibtimes.co.in/articles/423454/20130112/dilwale-dulhania-le-jayenge-completes-historic-900.htm> (last accessed 3 March 2014).
Mehta, Monika (2007) 'Globalizing Bombay Cinema: Reproducing the Indian State and Family', in Gurbir Jolly, Zenia Wahwani and Deborah Barretto (eds), *Once Upon a Time in Bollywood: The Global Swing in Hindi Cinema*, Ontario: TSAR Publications, pp. 20–42.
Mehta, Rini Battacharya and Rajeshwari V. Pandharipande (2010) *Bollywood and Globalization: Indian Popular Cinema, Nation and Diaspora*, London: Anthem.
Melville, Stephen (1994) 'Picturing Japan: Reflections on the Workshop', in Harry D. Harootunian and Miyoshi Masao (eds), *Postmodernism and Japan*, Durham, NC and London: Duke University Press, pp. 279–85.
Merchant, Ismail (2004) 'Foreword', in Dinesh Raheja and Jitendra Kothari (eds), *Indian Cinema: The Bollywood Saga*, New Delhi: Lustre Press Roli Books, pp. 9–11.
Miles, Alice (2009) 'Shocked by Slumdog's Poverty Porn', *The Times*, 14 January, p. 26.

Mishra, Vijay (1985) 'Towards a Theoretical Critique of Bombay Cinema', in Rajinder Dudrah and Jigna Desai (eds), *The Bollywood Reader*, Maidenhead: McGraw-Hill/Open University Press, pp. 32–44.
Mishra, Vijay (2002) *Bollywood Cinema: Temples of Desire*, London and New York: Routledge.
Mishra, Vijay (2006) *Bollywood Cinema: A Critical Genealogy*, Wellington, New Zealand: Asian Studies Institute.
Mishra, Vijay (2008) 'Bollywood', in Wolfgang Donsbach (ed.), *The International Encyclopedia of Communication*, Oxford: Blackwell, pp. 349–53.
Mitra, Ananda (1999) *India through the Western Lens*, New Delhi, Thousand Oaks, London: Sage.
Miyoshi, Masao (1994) 'Against the Native Grain: The Japanese Novel and the "Postmodern" West', in Harry D. Harootunian and Miyoshi Masao (eds), *Postmodernism and Japan*, 1994, Durham, NC and London: Duke University Press, pp. 143–68.
Mulvey, Laura (1975) 'Visual Pleasure and Narrative Cinema', *Screen*, vol. 16, no. 3, pp. 6–18.
Murphy, Richard (1999) *Theorising the Avant-Garde*, Cambridge: Cambridge University Press.
Nair, P. K. (2002) 'The Devdas Syndrome in Indian Cinema', *Cinemaya*, 56/57, 1 December, pp. 82–7.
Nandy, Ashis (1995) 'An Intelligent Critic's Guide to Indian Cinema', *The Savage Freud and Other Essays on Possible and Retrievable Selves*, pp. 196–236.
Nandy, Ashis (1998) 'Introduction: Indian Popular Cinema as a Slum's Eye View of Politics', in Ashis Nandy (ed.), *The Secret Politics of Our Desires: Innocence, Culpability and Indian Popular Cinema*, London: Zed Books, pp. 1–18.
Nandy, Ashis (2003) 'Notes Towards an Agenda for the Next Generation of Film Theorists in India', *South Asian Popular Culture*, vol. 1, no. 1, pp. 79–84.
Naremore, James (2000) *Film Adaptation*, London: Athlone Press.
Nayar, Sheila (1997) 'The Values of Fantasy: Indian Popular Cinema Through Western Scripts', *Journal of Popular Culture*, vol. 31, no. 1, pp. 73–90.
Nayar, Sheila (2005) 'Dis-Orientalizing Bollywood', *New Review of Film and Television Studies*, vol. 3, no. 1, pp. 59–74.
Neale, Steve (1990) 'Questions of Genre', *Screen*, vol. 31, no. 1, spring, pp. 45–66.
Ning, Wang (2000) 'The Mapping of Chinese Postmodernity', in Arif Dirlik and Xudong Zhang (eds), *Postmodernism and China*, Durham, NC and London: Duke University Press, pp. 21–40.
Nygren, Scott (1989) 'Reconsidering Modernism: Japanese Film and the Postmodern Context', *Wide Angle*, vol. 11, no. 3, July, pp. 6–15.
Pauwels, Heidi (2007) *Indian Literature and Popular Cinema: Recasting the Classics*, London and New York: Routledge, pp. 201–17.
Pendakur, Manjunath (1990) 'India', in John A. Lent (ed.), *The Asian Film Industry*, London: Christopher Helm, pp. 229–52.
Pendakur, Manjunath (2003) *Indian Popular Cinema: Industry, Ideology and Consciousness*, Cresskill, NJ, London and Hampton: Eurospan.
Prasad, Madhava (2003) 'This Thing Called Bollywood', *Seminar 525*, <http://www.india-seminar.com/2003/525/525%20madhava%20prasad.htm> (last accessed 10 May 2009).
Prasad, Madhava (2008) 'Surviving Bollywood', in Anandam P. Kavoori and Aswin Punathambekar (eds), *Global Bollywood*, New York and London: New York University Press, pp. 41–51.

Propp, V.I. (1968) *Morphology of the Folktale*, 2nd edn, ed. L. A. Wagner, Austin, TX: University of Texas Press.
Pugsley, Peter C. (2013) *Tradition, Culture and Aesthetics in Contemporary Asian Cinema*, Farnham: Ashgate.
Radhakrishnan, R (2000) 'Postmodernism and the Rest of the World', in Fawzia Afzal-Khan and Kalpana Seshadri-Crooks (eds), *The Pre-occupation of Postcolonial Studies*, Durham, NC and London: Duke University Press, pp. 37–70.
Raghavendra, Nandini (2002) 'Setting Laws in Motion', in *Times News Network, The Economic Times Online*, 10 November, <http://economictimes.indiatimes.com/articleshow/277957 31.cms> (last accessed 12 June 2007).
Raheja, Dinesh and Jitendra Kothari (2004) 'The Post-millennial Period', *Indian Cinema: The Bollywood Saga*, New Delhi: Lustre Press Roli Books, pp. 133–46.
Rai, Amit S. (2009) *Untimely Bollywood: Globalization and India's New Media Assemblage*, Durham, NC and London: Duke University Press.
Raj, Ashok (2004) 'The Curse of Globalised Culture: The Fall of Indian Cinema Foretold', *Futures*, 36, pp. 797–809.
Rajadhyaksha, Ashish (1998) 'Indian Cinema', *The Oxford Guide to Film Studies*, ed. John Hill and Pamela Church Gibson, Oxford: Oxford University Press.
Rajadhyaksha, Ashish (2003) 'The "Bollywoodization" of the Indian Cinema: Cultural Nationalism in a Global Arena', *Inter-Asia Cultural Studies*, vol. 4, no. 1, pp. 25–39.
Rajadhyaksha, Ashish (2009) ' "Bollywood" 2004: The Globalized Freak Show of What Used to Be Cinema', in *Indian Cinema in the Time of Celluloid: From Bollywood to the Emergency*, Bloomington and Indianapolis: Indiana University Press, pp. 51–68.
Rajadhyaksha, Ashish and Kim Soyoung (2003) 'Introduction: Imagining the Cinema Anew', *Inter-Asia Cultural Studies*, vol. 4, no. 1, pp. 7–9.
Rajadhyaksha, Ashish and Paul Willemen (1999) *Encyclopaedia of Indian Cinema*, 2nd rev. and updated edn, London: BFI.
Ramachandran, Naman (2002) 'Reviews: Devdas', *Sight and Sound*, vol.12, no. 9, 1 September, p. 58.
Ray, Satyajit (1976) 'What Is Wrong with Hindi Films', *Our Films, Their Films*, Bombay: Orient Longman.
Robinson, Andrew (2004) 'Unmade Films: Ravi Shankar, The Mahabharata, A Passage to India, The Alien', in *Satyajit Ray: The Inner Eye*, London: Deutsch.
Sardar, Ziauddin (1998) *Postmodernism and the Other: The New Imperialism of Western Culture*, London: Pluto Press.
Sarkar, Bhaskar (2013) 'Metafiguring Bollywood: Brecht after *Om Shanti Om*', in Meheli Sen and Anustup Basu (eds), *Figurations in Indian Film*, Basingstoke: Palgrave Macmillan, pp. 205–35.
Sergi, Gianluca (2004) 'Tackling Sound: Suggestions for Sound Analysis', *The Dolby Era: Film Sound in Contemporary Hollywood*, Manchester and New York: Manchester University Press, pp. 136–62.
Sharma, Murli (1997) 'Is It Phantom of Just a Phantom?', *The Indian Express*, 16 June, <http://www.indianexpress.com/ie/daily/19970616/16750663.html> (last accessed 7 October 2008).
Singh, Anup (2002) 'Sanjay Leela Bhansali's Devdas and the Intensity of the Self', *Cinemaya*, nos 56/57, 1 December, pp. 88–91.
Singh, Harneet (2003), 'Jana Gana Mana Adhinaayaka, Jaya He . . .', *Times of India Online*, 23 January, <http://timesofindia.indiatimes.com/articleshow/35210761.cms> (last accessed 3 October 2008).

Singhal, Rahul (2002) *Devdas: The Eternal Saga of Love*, Delhi: Pentagon Press.
Srivastava, Sanjay (1998) 'Post-Coloniality, National Identity, Globalisation and the Simulation of the Real', *Constructing Post-colonial India: National Character and the Doon School*, London: Routledge, pp. 190–220.
Stam, Robert (2000) 'Beyond Fidelity: The Dialogics of Adaptation', in James Naremore (ed.), *Film Adaptation*, London: Athlone Press, pp. 54–76.
Straubhaar, Joseph D (1991) 'Beyond Media Imperialism: Assymetrical Interdependence and Cultural Proximity', in *Critical Studies in Mass Communication*, vol. 8, no. 1 March, pp. 39–59.
Stringer, Julian (2003) *Movie Blockbusters*, London: Routledge.
Thomas, Rosie (1985) 'Indian Cinema: Pleasures and Popularity', *Screen*, vol. 26, no. 3–4, pp. 116–31.
Tiffin, Helen (1988) 'Post-colonialism, Post-modernism and the Rehabilitation of Post-colonial History', *Journal of Commonwealth Literature*, vol. 23, no. 1, pp. 169–81.
Tyrrell, Heather (1999) 'Bollywood versus Hollywood: The Battle of the Dream Factories', in Tracey Skelton and Tim Allen (eds), *Culture and Global Change*, London: Routledge, pp. 260–73.
Unauthored (2002) 'Reviews: Devdas', *Trade Guide*, vol. 48, no. 41, 13 July, pp. 1–2, 6.
Unauthored (2003a) 'Kaante/Thorns Review', *Sight and Sound*, vol. 13, no. 4, April, pp. 54–5.
Unauthored (2003b) *Time* (Asia Edition), vol. 162, no. 16, Oct.
Verevis, Constantine (2006) *Film Remakes*, Edinburgh: Edinburgh University Press.
Virdi, Jyotika (2003) *The Cinematic [Imagi]Nation: Indian Popular Film as Social History*, New Brunswick, NJ: Rutgers University Press, pp. 205–14.
Vitali, Valentina (2006) 'Not a Biography of the "Indian Cinema": Historiography and the Question of National Cinema in India', in Paul Willeman (ed.), *Theorising National Cinema*, London: BFI, pp. 262–73.
Vitali, Valentina (2008) *Hindi Action Cinema: Industries, Narratives, Bodies*, Delhi: Oxford University Press.
Wax, Emily (2009) 'Hollywood Finally Challenging India's Booming Bollywood Over Knockoffs', *Washington Post Foreign Service*, 26 August, <http://www.washingtonpost.com/wp-dyn/content/article/2009/08/25/AR2009082503104.html> (last accessed 24 March 2014).
White, Hayden (1978) 'The Historical Text as Literary Artifact', *Tropics of Discourse: Essays in Cultural Criticism*, Baltimore, MD: The Johns Hopkins University Press, pp. 81–100.
White, Hayden (1996) 'The Modernist Event', in Vivian Sobchak (ed.), *The Persistence of History: Cinema, Television, and the Modern Event*, New York and London: Routledge, pp. 17–38.
Willemen, Paul (2006) 'The National Revisited', Paul Willemen (ed.), *Theorising National Cinema*, London: BFI, pp. 29–43.
Williams, Patrick and Laura Chrisman (1993) 'Colonial Discourse and Postcolonial Theory: An Introduction', in *Colonial Discourses and Postcolonial Theory: A Reader*, New York, London, Toronto, Sydney, Tokyo and Singapore: Harvester Wheatsheaf, pp. 1–20.
Willis, Andrew (2003) 'Locating Bollywood': Notes of the Hindi Blockbuster, 1975 to the Present', in Julian Stringer (ed.), *Movie Blockbusters*, London and New York: Routledge, pp. 255–67.
Wills, David (1998) 'The French Remark: Breathless and Cinematic Citationality', in Andrew Horton and Stuart McDougal (eds), *Play It Again, Sam: Retakes on Remakes*, Berkeley, CA and London: University of California Press, pp. 147–61.

Wollen, Peter (1986) 'Godard and Counter-Cinema: Vent d'Est', in P. Rosen (ed.), *Narrative, Apparatus, Ideology: A Film Theory Reader*, Chichester and New York: Columbia University Press, pp. 120–9.
Wong, Silvia (2005) '*Krrish* Rolls in Singapore Under Incentive Scheme', *Screen Daily Online*, 16 September, <http://www.screendaily.com/krrish-rolls-in-singapore-under-incentive-scheme/4024398.article> (last accessed 11 March 2009).
Worton, Michael and Judith Still (1990) *Intertextuality: Theories and Practices*, Manchester: Manchester University Press.
Wright, Neelam Sidhar (2009) '"Tom Cruise? Tarantino? E.T.? . . . Indian!" Innovation through Imitation in the Cross-Cultural Bollywood Remake', in Iain Robert Smith (ed.), *Cultural Borrowings: Appropriation, Reworking, Transformation* [e-book], *Scope*, no. 15, October, pp. 194–210.
Wright, Neelam Sidhar (2010) 'Bollywood Eclipsed: The Postmodern Aesthetics, Scholarly Appeal, and Remaking of Contemporary Popular Indian Cinema', doctoral thesis, University of Sussex.
Wyatt, Andrew (2005) 'Building the Temples of Postmodern India: Economic Constructions of National Identity', in *Contemporary South Asia*, vol. 14, no. 4, December, pp. 465–80.
Yoshimoto, Mitsuhiro (1991) 'The Difficulty of Being Radical: The Discipline of Film Studies and the Postcolonial World Order', *Boundary 2, Japan in the World*, vol. 18, no. 3, autumn, pp. 242–57.
Yoshimoto, Mitsuhiro (1993) 'Melodrama, Postmodernism and Japanese Cinema', in Wimal Dissanayake (ed.), *Melodrama and Asian Cinema*, New York: Cambridge University Press, pp. 101–26.
Yoshimoto, Mitsuhiro (2006) 'National/International/Transnational: The Concept of Trans-Asian Cinema and the Cultural Politics of Film Criticism', in Paul Willemen (ed.), *Theorising National Cinema*, London: BFI, pp. 254–61.
Zhang, Xudong (2000) 'Epilogue: Postmodernism and Postsocialist Society: Historicizing the Present', in Arif Dirlik and Xudong Zhang (eds), *Postmodernism and China*, Durham, NC and London: Duke University Press, pp. 399–442.

WEBSITES

Bhagavad Gita Online: <http://www.bhagavad-gita.org> (last accessed 10 May 2009).
Box Office Mojo (film box office statistics): <http://www.boxofficemojo.com> (last accessed 4 March 2014).
British Film Institute (2007) *BFI Southbank Season: Indian Cinema Now press release*, 25 July, <http://www.bfi.org.uk/about/media/releases/2007-07-25-indian-cinema.pdf> (last accessed 10 May 2009).
British Film Institute: '"Long List" for Top Indian Films Poll', <http://www.bfi.org.uk/features/imagineasia/guide/poll/india/long_list.html> (last accessed 20 December 2007).
Devdas official website: 'The Making', <http://devdas.indiatimes.com/making.htm> (last accessed 1 March 2006).
Internet Movie Database: <http://www.imdb.com> (last accessed 1 April 2014).
London Indian Film Festival: <http://www.londonindianfilmfestival.co.uk> (last accessed 24 March 2014).
Oxford English Dictionary Online: <http://dictionary.oed.com> (last accessed 5 February 2009).

Saawariya official website: <http://www.saawariyafilm.com> (last accessed 8 June 2009).
The DEVDAS Phenomenon (Corey Creekmur): <http://www.uiowa.edu/~incinema/DEVDAS.html> (last accessed 12 May 2006).

Additional Reading

The publications cited below are not mentioned in the main text of the book, but are listed here as being of value and interest to students of Indian cinema in relation to the issues discussed in the book.

Bertens, Hans (1995) 'Introduction', in *The Idea of the Postmodern: A History*, London and New York: Routledge.
Biguenet, John (1998) 'Double Take: The Role of Allusion in Cinema', in Andrew Horton and Stuart McDougal (eds), *Play It Again, Sam: Retakes on Remakes*, Berkeley, CA and London: University of California Press, pp. 131–43.
Boggs, Carl and Thomas Pollard (2003) *A World in Chaos: Social Crisis and the Rise of Postmodern Cinema*, Lanham, Oxford: Rowman & Littlefield.
Cartmell, Deborah and Imelda Whelehan (1999) *Adaptations: From Text to Screen, Screen to Text*, London: Routledge.
Cooke, Paul (2007) *World Cinema 'Dialogues' with Hollywood*, Basingstoke and New York: Palgrave Macmillan.
Creekmur, Corey K. and Jyotika Virdi (2006) 'India: Bollywood's Global Coming of Age', in Anne Tereska Ciecko (ed.), *Contemporary Asian Cinema*, Oxford and New York: Berg, pp. 133–43.
Deckha, Nitin (2007) 'From Artist to Hero to the Creative Young Man: Bollywood and the Aestheticization of Indian Masculinity', in Gurbir Jolly, Zenia Wahwani and Deborah Barretto (eds), *Once Upon a Time in Bollywood: The Global Swing in Hindi Cinema*, Ontario: TSAR Publications, pp. 61–9.
Derne, Steve (2000) *Movies, Masculinity, and Modernity: An Ethnography of Men's Film Going in India*, Westport, CT and London: Greenwood Press.
Desai, Radhika (2007) 'Imagi Nation: The Reconfiguration of National Identity in Bombay Cinema in the 1990s', in Gurbir Jolly, Zenia Wahwani and Deborah Barretto (eds), *Once Upon a Time in Bollywood: The Global Swing in Hindi Cinema*, Ontario: TSAR Publications, pp. 43–60.
Doniger, Wendy (2005) *The Woman Who Pretended to Be Who She Was: Myths of Self-Imitation*, New York: Oxford University Press.
Dudrah, Rajinder and Jigna Desai (2008) 'The Essential Bollywood', *The Bollywood Reader*, Maidenhead: Open University Press, pp. 1–17.

Eten, Faria (2002) 'Seen from Bangladesh: No Borders for Devdas', in *Cinemaya*, 56/57, December, pp. 92–6.
Ganpatye, Pramod (1994) *A Guide to the Indian Miniature*, National Museum, New Delhi: Janpath.
Gopal, Sangita (2010) 'Sentimental Symptoms: The Films of Karan Johar and Bombay Cinema', in Rini Battacharya Mehta and Rajeshwari V. Pandharipande (eds), *Bollywood and Globalization: Indian Popular Cinema, Nation and Diaspora*, London: Anthem, pp. 15–34.
Hutchinson, Rachel (2007) 'A Fistful of Yojimbo: Appropriation and Dialogue in Japanese Cinema', in Paul Cooke (ed.), *World Cinema 'Dialogues' with Hollywood*, Basingstoke and New York: Palgrave Macmillan, pp. 172–87.
Ken, Inoue and Kodama Sanehide (1997) 'Postmodernism in Japan', in Hans Bertens and Douwe Fokkema (eds), *International Postmodernism: Theory and Literary Practice*, Amsterdam: John Benjamins, pp. 511–16.
Kumar, Shanti (2008) 'Hollywood, Bollywood, Tollywood: Redefining the Global in Indian Cinema', in Anandam P. Kavoori and Aswin Punathambekar (eds), *Global Bollywood*, New York and London: New York University Press, pp. 79–96.
Mercer, John and Martin Shingler (2004) *Melodrama: Genre, Style and Sensibility*, London and New York: Wallflower.
Ninian, Alex (2003) 'Bollywood', *Contemporary Review*, October, vol. 283, no. 1,653, pp. 235–40.
Rajagopal, Arvind (2008) 'Afterword – Fast-forward into the Future, Haunted by the Past: Bollywood Today', in Anandam P. Kavoori and Aswin Punathambekar (eds), *Global Bollywood*, New York and London: New York University Press, pp. 300–6.
Rao, Raja (1949) 'The Artistic Revival in India: Music, the Dance, Painting', *UNESCO Courier Supplement*, vol. 2, no. 4, May, p. 8.
Skillman, Terry (1998) 'Songs in Hindi Films: Nature and Function', in Wimal Dissanayake (ed.), *Cinema and Cultural Identity: Reflections on Films from Japan, India and China*, Lanham: University Press of America, pp. 149–58.
Sobchak, Vivian (1997) 'Postmodern Modes of Ethnicity', in Peter Brooker and Will Brooker (eds), *Postmodern After Images: A Reader in Film, Television and Video*, London, New York, Sydney and Auckland: Arnold, pp. 113–45.
Sumahendra, D. (1990) *Miniature Painting Technique*, Jaipur: Rooprang Publications.
Thussu, Daya Kishan (2008) 'The Globalisation of "Bollywood": The Hype and the Hope', in Anandam P. Kavoori and Aswin Punathambekar (eds), *Global Bollywood*, New York and London: New York University Press, pp. 97–113.
Whelehan, Imelda (1999) 'The Contemporary Dilemmas', in Deborah Cartmell and Imelda Whelehan (eds), *Adaptations: From Text to Screen, Screen to Text*, London and New York: Routledge.

Appendix: Popular Indian Film Remakes

Film Remake	Year	Original Source(s)	Year
1920	2008	*The Exorcist*	1973
		The Exorcism of Emily Rose	2005
3 Deewarein	2003	*Shawshank Redemption*	1994
36 China Town	2006	*Once Upon a Crime…*	1992
7 1/2 Phere	2005	*Ed TV*	1999
Aap Ki Khatir	2006	*The Wedding Date*	2005
Aapko Pehle Bhi Kahin Dekha Hai	2003	*Father of the Bride / Meet the Parents*	1991/2000
Aamir	2008	*Cavite*	2005
Aashiqui 2	2013	*A Star Is Born*	1976
Abraa Ka Daabra	2004	*Harry Potter and the Philosopher's Stone*	2001
Agneepath	1990	*Scarface*	1983
Agneepath	2012	*Agneepath*	1990
Agni Sakshi	1996	*Sleeping with the Enemy*	1991
Aitraaz	2004	*Disclosure*	1994
Ajnabee	2001	*Consenting Adults*	1992
Akele Hum, Akele Tum	1995	*Kramer versus Kramer*	1979
Alag	2006	*Powder*	1995
Anamika	2008	*Rebecca*	1940
Anjaane: The Unknown	2005	*The Others*	2001
Aunty No.1	1998	*Mrs Doubtfire*	1993
Awara Paagal Dewaana	2002	*The Whole Nine Yards*	2000
Baazigar	1993	*A Kiss Before Dying*	1991
Bachke Raina Babu	2005	*Heartbreakers*	2001
Bewafaa	2005	*Gumrah*	1963
Bhagham Bhag	2006	*Mannar Mathai Speaking*	1995
Bheja Fry	2007	*Le Dinner De Cons*	1998
Bichhoo	2000	*Leon*	1994
Black	2005	*The Miracle Worker*	1962
Blue	2009	*Into the Blue*	2005

Film Remake	Year	Original Source(s)	Year
Bluffmaster	2005	*Matchstick Men*	2003
Bunty Aur Babli	2005	*Bonnie and Clyde*	1967
Chachi 420	1998	*Mrs Doubtfire*	1993
Chak De India	2007	*Miracle*	2004
Chocolate: Deep Dark Secrets	2005	*The Usual Suspects*	1994
Chori Chori	2003	*Housesitter*	1992
Chor Machaaye Shor	2002	*Blue Streak*	1999
Chura liyaa Hai Tumne	2003	*The Truth About Charlie / Charade*	2002 / 1963
Commando	1988	*American Ninja*	1985
Criminal	1995	*The Fugitive*	1993
Daddy Cool	2009	*Death at a Funeral*	2007
Dansh	2005	*Death and the Maiden*	1994
Daraar	1996	*Sleeping with the Enemy*	1991
Darr	1993	*Dead Calm*	1989
Devdas	2002	*Devdas*	1955
Dewaangee	2002	*Primal Fear*	1996
Dewane Huye Paagal	2005	*There's Something About Mary*	1998
Dhamaal	2007	*It's a Mad, Mad, Mad, Mad World*	1963
Dhoom	2004	*Point Break / The Fast and the Furious*	1991 / 2001
Dil Hai Ke Manta Nahin	1991	*It Happened One Night*	1934
Dil Ka Rishta	2003	*Magnificent Obsession*	1954
Do Knot Disturb	2009	*The Valet*	2006
Don Muthu Swami	2008	*Oscar*	1991
Don: The Chase Begins	2006	*Don*	1978
Dostana	2008	*I Now Pronounce You Chuck and Larry*	2007
Duplicate	1998	*Desperado / Multiplicity*	1995 / 1996
Dus	2005	*Usual Suspects / Sum of All Fears*	1994 / 2002
Ek Ajnabee	2005	*Man On Fire*	2004
Ek Din 24 Ghante	2003	*Run Lola Run*	1998
Ek Chhotisi Love Story	2002	*Krotki Film O Milosci*	1988
Fareb	1996	*Unlawful Entry*	1992
Fight Club	2006	*Fight Club*	1999
Ghajini	2008	*Memento*	2000
Ghulam	1998	*On the Waterfront*	1954
God Tussi Great Ho	2008	*Bruce Almighty*	2003
Hari Puttar	2008	*Home Alone*	1990
Hawa	2003	*The Entity*	1981
Heyy Baby	2007	*3 Men and a Baby*	1987
Hiss	2009	*Nagin / Nagina*	1976 / 1986
Hum Hai Kamaal Ke	1993	*See No Evil, Hear No Evil*	1989
Hum Hai Rahi Pyaar Kain	1993	*Houseboat*	1958
Hum Kaun Hai	2004	*The Others*	2001
Hum Kisi Se Kum Nahin	2002	*Analyze This*	1999
Humraaz	2002	*Dial M For Murder*	1954

APPENDIX: POPULAR INDIAN FILM REMAKES 217

Film Remake	Year	Original Source(s)	Year
Hum Tum	2004	*When Harry Met Sally*	1989
Inteha	2003	*Fear*	1996
Jaani Dushman: Ek Anokhi Kahani	2002	*Nagin/Jaani Dushman*	1976/1979
Jism	2003	*Double Indemnity/Body Heat*	1944/1981
Jo Bole So Nihaal	2005	*Crocodile Dundee*	1986
Jo Geeta Woi Sikander	1992	*Breaking Away*	1979
Josh	2000	*West Side Story*	1961
Judaii	1997	*Indecent Proposal*	1993
Jung	2000	*Desperate Measures*	1998
Kaante	2002	*Reservoir Dogs*	1992
Kahin Pyaar Na Hon Jaye	2000	*The Wedding Singer*	1998
Karobaar: The Business of Love	2000	*Indecent Proposal*	1993
Karzzzz	2008	*Karz*	1980
Kasoor	2001	*Jagged Edge*	1985
Khal Naaikaa	1993	*The Hand That Rocks the Cradle*	1992
Kismat Konnection	2008	*Just My Luck*	2006
Koi Mil…Gaya	2003	*E.T.: The Extra Terrestrial*	1982
Krazzy 4	2008	*The Dream Team*	1989
Krishna Cottage	2004	*The Ring*	1998
Krrish	2006	*The Matrix/Daredevil/Paycheck*	1999/2003/2003
Kuch Khatti Kuch Meethi	2001	*The Parent Trap*	1961
Kucch To Hai	2003	*I Know What You Did Last Summer*	1998
Kyon Ki…	2005	*One Flew Over the Cuckoo's Nest*	1975
Kyo Kii… Main Jhuth Nahin Bolta	2001	*Liar Liar*	1997
Mahakaal	1993	*Nightmare on Elm Street*	1984
Main Aisan Hi Hoon	2005	*I Am Sam*	2001
Main Azaad Hoon	1989	*Meet John Doe*	1941
Main Hoon Na	2004	*MI2/The Matrix*	1996/1999
Maine Pyar Kyun Kiya	2005	*Cactus Flower*	1969
Malamaal Weekly	2006	*Waking Ned*	1998
Mann	1999	*An Affair to Remember*	1957
Manorama 6 Feet Under	2007	*Chinatown*	1974
Masti	2004	*The Seven Year Itch*	1955
Mazaa Mazaa	2004	*13 Going On 30*	2004
Mere Yaar Ki Shaadi	2002	*My Best Friend's Wedding*	1997
Mohabbatein	2000	*Dead Poets Society*	1989
Mother India	1957	*Aurat*	1940
Mr India	1987	*Indiana Jones and the Temple of Doom*	1984
Mr Ya Miss	2005	*The Hot Chick*	2002
Munna Bhai	2003	*Patch Adams/Analyze This*	1998/1999
Murder	2004	*Unfaithful*	2002
Musafir	2004	*U-Turn*	1997

Film Remake	Year	Original Source(s)	Year
Naina	2002	*The Eye*	2002
Naksha	2006	*The Rundown / Indiana Jones and the Last Crusade*	2003/1989
Naqaab	2007	*Dot the I*	2003
Om Shanti Om	2007	*Karz*	1980
One Two Three	2008	*Blame It on the Bellboy*	1992
Padmashree Laloo Prasad Yadav	2005	*A Fish Called Wanda*	1998
Paheli	2005	*Duvidha*	1973
Parineeta	2005	*Parineeta*	1953
Partner	2007	*Hitch*	2005
Phir Hera Phiri	2006	*Lock, Stock and Two Smoking Barrels*	1998
Plan	2004	*Suicide Kings*	1997
Pyaar To Hona Hi Ta	1998	*French Kiss*	1995
Pyaar Tune Kya Kiya	2001	*Fatal Attraction*	1987
Qayamat	2003	*The Rock*	1996
Raaz	2002	*What Lies Beneath*	2000
Race	2008	*Goodbye Lover*	1998
Raghu Romeo	2003	*Tie Me Up, Tie Me Down*	1990
Rakht	2004	*The Gift*	2000
Ram Gopal Varma Ki Aag	2007	*Sholay*	1975
Ru Ba Ru	2008	*If Only*	2004
Saaya	2003	*Dragonfly*	2002
Sadak	1991	*Taxi Driver / Lethal Weapon / Cyborg*	1976/1987/1989
Salaam-E-Ishq	2007	*Love Actually*	2003
Salaam Namaste	2005	*Nine Months*	1995
Samay	2003	*Seven*	1995
Sangharsh	1999	*Silence of the Lambs*	1991
Sarkar	2005	*The Godfather*	1972
Sauda – The Deal	2005	*Indecent Proposal*	1993
Sholay	1975	*The Magnificent Seven*	1960
Singh is Kinng	2008	*Miracles*	1989
Soch	2002	*Strangers on a Train*	1951
Speed	2007	*Cellular*	2004
Taarzan: The Wonder Car	2004	*Christine*	1983
Ta Ra Rum Pum	2007	*Days of Thunder*	1990
Tathastu	2006	*John Q*	2002
Teen Patti	2009	*21*	2008
Tees Maar Khan	2010	*After the Fox*	1966
The Killer	2006	*Collateral*	2004
The Train	2007	*Derailed*	2005
Thoda Pyaar Thoda Magic	2008	*Mary Poppins*	1964
Ugly Aur Pagli	2008	*My Sassy Girl*	2001
U, Me Aur Hum	2008	*A Moment to Remember*	2004
Umrao Jaan	2006	*Umrao Jaan*	1981
Viruddh	2005	*In the Bedroom*	2001

Film Remake	Year	Original Source(s)	Year
Yaarana	1995	*Sleeping with the Enemy*	1991
Ye Dil Lagi	1994	*Sabrina*	1954
Yeh Kya Ho Raha Hai	2002	*American Pie*	1999
Yes Boss	1997	*For Love or Money*	1993
Yuvraaj	2008	*Rain Man*	1988
Zamaanat	2009	*Justice Chowdhary / Scent of a Woman*	1982 / 1992
Zeher	2005	*Out of Time*	2003
Zinda	2006	*Oldboy*	2003

Filmography

36 China Town, dir. Abbas and Mastan Alibhai Burmawalla. India: Mukta Arts, 2006
Aa Ab Laut Chalein, dir. Rishi Kapoor. India: R. K. Films Ltd, 1999
Abhay [aka *Aalavandhan*], dir. Suresh Krishna. India: V. Creations, 2001
Action Replay, dir. Vipul Amrutlal Shah. India: PVR Pictures, 2009
Agneepath, dir. Mukul Anand. India: Dharma Productions, 1990
Agneepath, dir. Karan Malhotra. India: Dharma Productions, 2012
Amores Perros, dir. Alejandro González Iñárritu. Mexico: Altavista Films, 2000
Amrapali, dir. Lekh Tandon. India: Eagle Films, 1966
An Evening in Paris, dir. Shakti Samanta. India: Shakti Films, 1967
Asoka, dir. Santosh Sivan. India: Dreamz Unlimited, 2001
Awara Paagal Deewana, dir. Vikram Bhatt. India: Base Industries Group, 2002
Bang Bang, dir. Siddharth Anand. India: Fox STAR Studios, 2014
Being John Malkovich, dir. Spike Jonze. USA: Astralwerks, 1999
Billu Barber, dir. Priyadarshan. India: Red Chillies Entertainment, 2009
Black, dir. Sanjay Leela Bhasali. India: SLB Films, 2005
Blue, dir. Anthony D'Souza. India: Shree Ashtavinayak Cine Vision, 2009
Blue, dir. Anthony D'Souza. India: Shree Ashtavinayak Cine Vision, 2009
Body Heat, dir. Lawrence Kasdan. USA: The Ladd Company, 1981
Bol Bachchan, dir. Rohit Shetty. India: Devgan Films, 2012
Bonnie and Clyde, dir. Arthur Penn. USA: Warner Bros Seven Arts, 1967
Bride and Prejudice, dir. Gurinder Chadha. UK/USA: Pathé Pictures, 2004
Bunty aur Babli, dir. Shaad Ali. India: Yash Raj Films, 2005
Cash, dir. Anubhav Sinha. India: Seven Entertainment, 2007
Cellular, dir. David R. Ellis. USA/Germany: LFG Filmproduktions & Co./New Line Cinema, 2004
Chak De India, dir. Shimit Amin. India: Yash Raj Films, 2007
Chand Par Chadayee, dir. T. P. Sundaram. India: Cauvery Productions, 1967
Chandni Chowk to China, dir. Nikhil Advani. India/USA: Warner Bros, 2009
Chashme Baddoor, dir. Sai Paranjpye. India: PLA Productions, 1981
Chashme Baddoor, dir. David Dhawan, India: Viacom18 Pictures, 2013
Chocolate: Deep Dark Secrets, dir. Vivek Agnihotri. India: Inspired Movies, 2005
City on Fire, dir. Ringo Lam. Hong Kong: Cinema City, 1987
Company, dir. Ram Gopal Varma. India: Varma Corporation, 2002

Coolie, dir. Manmohan Desai. India: Asia Films, 1983
Daredevil, dir. Mark Steven Johnson. USA: Marvel Enterprises, 2003
Darna Zaroori Hai, dir. Ram Gopal Varma/J. D. Chakravarthi/Manish Gupta/Sajid Khan/Jijy Philip/Prawal Raman/Vivek Shah. India: K Sera Sera, 2006
Dead Poets Society, dir. Peter Weir. USA: Touchstone, 1989
Dev. D, dir. Anurag Kashyap. India: UTV Motion Pictures, 2009
Devdas, dir. Bimal Roy. India: Bimal Roy Productions, 1955
Devdas, dir. Sanjay Leela Bhansali. India: Mega Bollywood, 2002
Dhoom, dir. Sanjay Gadhvi. India: Yash Raj Films, 2004
Dhoom 2, dir. Sanjay Gadhvi. India: Yash Raj Films, 2006
Dhoom 3, dir. Vijay Krishna Acharya. India: Yash Raj Films, 2013
Dil Chahta Hai, dir. Farhan Akhtar. India: Excel Entertainment, 2001
Dil Se, dir. Mani Ratnam. India: India Talkies, 1998
Dilwale Dulhaniya Le Jayenge, dir. Yash Chopra. India: Yash Raj Films, 1995
Don, dir. Chandra Barot. India: Nariman Films, 1978
Don: The Chase Begins, dir. Farhan Akhtar. India: Excel Entertainment, 2006
Dostana, dir. Tarun Mansukhani. India: Dharma Productions, 2008
Double Indemnity, dir. Billy Wilder. USA: Paramount Pictures, 1944
Dredd, dir. Peter Travis. USA: DNA Films, 2012
Dum Maaro Dum, dir. Rohan Sippy. India: Fox STAR Studios, 2011
Dus, dir. Anubhav Sinha. India: Neha Arts, 2005
Ek Ajnabee, dir. Apoorva Lakhia. India: G. S. Entertainment, 2005
Eklavya: The Royal Guard, dir. Vidhu Vinod Chopra. India: Vinod Chopra Productions, 2007
Elaan, dir. K. Ramanlal. India: United Producers, 1971
E.T.: The Extra Terrestrial, dir. Steven Spielberg. USA: Universal Pictures, 1982
ExTerminators, dir. John Inwood. USA: UTV Motion Pictures, 2009
Face/Off, dir. John Woo. USA: Permut Presentations, 1997
Fight Club, dir. David Fincher. USA: Fox 2000 Pictures, 1999
Fight Club: Members Only, dir. Vikram Chopra. India: Rising Star Entertainment, 2006
Gaja Gamini, dir. M. F. Hussain. India: Dashaka Films, 2000
Ghajini, dir. A. R. Murugadoss. India: Geetha Arts, 2008
Ghostbusters, dir. Ivan Reitman. USA: Black Rhino Productions, 1984
Ghost World, dir. Terry Zwigoff. USA: United Artists, 2001
Girlfriend, dir. Karan Razdan. India: MIG Film, 2004
Goliyon Ki Rasleela Ram-Leela, dir. Sanjay Leela Bhansali. India: SLB Films, 2013
Gol Maal, dir. Hrishikesh Mukherjee. India: Rupam Chitra, 1979
Golmaal Returns, dir. Rohit Shetty. India: Indian Films, 2008
Gone with the Wind, dir. Victor Fleming. USA: Selznick International, 1939
Guide, dir. Vijay Anand. India: Navketan International, 1965
Guzaarish, dir. Sanjay Leela Bhansali. India: SLB Films/UTV Motion Pictures, 2010
Hanuman, dir. V. G. Samant and Milind Ukey. India: Percept Picture Company, 2005
Hey Ram!, dir. Kamal Haasan. India: Raajkamal Films International, 2000
Himmatwala, dir. K. Raghavendra Rao. India: Padmalaya Films, 1983
Himmatwala, dir. Sajid Khan. India: UTV Motion Pictures, 2013
Hindustani [aka *Indian*], dir. S. Shankar. India: Jhamu Sughand Productions, 1996
Hisss, dir. Jennifer Lynch. India/USA: Split Image Pictures, 2010
Hitch, dir. Andy Tennant. USA: Columbia Pictures, 2005
Hum Aapke Hai Kaun, dir. Sooraj R. Barjatya. India: Rajshri Productions, 1994
Hum Dil De Chuke Sanam, dir. Sanjay Leela Bhansali. India: Bhansali Films, 1999

Humjoli, dir. Ramanna. India: Tirupati Pictures, 1970
Hum Tum, dir. Kunal Kohli. India: Yash Raj Films, 2004
Hyderabad Blues, dir. Nagesh Kukunoor. India: Kukunoor Movies, 1998
Indiana Jones and the Temple of Doom, dir. Steven Spielberg. USA: Paramount, 1984
It Happened One Night, dir. Frank Capra. USA: Columbia, 1934
Jaani Dushman: Ek Anokhi Kahani, dir. Rajkumar Kohli. India: Shankar Films, 2002
Jai Vejay, dir. L. V. Prasad. India: Prasad Productions, 1977
Jewel Thief, dir. Vijay Anand. India: Navketan, 1967
Jhoom Barabar Jhoom, dir. Shaad Ali. India: Yash Raj Films, 2007
Jism, dir. Amit Saxena. India: Fish Eye Network, 2003
Jodha Akbar, dir. Ashutosh Gowariker. India: UTV Motion Pictures, 2008
Kaante, dir. Sanjay Gupta. India: Pritish Nandy Communications, 2002
Kabhi Alvida Naa Kehna, dir. Karan Johar. India: Dharma Productions, 2006
Kabhi Kabhie, dir. Yash Chopra. India: Yash Raj Films, 1976
Kabhi Kushi Kabhie Gham, dir. Karan Johar. India: Dharma Productions, 2001
Kaho Naa . . . Pyaar Hai, dir. Rakesh Roshan. India: Film Kraft, 2000
Kal Ho Naa Ho, dir. Karan Johar. India: Dharma Productions, 2003
Kambakkht Ishq, dir. Sabbir Khan. India: Eros International, 2009
Karz, dir. Subhash Ghai. India: Mukta Arts, 1981
Khal Nayak, dir. Subhash Ghai. India: Mukta Arts, 1993
Kites, dir. Rakesh Roshan. India: Bollywood Hollywood Production, 2009
Knight and Day, dir. James Mangold. USA: Twentieth Century Fox, 2010
Koi . . . Mil Gaya, dir. Rakesh Roshan. India: Film Kraft, 2003
Krishna Cottage, dir. Santram Varma. India: Balaji Films, 2004
Krrish, dir. Rakesh Roshan. India: Film Kraft, 2006
Krrish 3, dir. Rakesh Roshan. India: Film Kraft, 2013
Kuch Kuch Hota Hai, dir. Karan Johar. India: Yash Raj Films, 1998
Lagaan: Once Upon a Time in India, dir. Ashutosh Gowariker. India: Aamir Khan Productions, 2001
Lage Raho Munna Bhai, dir. Rajkumar Hirani. India: Vinod Chopra Productions, 2006
Life of Pi, dir. Ang Lee. USA: Fox 2000 Pictures, 2012
Love, Sex Aur Dhokha, dir. Dibakar Banerjee. India: ALT Entertainment, 2010
Luck by Chance, dir. Zoya Akhtar. India: Excel Entertainment/Reliance Big Pictures, 2009
Lust, Caution, dir. Ang Lee. USA/China/Taiwan: Haishang Films, 2007
Maine Pyar Kiya, dir. Sooraj R. Barjatya. India: Rajshri Productions, 1989
Main Hoon Na, dir. Farah Khan. India: Red Chillies Entertainment, 2004
Main, Meri Patni . . . Aur Woh!, dir. Chandan Arora. India: UTV Motion Pictures, 2005
Mamma Mia!, dir. Phyllida Lloyd. UK/USA/Germany: Universal, 2008
Mary Poppins, dir. Robert Stevenson. USA: Walt Disney, 1964
Mast, dir. Ram Gopal Varma. India: Varma Corportation, 1999
Matchstick Men, dir. Ridley Scott. USA: Warner Bros, 2003
Memento, dir. Christopher Nolan. USA: Newmarket Capital Group, 2000
Milenge Milenge, dir. Satish Kaushik. India: Eros International, 2010
Mission: Impossible – Ghost Protocol, dir. Brad Bird. USA: Skydance Productions, 2011
Mohabbatein, dir. Aditya Chopra. India: Yash Raj Films, 2000
Monsoon Wedding, dir. Mira Nair. India/USA/Italy/Germany/France: IFC Productions, 2001
Mother India, dir. Mehboob Khan. India: Mehboob Productions, 1957
Moulin Rouge, dir. Baz Luhrmann. USA/Australia: Twentieth Century Fox/Bazmark, 2005

Mr India, dir. Boney Kapoor. India: Narsimha Enterprises, 1987
Mujhse Shaadi Karogi, dir. David Dhawan. India: Nadiadwala Grandsons, 2004
Munna Bhai M.B.B.S, dir. Rajkumar Hirani. India: Vinod Chopra Productions, 2003
Murder, dir. Anurag Basu. India: Vishesh Films, 2004
Musafir, dir. Sanjay Gupta. India: White Feather Films, 2004
My Cousin Vinny, dir. Johnathan Lynn. USA: Twentieth Century Fox, 1992
My Name Is Khan, dir. Karan Johar. India: Dharma Productions, 2010
Naach, dir. Ram Gopal Varma. India: K Sera Sera, 2004
Nagina, dir. Harmesh Malhotra. India: Eastern Films, 1986
Nigahen, dir. Harmesh Malhotra. India: Eastern Films, 1989
Oldboy, dir. Chan-wook Park. South Korea: Egg Films/Show East, 2003
Om Shanti Om, dir. Farah Khan. India: Red Chillies Entertainment, 2007
Our Hospitality, dir. John G. Blystone/Buster Keaton. USA: Joseph M. Schenck Productions, 1923
Oye Lucky! Lucky Oye!, dir. Dibakar Banerjee. India: UTV Motion Pictures, 2008
Paheli, dir. Amol Palekar. India: Red Chillies Entertainment, 2005
Parineeta, dir. Bimal Roy. India: Ashok Kumar Productions, 1953
Parineeta, dir. Pradeep Sarkar. India: Vinod Chopra Productions, 2005
Partner, dir. David Dhawan. India: K Sera Sera/Eros International, 2007
Perhaps Love, dir. Peter Chan. China/Hong Kong: Applause Pictures, 2005
Phir Bhi Dil Hai Hindustani, dir. Aziz Mirza. India: Dreamz Unlimited, 2000
Players, dir. Abbas Alibhai Burmawalla/Mastan Alibhai Burmawalla. India: Viacom18 Motion Pictures, 2011
Pleasantville, dir. Gary Ross. USA: New Line Cinema, 1998
Powder, dir. Victor Salva. USA: Caravan Pictures, 1995
Raaz, dir. Vikram Bhatt. India: Bhatt Productions, 2002
Raaz 3, dir. Vikram Bhatt. India: Fox STAR Studios, 2012
Rab Ne Bana Di Jodi, dir. Aditya Chopra. India: Yash Raj Films, 2008
Race, dir. Abbas and Mastan Alibhai Burmawalla. India: UTV Motion Pictures, 2008
Raja Harichandra, dir. Dhundiraj Govind Phalke. India: Phalke Films, 1913
Ram Gopal Varma's Aag, dir. Ram Gopal Varma. India: K Sera Sera, 2007
Rang De Basanti, dir. Rakesh Omprakash Mehra. India: UTV Motion Pictures, 2006
Rangeela, dir. Ram Gopal Varma. India: Jhamu Sughand Productions, 1995
Reservoir Dogs, dir. Quentin Tarantino. USA: Dog Eat Dog Productions, 1992
Return of the Jewel Thief, dir. Ashok Tyagi. India: Arshee Films, 1996
Ringu, dir. Hideo Nakata. Japan: Omega Project, 1998
Roadside Romeo, dir. Jugal Hansraj. India/USA: Yash Raj Films/Walt Disney, 2008
Saawariya, dir. Sanjay Leela Bhansali. India: SLB Films, 2009
Sachaa Jhuta, dir. Manmohan Desai. India: V. R. Films, 1970
Salaam Namaste, dir. Siddharth Anand. India: Yash Raj Films, 2005
Sarkar, dir. Ram Gopal Varma. India: K Sera Sera, 2005
Sarkar Raj, dir. Ram Gopal Varma. India: K Sera Sera/Adlabs, 2008
Satya, dir. Ram Gopal Varma. India: Varma Corporation, 1998
Serendipity, dir. Peter Chelsom. USA: Miramax/Tapestry Films, 2001
Shabd, dir. Leena Yadav. India: Pritish Nandy Communications, 2005
Shahenshah, dir. Tinnu Anand. India: Film Vision, 1988
Shiva Ka Insaaf, dir. Raj N. Sippy. India: Shemaroo, 1985
Shoeshine, dir. Vittorio De Sica. Italy: Società Cooperativa Alfa Cinematografica, 1946
Sholay, dir. Ramesh Sippy. India: United Producers, 1975

Silver Linings Playbook, dir. David O. Russell. USA: The Weinstein Company, 2012
Singh Is Kinng, dir. Anees Bazmee. India: Blockbuster Movie Entertainers, 2008
Slumdog Millionaire, dir. Danny Boyle. UK: Celador Films/Pathé/Film4, 2008
Son of Sardaar, dir. Ashwani Dhir. India: Viacom18 Motion Pictures, 2012
Stepmom, dir. Chris Columbus. USA: Tristar/1492 Pictures, 1998
Superman, dir. Richard Donner. USA/UK: Dovemead Films, 1978
Swades, dir. Ashutosh Gowariker. India: UTV Motion Pictures, 2004
Sweeney Todd: The Demon Barber of Fleet Street, dir. Tim Burton. USA/UK: Warner Bros/Dreamworks, 2007
Tashan, dir. Vijay Krishna Acharya. India: Yash Raj Films, 2008
Teen Patti, dir. Leena Yadav. India: Hinduja Ventures, 2009
Tees Maar Khan, dir. Farah Khan. India: UTV Motion Pictures, 2010
The Amazing Spider-Man, dir. Mark Webb. USA: Columbia/Marvel, 2012
The Curious Case of Benjamin Button, dir. David Fincher. USA: Warner Bros/Paramount, 2008
The Dark Knight, dir. Christopher Nolan. USA/UK: Warner Bros, 2008
The Eye, dir. Oxide Pang Chun and Danny Pang. Hong Kong/Singapore: Applause Pictures, 2002
The Gift, dir. Sam Raimi. USA: Lakeshore Entertainment, 2000
The Godfather, dir. Francis Ford Coppola. USA: Paramount, 1972
The Great Gatsby, dir. Baz Luhrmann. USA/Australia: Warner Bros/Bazmark, 2013
The Guru, dir. Daisy von Scherler Mayer. UK/France/USA: Studio Canal/Working Title Films, 2002
The Italian Job, dir. Peter Collinson. UK: Paramount, 1969
The Matrix, dir. Andy and Larry Wachowski. USA/Australia: Warner Bros, 1999
The Pink Panther 2, dir. Harald Zwart. USA: Metro-Goldwyn-Mayer/Columbia, 2009
The Ring, dir. Gore Verbinski. USA: Dreamworks, 2002
The Sound of Music, dir. Robert Wise. USA: Argyle Enterprises, 1965
The Truman Show, dir. Peter Weir. USA: Paramount, 1998
The Usual Suspects, dir. Byan Singer. USA: PolyGram Filmed Entertainment, 1995
The Wizard of Oz, dir. Victor Fleming. USA: Metro-Goldwyn-Mayer, 1939
Three Men and a Baby, dir. Leonard Nimoy. USA: Touchstone, 1987
Titanic, dir. James Cameron. USA: Twentieth Century Fox/Paramount, 1997
Toofan, dir. Ketan Desai. India: M. K. D. Films Combine, 1989
Umrao Jaan, dir. Muzaffar Ali. India: Integrated Films, 1981
Umrao Jaan, dir. J. P. Dutta. India: J. P. Films, 2006
U-Turn, dir. Oliver Stone. USA/France: Phoenix Pictures/Illusion Entertainment Group, 1997
Vaastav: The Reality, dir. Mahesh Manjrekar. India: Adishakti Films, 1999
Walking with Dinosaurs 3D, dir. Barry Cook/Neil Nightingale. UK/USA: BBC Earth, 2013
Waqt, dir. Yash Chopra. India: United Producers, 1965
We Are Family, dir. Siddharth Malhotra. India: Columbia/Dharma Productions, 2010
What Lies Beneath, dir. Robert Zemekis. USA: Twentieth Century Fox, 2000
When Harry Met Sally, dir. Rob Reiner. USA: Castle Roch Entertainment, 1989
Zanjeer, dir. Prakash Mehra. India: Prakash Mehra Productions, 1973
Zanjeer, dir. Apoorva Lakhia. India: Prakash Mehra Productions, 2013
Zinda, dir. Sanjay Gupta. India: White Feather Films, 2006

Index

Abhay, 17, 20n, 62n, 93, 114, 116–24, 126, 127, 151, 178, 198
adaptation, 3, 4, 18, 56, 57, 111, 130–3, 146n, 149, 152, 160, 163, 165, 182, 185, 188n
advertising, 4, 20n, 64, 95, 106, 173; *see also* consumerism
ahistorical, 88–9, 149, 165–6; *see also* metahistory
Akhtar, Farhan, 3, 9, 168, 170, 172
alternative modernism, 68
alternative postmodernism, 75
animation, 3, 111, 119–21, 167, 188n, 195; *see also* cartoon
apolitical *see* depthless
asian cinema, 37, 51, 52
aura (lost), 13, 82, 151, 186
Australia (and Bollywood), 5, 38, 50, 55, 62n, 169
auteur, 17, 45, 46, 100, 126
avant-garde, 2, 17, 53, 71, 83, 84, 116, 117, 124, 151, 189n, 195
   expressionist, 116

Bachchan, Abhishek, 8, 143–5
Bachchan, Amitabh, 2, 4, 19n, 23, 33, 143–5, 146n, 184, 198
Baudrillard, Jean, 13–14, 16, 59, 79, 84, 92, 93, 99; *see also* hyper and simulacra
Bertens, Hans (and Douwe Fokkema), 66–7, 69–70
Betaal, 118, 123
Bhagavad Gita, 97, 126n

Bhansali, Sanjay Leela, 3, 32, 134, 148, 149, 158, 160, 162, 163, 164, 165
Bhatt, Vikram, 134, 140, 182, 198
blank parody *see* parody
blank pastiche *see* pastiche
Blu-ray, 165
Bollywood (definition), 32–6
Bollywood-Hollywood (remake), 35, 136, 173–82
Bollywoodisation, 33, 37
Bombay *see* city
boundary blurring, 15, 82, 85–6, 100, 102, 116
bricolage, 80, 82, 85, 87, 91, 140, 187, 195
British Film Institute (BFI), 6, 20n, 46, 61–2n
Bunty aur Babli, 143, 145, 183, 197

canon (Indian cinema), 18, 26, 36, 53, 91, 94, 135, 195
capitalism, 5, 9, 13, 35, 36, 40, 59, 64, 66, 77, 192
cartoon, 119, 120, 121, 122, 167; *see also* animation
casting (global), 2, 4–5, 62n, 92, 94, 129, 144, 156, 168, 171, 197, 198; *see also* genetic textuality
celebrity intertextuality *see* intertextuality
Chinese postmodernism, 39, 73–4
cinephilia, 12, 84, 85, 99, 166
circular narrative, 97–9
city
   Delhi, 63–4, 78n
   Mumbai (Bombay), 64–5, 78n, 144

cognitive (scientific theory), 32, 58–9
colonial, 3, 29, 70, 71, 73, 106, 149, 180
　postcolonial, 23, 24, 25–6, 29, 69–70, 87, 103–9
　see also reverse colonialism
comic book aesthetics, 17, 62n, 118–23, 167
commodification, 5, 73
commoditisation, 30, 35, 105, 144, 154, 194, 195, 199
conjugation, 5
consumerism, 5, 7, 39, 64–5, 67, 73, 77, 83, 95–6, 105–6; *see also* advertising
contemporary Bollywood, 8, 16, 20n, 28, 31, 46, 50, 55–61
cool (aesthetic), 129, 141, 172, 174–9, 186–7, 191
copyright, 138, 181
costume, 27, 48, 91, 92, 97, 106, 113, 115, 118, 143, 149, 152, 156, 158–9, 165–6, 169, 174, 176, 195
cultural proximity, 50, 134, 174

de-differentiation, 5, 15, 86, 151
Delhi *see* city
depthless, 13, 41, 42, 79, 81–3, 149
Devdas, 3, 18, 32, 47, 51, 58, 60, 94, 134, 146n, 148–54, 156–65, 186, 188n
Dhoom, 4, 52, 92, 94, 99, 173, 176, 184, 195–6
diaspora, 6, 10, 12, 22, 25–9, 37, 38, 45n, 51, 53, 56, 61, 135, 153–4, 196; *see also* non-resident Indian
Dil Chahta Hain, 3, 9, 166–72, 184
Dilwale Dulhania Le Jayenge, 9, 26, 27, 50, 168
Dirlik, Arif (and Zhang, Xudong), 72–4
Disney, 38, 45n, 52
displeasure, 39, 41, 44, 45n, 50, 55, 154, 190
Druxman, Michael, 130, 132–4, 137
Dudrah, Rajinder, 61, 179, 180, 186, 187
Dutt, Sanjay, 142, 146n, 167

economic liberalisation (Indian film industry), 1–2, 5, 6, 25, 38, 54, 57, 81, 190
Ek Ajnabee, 94, 141, 173, 183
endorsement (celebrity), 12n, 64, 95–6
E.T.: The Extra Terrestrial, 100–3, 109–13, 132

excess, 2, 18, 30, 42–3, 55, 59, 82, 90, 98, 113, 140, 149, 151–6, 158–61, 164–5, 178–80, 188n, 190, 195

femininity *see* gender
fidelity, 18, 129–30, 132
figural, 42, 77, 79, 83–4, 90, 148–52, 159–66, 178, 182, 188n, 194, 195; *see also* Lash, Scott
film education, 30, 48–55
film festival, 3, 15–16, 46, 61, 62n, 149
film financing, 1, 5, 25, 38, 61n, 147n, 172, 181–2, 199
film studies *see* film education
Fokkema, Douwe *see* Bertens, Hans
fragmentation, 26, 28, 34, 41, 42, 64, 82, 86–7, 90, 149, 152, 179–80, 196
franchise, 4, 52, 132, 173
　cultural, 135, 146n, 186
　Dhoom, 52, 173

Gaja Gamini, 1, 2, 20n
Ganti, Tejaswini, 24, 31–3, 57–8, 134
gender, 8, 94, 156–8, 172, 176–7, 184
　femininity, 2, 156, 171, 176
　masculinity, 2, 173, 176–7, 184
genetic textuality *see* intertextuality
Genette, Gerard, 85, 130–2, 146n, 189n
genre (film), 10, 27–8, 30, 35, 43, 60, 100–14
global cinema, 37–8
global postmodernism *see* international postmodernism
globalisation, 25, 37, 39, 65, 81, 179, 181, 182, 185
Godfather, The, 18, 132, 143–4, 183–5; *see also* Sarkar
Goliyon Ki Raasleela Ram-Leela, 165–6
grand narrative, 14, 70, 82, 86, 89, 194; *see also* Lyotard, Jean-François
guidebook (Indian cinema), 23, 24–5, 30–1, 44n
Gupta, Sanjay, 3, 167, 174; *see also Kaante, Musafir, Zinda*
Guzaarish, 165

Haasan, Kamal, 116–17; *see also Abhay*
Hatke, 5, 6, 134, 197–8
[H]indianisation, 57–8, 182
Hinglish, 5, 48

Hong Kong (cinema, aesthetic), 37, 38, 39, 51, 172, 131, 141
Hutcheon, Linda, 8, 11, 12, 15, 16, 20n, 79, 81, 138
hybridity, 3, 29, 30, 31, 35, 60, 82, 85, 107, 131, 140, 174, 179, 184, 194; *see also* bricolage
hyper
  -feminine, 2, 156
  -masculine, 2
  -performativity, 60
  -realism, 14, 59, 79, 82, 87–8, 92, 118–23, 136, 156, 171, 190, 195
  -textual, 130, 138

imitation, 42, 56, 75, 98, 140–2, 169, 186; *see also* parody, mimicry
Indian film studies *see* film studies
industry status *see* economic liberalisation
intentionality, 12, 76, 82, 83, 138–42, 166, 184–5, 188n, 193
international postmodernism, 66–76, 136, 192; *see also* Bertens, Hans
intertextuality, 11, 18, 35, 76, 80, 82, 85, 99, 130–1, 137, 139, 140, 142, 181, 187, 199
  celebrity, 131, 142–5
  genetic, 131, 142–5
irony (postmodern), 9, 11, 93, 125, 140–1

Jameson, Fredric, 11, 13, 14, 15, 16, 65, 79, 80, 81, 83, 91, 99; *see also* parody, pastiche, depthless
Jhoom Barabar Jhoom, 61
Johar, Karan, 2, 7, 26, 28; *see also Kabhi Kushi Kabhie Gham, Kal Ho Naa Ho, My Name is Khan*

Kaante, 38, 86, 132, 172–6, 177–81, 183, 187, 191
Kabhi Kushi Kabhie Gham (K3G), 2, 6, 26, 28, 61, 168
Kal Ho Naa Ho (KHNH), 28, 168
Kapur, Geeta, 11, 12, 20n
Khan, Farah, 3, 7, 8, 17, 38, 91, 93, 95, 99–100, 136, 193; *see also Main Hoon Na, Om Shanti Om*
Khan, Shah Rukh, 2, 4, 7–9, 20n, 33, 91, 92, 94, 95, 99, 136, 145, 159, 164, 168, 184, 188n, 196, 199–200

kitsch, 33, 39, 49, 51, 149, 164
Koi Mil Gaya, 3, 17, 39, 100–14, 126n, 132, 135, 136
Krishna (*KMG*), 103–4, 106
Krrish, 4, 38, 106–7, 114, 121–2, 126n, 136, 184

Lash, Scott, 15, 79, 84, 86, 150–2, 163, 188n; *see also* figural, de-differentiation
literacy (film), 12, 71, 73, 185
Luhrmann, Baz, 3, 126n, 165
Lyotard, Jean-François, 11, 13, 14, 16, 65, 79, 89, 116, 150, 192; *see also* boundary blurring, grand narrative, sublime

Mahabharata, 21, 101, 104, 134
Marks, Laura, 153–4
masala (film genre), 5, 22, 23, 44n, 94, 100, 101, 133, 140, 171, 183, 195
masculinity *see* gender
melodrama, 2, 30, 40, 83, 92, 99, 114, 149, 176, 183
metahistory, 88–9; *see also* ahistorical
mimicry (cultural), 12, 48, 72, 180–1, 184; *see also* reverse colonialism
miniature (painting), 154–9
mise en abyme, 82, 87, 98
Mishra, Vijay, 12, 59–60, 143–5
modernism, 11–12, 23, 37, 64, 65–9, 70–2, 77, 78n, 86, 87, 101, 124, 150
  Japanese, 67–7, 70, 78n
  see also modernity
modernity, 29, 31, 60, 67–9, 71–2, 103–8
Mona Lisa, 1, 2, 19n, 179
MTV, 2, 31, 39, 55, 62n, 152, 174, 176
multiplex (cinema), 12, 65, 78n, 196–7, 198
Mumbai *see* city
Musafir, 167
musical (film genre), 3, 38, 43, 51, 91, 97, 101, 106, 111, 113, 163, 174
My Name is Khan, 28, 38
mythology, 2, 21, 29, 72, 88, 101, 104, 114, 118, 133, 146n
mythological film, 21, 30, 40, 98

Nandy, Ashis, 53–4, 59
narrative (film), 8, 17, 31, 34, 39, 41, 42, 48, 49, 57, 58, 80, 82, 83–4, 88, 95, 97–100, 101, 103, 109, 111, 114, 131–2, 137, 144, 150, 152, 161–4, 167, 171, 176, 186

nation, 23, 26, 27, 32, 34, 36, 39, 73–4, 133
   national cinema, 25–6, 36–8, 39, 87, 114, 131
   nationalism (and identity), 6, 23, 25, 27, 29, 61, 87, 89, 104, 105, 117, 190, 196
Nayar, Sheila, 52, 57, 128, 132, 182
New Bollywood (definition), 5–6
non-resident Indian, 45n, 8, 22, 23, 26–8, 51, 53, 94, 135, 175, 196; see also diaspora
nostalgia (postmodern), 15, 82, 88

Om Shanti Om, 4, 8, 9, 17, 90–100
orientalism, 38, 52
ornamenting the frame, 25, 159, 165, 195
otherisation, 37, 41, 70, 72, 73, 75, 86, 87, 89, 102, 178–9, 180, 186, 190

painting *see* miniature
Palakunnathu, Anna, 11
paradiegetic, 48
parallel cinema *see* social films
paratextuality, 171, 189n
parody, 12, 14, 18, 35, 38, 59
   blank, 13, 82, 83
pastiche
   blank, 12, 15, 99, 178
   pasticcio, 140
pedagogy (and Indian cinema), 21–44, 46–61
picturisations, 27, 45n, 55
piracy (DVD), 22, 45n
plagiarism, 13, 30, 35, 83, 100, 106, 129, 138, 184, 187, 189n, 191
pleasure (audience), 7, 12, 18, 27, 53, 58, 84–5, 98, 125, 138, 139, 150–2, 166, 170–2, 184, 185, 190–2; see also displeasure, cinephilia
politics of representation, 70, 79, 81, 83, 90, 95, 105, 109, 117, 154, 185; see also Hutcheon, Linda
postcolonial *see* colonial
postmodernisms, 74–5
postmodernity, 64, 65, 66, 73, 75
Prasad, Madhava, 32–3, 34, 35

Rai, Aishwarya, 2, 5, 19n, 94, 156–8, 196
Rajadhyaksha, Ashis, 23, 24, 25, 33, 59, 60, 64; see also Bollywoodisation

Ramayana, 21, 22, 101, 133, 134
Ram-Leela *see Goliyon Ki Raasleela Ram-Leela*
Ray, Satyajit, 26, 30, 31, 46–7, 50, 52–3, 100, 146n
realism, 40–1, 42, 44, 47, 50, 52, 55, 56, 87–8, 90, 92–3, 114–25, 151, 152, 158–9, 168–88; see also hyper, *Abhay*, *Hatke*
rebirth *see* reincarnation
reception (film audience), 18, 55, 137–8, 140
recursive imaging *see mise en abyme*
reincarnation, 97–100
religion, 14, 22, 28, 31, 45n, 54, 64, 78n, 89, 95, 97–9, 103–4, 108, 112, 114, 126n, 194; see also mythology
remake *see* unofficial remake, Hollywood-Bollywood remake, self-remake
renaissance (Bollywood), 10, 59, 196
repetition (Indian cinema), 99, 125, 133, 191–2, 194
Reservoir Dogs, 3, 18, 132, 140, 174, 175, 183, 186; see also *Kaante*
reverse engineering, 134, 140
Roshan, Hrithik, 2, 4, 8, 102, 184

Saawariya, 38, 164–5
samsara *see* rebirth
Sarkar, 4, 132, 143–5, 167, 183–4
schizophrenia (postmodern), 82, 86–7, 174, 185; see also fragmentation and bricolage
science-fiction, 100–6, 108–14, 198
self-referentiality *see* self-reflexivity
self-reflexivity, 20n, 35–6, 59–61, 82, 84–5, 93–5, 98, 100, 115, 166–72, 188n, 191, 199–200
self-remake (Bollywood), 19n, 58, 132, 135, 198
sensory, 82, 84, 152–4, 159, 162–5, 173
sequel (Bollywood), 4, 58, 132, 134, 198
sexuality, 8, 31, 57, 94, 112, 152, 174, 195–6, 200n
signification (regime of), 84, 150–2; see also Lash, Scott, figural
simulacra, 13–14, 79, 88, 93, 99, 124, 200
social (socio-realist) films, 22, 25–6, 40, 50, 53, 114, 148, 188n, 162
sociologist *see* sociology

sociology (and film), 24–7, 53, 61
spectacle (Geoff King), 111–12
Stam, Robert, 130–1, 149, 166
stardom (film), 2, 3, 4, 5, 7, 8, 49, 91, 92, 94, 142–5, 168, 195, 198, 199–200
students (Indian cinema), 48–54
sublime, 82, 89–90, 151, 164
superhero (film), 94, 106, 107, 121, 126n, 183, 198
suspension of disbelief, 49, 88, 126n, 135, 185
synaesthesia, 152–4

Tarantino, Quentin, 17, 80, 178, 186–7, 191
Tashan, 179
technology, 5, 60, 67, 69, 72, 100, 103, 105–7, 114, 126n, 135–6, 172; *see also* Blu-ray
technorealism, 60, 136, 172
Thomas, Rosie, 40–3, 55, 133
3D cinema, 165, 188n, 198, 199
transgressive postmodernism, 151
transnational, 5, 25, 32, 34, 36, 38–9, 198–9

transtextuality, 130–1
Twentieth Century Fox, 38, 186, 189n

underworld (Mumbai), 1, 61n, 142, 144, 145, 147n
unfine cinema, 43
unpresentable, 79, 82, 90, 164; *see also* sublime

Varma, Ram Gopal, 45n, 58, 143–4, 167, 188n
verisimilitude, 85, 114–15, 124, 126n, 138, 146n, 166, 171–2
violence, 120–3

Warner Bros, 4, 38
world cinema, 36–7, 39, 46

Zhang, Xudong *see* Dirlik, Arif; *see also* international postmodernism
Zinda, 173, 183, 184, 185, 186, 189n

EU representative:
Easy Access System Europe
Mustamäe tee 50, 10621 Tallinn, Estonia
Gpsr.requests@easproject.com

www.ingramcontent.com/pod-product-compliance
Lightning Source LLC
Chambersburg PA
CBHW062215300426
44115CB00012BA/2073